The International
Political Economy
of the Environment

International Political Economy Yearbook
Volume 12

Kurt Burch, Robert A. Denemark,
Mary Ann Tétreault, and Kenneth P. Thomas
Series Editors

Board of Editors

The International Political Economy of the Environment

Critical Perspectives

edited by
Dimitris Stevis
Valerie J. Assetto

LYNNE
RIENNER
PUBLISHERS

BOULDER
LONDON

Published in the United States of America in 2001 by
Lynne Rienner Publishers, Inc.
1800 30th Street, Boulder, Colorado 80301
www.rienner.com

and in the United Kingdom by
Lynne Rienner Publishers, Inc.
3 Henrietta Street, Covent Garden, London WC2E 8LU

Library of Congress Cataloging-in-Publication Data
The international political economy of the environment : critical perspectives / edited
by Dimitris Stevis and Valerie J. Assetto.
     p. cm.—(International political economy yearbook; v. 12)
    Includes bibliographical references and index.
    ISBN 1-55587-922-5 (hc : alk. paper)
    ISBN 1-55587-980-2 (pb : alk. paper)
    1. Environmental policy—Economic aspects. 2. Economic
development—Environmental aspects. 3. International economic relations.
I. Stevis, Dimitris. II. Assetto, Valerie J. III. Series.
HF1410.I579 v. 12
[HC79.E5]
337.05s—dc21
[333.7]   00-042553

British Cataloguing in Publication Data
A Cataloguing in Publication record for this book
is available from the British Library.

Printed and bound in the United States of America

The paper used in this publication meets the requirements
of the American National Standard for Permanence of
Paper for Printed Library Materials Z39.48-1984.

5   4   3   2   1

Contents

Preface

Before the late 1980s, the range of conceptual approaches in the literature on the international relations of the environment in general, and the international political economy (IPE) of the environment in particular, was quite limited. During the past ten years or so, however, the literature has grown in quantity and quality. The goal of this book is to introduce a critical approach to the IPE of the environment—an approach that focuses on the historical development and framing of environmental problems and solutions and that seeks to understand the social priorities or purpose that differing problems and solutions reflect.

This effort is motivated by our sense that many scholars and practitioners assume that, while there may be some disagreement about solutions, we do know what the problems are. The authors of this book agree with other critical thinkers who argue that the investigation of the emergence and framing of both problems and solutions remains a central endeavor of the IPE of the environment. In our view, problems and solutions are intimately related. The ways in which problems are framed delineate the kinds of solutions that will be entertained; complementarily, the kinds of solutions that are deemed desirable often shape the ways in which problems are framed. Moreover, a closer investigation of the politics associated with the historical emergence and framing of environmental problems and solutions will help reveal which standpoints, values, and preferences shape international environmental politics and policies and which are marginalized—in short, will help us to understand their social purpose.

In late 1997, we called for chapter proposals. Those who expressed interest received a précis specifying the general directions and goals of the book. During the early part of 1998, the selection process was completed and the contributors were asked to prepare their individual chapters. These chapters were circulated to all contributors before the 1999 International Studies Association (ISA) convention and were discussed in two panels and in an ISA workshop that took place during the convention. The fact that each contributor read most or all of the draft chapters and that we had the chance to discuss them individually as well as collectively has given the book cohesion and synergies.

We reviewed the first drafts, as did Kurt Burch (representing the series editors) and one or more anonymous reviewers. We want to thank Kurt for his crucial advice at this stage. The revised chapters were also reviewed. Finally, the full manuscript was reviewed by the series editors and by an anonymous reviewer. We are grateful to Mary Ann Tétreault for her detailed editorial and substantive comments and to the anonymous reviewer for providing us with a well-informed and constructive report.

A great number of people have our appreciation. We first want to thank the series editors—Kurt Burch, Bob Denemark, Mary Ann Tétreault, and Kenny Thomas—for entrusting us with this book. We want to recognize the ISA for its support and ISA's International Political Economy Section for its continued sponsorship of the *Yearbook* series. The participants in the fall 1998 International Environmental Politics research seminar at Colorado State University—Sasha Charney, Lisa Dale, Julie Payne, Lori Poloni-Staudinger, and Christina Sherman—and the anonymous reviewers of the chapters and the full manuscript also deserve our thanks. Our colleagues Kathryn Hochstetler, Brad Macdonald, Stephen Mumme, and Mary Van Buren were always willing to discuss various issues throughout this process. Susan Smith, the graduate secretary of the Political Science Department at Colorado State University, went well beyond the call of duty in preparing the manuscript; we are in her debt for making this a better book. We also wish to extend our appreciation to Earlene Bell, the secretary of the department, who assisted Susan and shouldered additional departmental work while we claimed Susan's time. Our thanks to Lynne Rienner, Sally Glover, Lesli Athanasoulis, Liz Miles, Dorothy Brandt, and Kate Bowman of Lynne Rienner Publishers, for their help and advice in preparing the book. Finally, Dimitris Stevis would like to extend his deep gratitude to his parents, and Valerie Assetto to her family, for their support and love.

—D. S.
—V. J. A.

Dimitris Stevis
Valerie J. Assetto

1

Introduction: Problems and Solutions in the International Political Economy of the Environment

During the past fifty years, the environment has increasingly become the subject of international politics. In the years immediately after World War II, conservation issues led to major international conferences. During the 1950s and early 1960s, accidents and pesticides generated a sense of urgency leading to heated domestic and international debates. Scarcity and population issues took center stage once again during the late 1960s and early 1970s. The 1972 Stockholm Conference brought environment and development together, reflecting the South's assertiveness at the time. Fifteen years later, sustainable development officially represented this fusion, while these same years witnessed a proliferation of international policies and debates. By the end of the 1980s, global environmental issues dominated environmental debates. The 1992 Rio Conference brought together environment, development, and global environmental problems. Ever since, relations between the economy and the environment have received increased attention, as reflected in the debates over the World Trade Organization (WTO) and the proposed Multilateral Agreement on Investment (MAI). More recently, efforts to privatize environmental policy (among other policies) have become an important issue. In short, the international political economy of the environment has now taken center stage (for overviews see Boardman 1981; McCormick 1989; Chatterjee and Finger 1994; Caldwell 1996; Elliott 1998).

Along with the growth of environmental issues there has also been a surge in the social science literature on the subject, best reflected by the publication of a number of new journals such as *Environmental Politics, Global Environmental Change, Global*

1

Environmental Politics, International Environmental Affairs, Journal of Environment and Development, Organization and Environment, and *Capitalism, Nature and Socialism,* to name just a few. At a somewhat slower pace, international relations (IR) and international political economy (IPE) have also joined this trend. With notable exceptions, the IR literature on the environment, and its IPE subset, do not investigate how environmental problems and solutions emerge and are framed, except in relation to intergovernmental negotiations and, more recently, implementation. Equally important, most of this literature does not address questions of social purpose—that is, the ways in which the framing of environmental problems and solutions reflects particular standpoints, values, and preferences.

As a result, our overarching goal in this book is to contribute to a broader debate over the IPE of the environment by employing a critical approach to investigate the framing and social purpose of environmental problems and solutions.[1] The remainder of this introduction clarifies the critical approach employed, situates the volume in the existing literature, and summarizes the contributions. In the conclusion to this book we provide a more theoretical synthesis of our approach and that of our collaborators.

A Critical Perspective

A critical perspective on any issue is not simply one that criticizes the works of others. Rather, a critical perspective is one that questions our understandings of the world around us, particularly those we take for granted, in order to identify who is served by them and who is marginalized. Such an enterprise can take place at different levels and requires both theoretical and empirical investigations. Moreover, one does not have to call oneself a critical analyst to engage in critical investigations as we broadly define them.

The measure of the success of critical analysis is the degree to which it can provide more inclusive accounts of how the world is organized, what its dynamics are, and how it can be changed toward more democracy and equity. From this angle, the worth of critical analyses is not limited to their utility in deconstructing what we take for granted and, as a result, in exciting the political imagination—although they do that. More significant is the capacity of various critical theories to offer descriptions, interpretations, and predictions that are at least as powerful as those offered by the other, well-known IPE perspectives.[2] In short, critical perspectives do not differ from other perspectives solely over what "should" be; they also differ in their understandings of what is.

In the rest of this subsection we identify a simple scheme for engaging in critical analysis, centered on the investigations of problems and solutions.[3] We suggest that a critical investigation of problems and solutions, and their social content or purpose, can proceed at various levels, starting from the more apparent to the least obvious but no less important.

Posing Problems

In looking at the history of international environmental politics during the last few decades, we note that particular issues tend to dominate different periods. In the early post–World War II period, for instance, there was much concern about the availability of natural resources; during the 1960s, the impacts of industrial practices and of population received a great deal of attention; more recently, the focus has been on global problems and the interplay of economic integration and environmental regulation. It is all a matter of degree, of course, since various issues can share the stage at any time. A critical analysis should examine the reasons why some issues receive more attention than others, rather than accept facile explanations. One may be tempted to argue that issues become prominent simply because they are important. Yet, many important issues do not receive much attention, while interest in others fluctuates a great deal. These observations suggest that other forces may be at work. Identifying these forces is essential to understanding why problems and solutions are framed in the ways that they are and the implications this has for various stakeholders.

Critical analysis, however, must go a step further. Even though a wide variety of groups may agree that scarcities, population, or global warming are important issues, they may disagree as to what makes them so. In dealing with climate change or population, for example, should we focus on their possible aggregate impacts or on the ongoing behavior of certain groups? Clearly both are important, but where we choose to put the emphasis does have important implications. If we choose an aggregate approach, then rich and poor alike seem to share some of the responsibility; if we focus on the impacts of particular groups, then some groups seem much more responsible than others in the production of environmental problems.

The closer we get to understanding the different ways in which problems are framed, the closer we get to the social forces involved, their unequal capacities, and their different values and preferences. A critical approach, in fact, takes into account that structural inequities among social groups play a dominant role in the creation and framing of problems. This is not to dismiss the significance of opportunities, negotiating forums, or tactics; rather, it aims to place them in their broader contexts in order to make better sense of their dynamics and outcomes.

Posing Solutions

Solutions can also be analyzed in a similar fashion. Sustainable development, for instance, has become the dominant concept during the last few years. How sustainable development came to fuse development and sustainability reveals a great deal about the environmental politics of the last thirty years (Peet and Watts 1996). Also, why sustainable development means different things to different groups and why alternatives such as sustainability have been marginalized are important questions (Dobson 1996).

Recent IR literature contains a number of compelling discussions of various policy instruments and the crafting of better organizations and rules to deal with the environment (Haas et al. 1993; Young 1997). These instruments and institutions are important in their own terms, and a great deal of work remains to be done in this regard.

Instruments and institutions, however, are not separate from the broader political economy within which they emerge (Eckersley 1995a). A market-based policy instrument, for instance, will have different results if it is used to prevent an environmental problem from occurring than if it is used to correct an environmental problem after it has occurred. More broadly, the move away from state-based and toward market-based instruments and institutions in environmental politics does not take place in a vacuum. Rather, it reflects the pressures of the last twenty years toward a more liberal world political economy.

As with the creation and posing of problems, the closer we get to the creation and posing of solutions, the closer we get to the social forces involved and the competing visions of the world that they promote—in short, the better we can identify who is served by particular solutions and who is excluded.

A critical approach to the international political economy of the environment, therefore, is sensitive to the structural dynamics that engender, constrain, or empower social forces with different resources, interests, and preferences. By focusing on social forces, moreover, it is also sensitive to their agency—that is, to politics.

Situating the Book

The discourse over the IPE of the environment can be broadened by casting our spatial, temporal, and issue criteria as widely as possible. Moving from natural media to social media or from products to production processes are positive steps in this direction. This book does address a number of substantive areas that have not yet received much attention by IR scholars, including radical ecology, environmental effectiveness, the MAI, and the impacts of international development policies at the local level. Our strategy, however, is not to provide an exhaustive discussion of issues that should receive more attention by IR scholars. Alternatively, broadening the discourse could also be well served by bringing together a variety of theoretical approaches (Vogler and Imber 1996) by examining a whole host of issues and forces (Hurrell and Kingsbury 1992; Kamieniecki 1993; Elliott 1998; Chasek 2000) or by covering a broad range of institutions and policies (Hurrell and Kingsbury 1992; Bartlett et al. 1995; Elliot 1998; Vig and Axelrod 1999; Chasek 2000). We have chosen, instead, to include a cohesive set of contributions that provide an overview of the IPE of the environment and that are individually and collectively sensitive to the implications of environmental problem posing and problem solving in their theoretical assumptions and their applied investigations. All of the chapters address important and complementary theoretical issues and, with few exceptions, are based on original empirical research. The measure of our success or failure, therefore, is not whether we are comprehensive, but whether we collectively contribute to broadening the scope of the IPE of the environment in the direction of a critical analysis of both problems and solutions.

Given our goals, perspective, and editorial strategy, where does this collective effort stand within the related bodies of literature? We cannot offer here a literature review, nor do we think it is necessary. Rather, we first situate ourselves within the broader social science literature and, then, within that on the IPE of the environment.

As we have noted, understanding how particular problems and solutions emerge and are posed or framed is both theoretically and practically necessary. Theoretically, it provides a more complete account of environmental politics. A closer look at how global warming has emerged as a dominant issue, for example, can help us understand whether it will remain so and what kinds of solutions are feasible. It makes a great deal of difference to know whether the fate of global climate policy is driven by scientists or energy concerns. In addition, and without denying the role of scientific advice, it makes for a much more accurate analysis to know how scientific networks are themselves engaged in politics (Boehmer-Christiansen 1994a, 1994b) and that scientific knowledge is internally contested (Schrader-Frechette and McCoy 1993; Golley 1993; Barbour 1996; Jasannof 1996).

Our emphasis on problems and solutions comes with a very important caveat. Examining the ways in which problems and solutions emerge and are framed is not intended to cast doubt on the significance of environmental problems and thus lend credence to antienvironmentalists (Simon and Kahn 1984). Nor do we aim to highlight social problems (such as poverty) in order to make environmental problems seem a concern of the rich (Lewis 1992; Beckerman 1996). Our goal is to suggest that environmental problems and solutions—like all social problems and solutions—are the products of actual human beings with unequal capacities and diverse interests. We would suggest, in fact, that by focusing more closely on how various social forces are involved in the creation and posing of environmental problems and solutions, we will be more successful in understanding and exposing certain views that seek to pit the environment against human well-being.

This relates to our interest in giving social purpose the centrality that it deserves. By social purpose we mean that all environmental politics and policy reflect particular standpoints, values, and preferences. Even if nature challenges political economy, it does not render it unnecessary. From beginning to end, it is humans who interpret and speak for nature. And they speak in many voices. The reasons for focusing on social purpose are not solely moral. In fact, we would argue, it is not possible to make sense of the origins, impacts, and efficacy of policies, including environmental policies, without understanding how they organize and affect the universe of stakeholders involved (Sen 1981; Hampson and Reppy 1996; Harvey 1996; Low and Gleeson 1998).

The emphasis on social purpose comes with two important caveats. First, even though we suggest that environmental debates are about who determines, and how, the "nature" of nature, we do not believe that this gives us license to do with nature anything that we please. Rather, the challenge is to identify the implications of how environmental problems and solutions are framed for both people and nature (for various views, see Sessions 1995; Cronon 1996a, 1996b; Harvey 1996: part II). Second, we recognize that the relationship between socially just policies and environmentally sound policies is neither self-evident nor unproblematic. Our goal here is not to equate social purpose with social justice; rather, it is to suggest ways in which social purpose can be dissected, a process that can contribute to understanding social justice (Lynch 1993; Pepper 1993; Hampson and Reppy 1996; Di Chiro 1996; Wapner 1997a; Low and Gleeson 1998; Stevis 2000).

Analyses that do seek to disaggregate environmental problems and solutions, even when they adopt an undifferentiated North-South approach or utilize whole countries as their units of analysis, move us in the right direction but not far enough (United Nations 1972; WCED 1987; Rowlands 1995; World Resources Institute 1996). The North-South approach, for instance, allows Southern elites to justify nonenvironmental practices in the name of development. This also works for Northern elites, either because they can invest in the South or because they can use Southern opposition as an excuse for diluting their own obligations. A less aggregate approach should pay attention to the variable interests of a variety of stakeholders, recognizing that domestic and international politics are contested by actual social forces rather than undifferentiated "states."

In this vein, we agree that environmental politics, like all politics, affect the role and functions of states and societies in distinct ways (Lipschutz and Conca 1993a; Litfin 1998). In our view, the impacts of environmental problems on states should be the subject of more investigation because we think that states are internally and comparatively diverse.[4] Complementarily, we agree with those analysts who seek to investigate the role of additional social forces (Princen and Finger 1994; Wapner 1996; Lipschutz with Mayer

1996). We are concerned, however, with analyses that do not differentiate among "civil society" forces, particularly since there is clear evidence of important differences, even among environmental organizations (Wapner 1996; Audley 1997).

The examination of the trade-environment relationship (Vogel 1995; Audley 1997) and of the role of economic organizations (Esty 1994) are important and growing research agendas. But, as various contributions to the book suggest, it is necessary to recognize that economic integration and the associated rules and international governmental organizations (IGOs) are not devoid of social priorities. During the April 2000 demonstrations against the International Monetary Fund (IMF) and the World Bank, for instance, the president of the World Bank expressed surprise that the Bank's work in favor of social justice was not recognized by those demonstrating. Without getting into the merits of the Bank's work, it is clear that his surprise is evidence of the competing visions of justice at play.

Our belief in the significance of understanding the ways in which problems and solutions emerge and are framed also colors our view of two additional, often overlapping, research programs—that is, the international environmental policy process and regime analysis.

In light of the proliferation of international policymaking, we believe that systematic accounts of various aspects of the policy process are invaluable (Soroos 1986; Benedick 1991; Caldwell 1996). Such accounts, should be sensitive to the fact that many stakeholders are excluded while participants do not have equal access. Moreover, policymaking forums and processes are neither procedurally nor substantively neutral. Even though more environmental nongovernmental organizations (ENGOs) than businesses participated in the 1992 Rio Conference, for instance, business is more influential than ENGOs (Chatterjee and Finger 1994).

Regime analysis holds a prominent position in the IR literature on the environment. Its advantage is that it aims at comprehensive and dynamic accounts of how particular issue areas are organized and governed (Young 1989, 1997; Zürn 1998). This is definitely an important move away from formalistic discussions of international policy that narrowly focus on organizations and legal rules. On balance, however, it has remained statist in the sense that it has not addressed how various social forces affect state interests and international policies and the cleavages within the state itself. In addition, it has tended to focus more on the mechanics of how regimes are negotiated and implemented and less on the social purpose that regimes embody.

This part has provided a very general account of how the book fits in the relevant literature. In our view, a broader discourse on the IPE of the environment requires that researchers with different agendas become familiar with and engage in dialogue with each other. At the very least, different research programs can benefit from each other's analytical insights and empirical evidence. But, in addition to engaging in constructive exchanges with other research programs, a critical IPE of the environment is well poised to generate its own research agendas and programs. We hope that our book contributes to this goal.

Summary of Contributions

The chapters in this book illustrate a cohesive story and one that illuminates our goals and our critical approach. We also hope that the contributions are indicative of additional lines of theoretical and substantive research. In Part 1, the chapters by Rosalind Irwin, Marc Williams, Daniel Egan and David Levy, and Peter Newell serve two goals. Collectively, they offer a historical account of the IPE of the environment from World War II to the present; individually, they examine in more depth various theoretical and political issues of the period.

Irwin traces the trajectory of the IPE of the environment from the debates between various conservationists and preservationists during the years shortly after World War II to the emergence of sustainable development in the 1980s as the core concept of environmental politics. She argues that this has been a contested process rather than one of convergence toward ever better and universally shared environmental standards. Williams underscores this argument and brings the discussion to the present, using the debates surrounding the rules and organization of the WTO and the emergence of managerial environmentalism. Egan and Levy focus on the politics of international regulation, using climate change and the MAI as their cases. They argue that the tactical preferences of particular actors depend on the characteristics of the policy arena as well as on their own longer-term interests. Thus, on the one hand, capital and its allies support international policies that enable further liberalization but resort to domestic politics in instances of policies that aim at social regulation. On the other hand, ENGOs are likely to follow the opposite strategy. Newell's chapter focuses on the strengths and limitations of voluntary arrangements between ENGOs and transnational corporations (TNCs). Like the other authors, his goal is to understand the implications of such arrangements for the IPE of the environment while providing insightful criticisms of the reasons for and efficacy of these attempts at private governance.

Turning to Part 2, the chapters by Marian A. L. Miller, Valérie de Campos Mello, and Barbara Lynch examine the impact of economic liberalization on the less industrialized world. The authors investigate connections between third world environmental politics and the current international political economy rather than make facile assumptions that cast all outsiders as equally devious and all insiders as equally pious. Miller's chapter discusses the increasing enclosure of space and knowledge under capitalism, from the earliest enclosures of land in Britain to the more recent enclosures of knowledge about nature, using the case of the neem tree in India. Her argument is that capitalist enclosure leads to tragedies for the commons, not because they result from collective irrationality in the use of open resources but because they are built into the historical unfolding of unregulated capitalism.

De Campos Mello's chapter examines environmental reform in postdictatorial Brazil. She argues that in order to understand the reasons for and limitations of environmental policy reform in Brazil, one must move beyond the partial accounts of realists and liberal institutionalists toward a more comprehensive account of the impacts of global neoliberal integration. This process, she suggests, has produced important changes in the nature of the Brazilian state but has not improved the lot of those most affected by environmental deterioration in the Amazon region. Along similar lines, Lynch's chapter analyzes the impacts of traditional developmentalist discourse and neoliberalism on the framing of local problems in the Dominican Republic and Cuba. She argues that the framing of environmental risk and danger reflects both external interests and domestic politics. As a consequence, Cuba's more inclusive politics casts both urban and industrial uses as the problem, while the Dominican Republic's more exclusive politics obscures the impact of industrial location and places the blame on the victims of environmental degradation.

The third part of the book consists of two chapters, two commentaries, and the conclusion. Collectively and individually they raise a number of theoretical challenges. Chapters 10 and 11 examine two important issues/challenges for contemporary environmental politics. Gabriela Kütting looks at the outcomes of international agreements and suggests that much of the research so far has focused on the institutional effectiveness of environmental organizations rather than on their environmental effectiveness. The key reason for this is the framing of both the problem and the solutions, as she demonstrates by using the Convention on Long-Range Transboundary Air Pollution (LRTAP), one of the most ambitious and effective international agreements. Eric Laferrière's chapter reconstructs the theoretical foundations of contemporary mainstream international relations. While he would not deny that such IR perspectives could deal with environmental issues, he suggests that they can do so only within the parameters of their mechanistic perspective, thus casting the environment as something to be managed. He argues that historical and relational approaches, such as dependency and historical materialism, are better suited to integrating the environment into their analyses. While they have not done so, and there is no guarantee that they will do so in the future, the relational approach of these perspectives is more promising than that of more mainstream approaches, such as liberalism or realism.

The commentators, Frederick Buttel and Timothy Luke, identify key themes in the book as well as issues that require more attention. Buttel finds that the contributors avoid simple arguments and pay close attention to the role of various social forces. He also suggests that more attention should be placed on the North-South dimension and on disputes internal to environmental science. Luke points to the book's emphasis on the "subpolitical" domain—that is, factors, such as science and technology and even economics, that are sometimes considered as outside of politics even though they are not, and suggests that this is an important line of critical research. The conclusion elaborates on the basic themes of the introduction and situates various literatures, as well as the contributions to this book, within these themes.

Notes

1. Our work adds to a growing body of literature. Some examples of general international environmental politics works with a critical bent or a substantial critical component include Lipschutz and Conca 1993a; Vogler and Imber 1996; Peet and Watts 1996; Hampson and Reppy 1996; Elliott 1998; and Laferrière and Stoett 1999.

2. We are referring, among others, to liberal (Keohane 1989), realist (Krasner 1985), and idealist (Wendt 1999) views. For an overview see Katzenstein, Keohane, and Krasner (1999).

3. Problems and solutions are intimately related. If one wishes to justify draconian population solutions, for instance, they are likely to pose population problems as the result of actions by unruly and selfish people whose freedoms must be curtailed. It is for analytical reasons, therefore, that we find this distinction useful.

4. We do not deny that physical processes do promote transboundary harm and that international policies may be desirable. We *are* denying the mechanistic assertion of cause and effect, however. Migrations and phytosanitary diseases (animal and plant diseases) are long-standing cross-border problems that have not led to the transcendence of the state. Policies, including global ones, are not simply the by-product of problems; rather they are the result of how problems and solutions are constructed, a deeply social process. In addition, we believe that the past autonomy of states has been quite exaggerated in conventional IR literature.

Part 1

The Politics of Global Policymaking

Rosalind Irwin # 2

Posing Global Environmental Problems from Conservation to Sustainable Development

Humanity's impact on the biosphere has become a major concern in recent decades, leading to the growth of multilateral environmental institutions. However, a contradiction persists between the institutionalization of the environment[1] and a continuing global environmental crisis evidenced by deforestation, soil erosion, loss of species diversity, pollution, depletion of fish stocks, and climate change, among other examples. The goal here is to understand this contradiction by exploring the limits of environmental institutionalization processes. The argument is that addressing environmental problems involves more than reactive problem solving (which would imply a kind of functional or instrumental response) or simple policy coordination (which emphasizes the limits placed by anarchical structures on the conditions of political action). It also requires the *construction* of global environmental problems and politics in particular ways in different historical contexts. In this chapter I evaluate how environmental paradigms have supported or subverted particular configurations of order and power by analyzing struggles over the definition of environmental politics and problems from the 1940s to the late 1980s.

In his essay "Social Forces, States, and World Orders," Robert Cox argues that critical theory can provide a perspective from which "the problematic becomes one of creating an alternative world" as opposed to solving the problems posed "within the terms of the particular perspective which was the point of departure" (Cox 1996b:88). Ultimately, the goal is to advance inquiries into "how developments in multilateralism can influence global structural changes in a normatively desirable direction" (Cox 1997:104).

Environmental problem solving assumes that international cooperation on environmental issues is a process of progressive convergence and integration around environmental concerns (Vogler and Imber 1996:7). While arrangements to deal with "market externalities, transboundary pollutants, and common-pool resources" (Lipschutz and Conca 1993b:7) may heighten awareness of particular environmental problems, such strategies primarily function to ensure that "relationships and institutions work smoothly by dealing effectively with particular sources of trouble" (Cox 1996b:88). These processes also involve fixing "limits or parameters to a problem area and . . . reduc[ing] the statement of a particular problem to a limited number of variables" (Cox 1996b:88).

The framing of environmental politics, in turn, is reduced to the terms of problem solving and produces solutions that are limited by their terms of reference. Institutional arrangements designed to deal with the ahistorical problem of "order-under-anarchy," for instance, may obscure the fact that institutions are "the particular historical consequences of social struggles which could have had very different outcomes" (C. Murphy 1994:37). Similarly, the "tragedy of the commons" as a model of the global environmental problematique is limited by the terms of rational-choice economic theory (Wendt and Duvall 1989:53).

Problem *posing* is a multilateral process through which ideas, institutions, and politics are linked to (re)define the social purposes of global environmental order. Using a sociological rather than an economic standpoint on global governance, problem posing involves inquiring into the normative constitution of multilateralism, asking how it is that "the social and political worlds of international relations are constructed" (Woods 1996:26). This approach emphasizes the role of collective and intersubjective knowledge, values, norms, and culture in configuring social relations of power.

Problem posing can be thought of as broadly similar to issue framing or agenda setting in that it involves a political process by which different definitions of "the problem to be solved" are articulated by agents (Haas 1991:3; Cobb and Ross 1997:3–24). However, while issue framing denotes specific political or ideological strategies, problem posing draws upon broader paradigms or worldviews. These are closer to what may be called discursive practices, which operate to "generate the categories of meaning by which reality can be understood and explained" (George 1994:29–30). Thus, this approach emphasizes the "intersubjective nature of social experience and its impact both on issue initiation and policy formulation" (Rochefort and Cobb 1993:57).

Problem posing, therefore, refers to the dominant discourse, worldviews, beliefs, and knowledge systems within which different framings or agendas can take place. For example, sustainable development as a paradigm gives rise to and draws upon important cultural and historical notions of development, ethics, economics, and politics but encompasses meanings much broader than a singular ideology, frame, or political program.

Two important post–World War II historical paradigms are analyzed in this chapter: the first is conservationist management, which dominated the period from the 1940s to the 1960s; and the second is sustainable development, encompassing the late 1960s to the Brundtland Report of 1987. The major concerns shifted from one era to the next, from natural resources management to pollution, scarcity, and development. These two periods, from the beginnings of globalization to its institutionalization, are chosen because they encompass a long enough span of history, allowing us to analyze changes in environmental ideas and meanings.

The developments during these periods are operationalized in terms of four stages or processes of problem posing: (1) the perception of the problem or crisis; (2) the political expression of the problem; (3) the globalization or internationalization of the political problem; and (4) the resolution of the conflict. The third and fourth steps embody the institutionalization of a particular form of problem posing. Organizationally, the analysis of these four problem-posing stages provides a framework on which to build comparisons of these two historical periods.

The Hegemony of Conservationist Management, 1930s–1960s

Perceptions of the Crisis

The construction of a post–World War II global environmental order involved the convergence of Keynesian economic thinking with U.S.

political conservationism. The management of global environmental problems took cultural cues from the modernist traditions of apolitical utilitarianism, scientific management, and engineering. However, the events that gave urgency to the political movement for global environmental concern were the Euro-American experiences of the Dust Bowl, the Depression, and World War II. The need for orderly resource management was underlined by the perception that unrestrained economic competition had contributed to the globalization of the Depression and the outbreak of World War II.

The starting point for modern economic science had been the advice of liberal classical economists such as Adam Smith to specifically exclude nature (i.e., biological and geographical factors) from consideration in the production of national wealth (Polanyi 1957:112). The Dust Bowl brought a new kind of thinking, exemplified in the report of the Great Plains Committee submitted to President Franklin Roosevelt in December 1936 (Worster 1994:230). The report concluded that the Dust Bowl was a wholly man-made disaster produced, in large part, by traditional U.S. attitudes that used self-interest, unregulated competition, and the conquest of nature as the basis for social harmony (Worster 1994:230). Therefore, newly developed Keynesian economics suggested that systems of social protection against unrestrained economic forces were necessary to preserve orderly development and equilibrium in the economy. A similar logic was applied to natural systems, which, like economies, required proper management to maintain their equilibrium.

In 1946, President Truman wrote to the U.S. representative on the UN Economic and Social Council that "[t]he real or exaggerated fear of resource shortages and declining standards of living has in the past involved nations in warfare. . . . [C]onservation can become a major basis of peace" (United Nations 1956:vii). Detlev Bronk, president of Johns Hopkins University and chairman of the National Research Council, implied in a speech to a UNESCO conference that the link between natural and social equilibria could be made by technology in the service of economics: "[N]ations can, through science, peacefully gain those material benefits which they have sought in vain to acquire through armed conflict" (United Nations 1956:4). Nature was incorporated into political order as an object of explicit control whose management was necessary to prevent both "natural" disasters, such as the Dust Bowl, and human disasters, such as global war.

Political Expression of the Problem

Prior to World War II, the problem of the environment was posed in two major, competing ways: conservation or preservation. The goal of conservation was planned and efficient progress (Switzer and Bryner 1998:5) to "maximize the efficient use of a resource while preventing its overexploitation" (Gottlieb 1993:22). Two resources were a particular focus: water and forests. The utilitarian principles of forest science emphasized the need for "development (the use of existing resources for the present generation) and the prevention of waste" (Nash and Pinchot 1967:121). Gifford Pinchot, a chief lieutenant of Theodore Roosevelt, a Progressive activist and forester trained at the French National School of Forestry (Nash and Pinchot 1967:xii), brought together populist political activism with the discourse of modern scientific management of natural resources.[2] U.S. conservationism thus represented an uneasy blending of managerial and populist themes.

As Gottlieb argues, U.S. government agencies and their resource strategies were key in framing conservationist politics and in veiling tensions between the Progressives' political agenda of economic democracy and the scientific management of resources (1993:2). During the 1920s, with the expansion of the involvement of resource industries and industrial interests (Gottlieb 1993:25–26), environmental problems were increasingly posed in conservationist terms, emphasizing the orderly development and marketing of natural resources (McCormick 1989:25–26).

The managerial aspect of conservation was epitomized in the Tennessee Valley Authority (TVA), an example of spectacular engineering know-how and an "integrated" approach to environmental resource management.[3] The TVA embodied the Keynesian approach of Roosevelt's New Deal, a living example of the power of technological and scientific resource management principles to solve problems of scarcity or inefficiencies using economic science.[4]

Preservationism offered an alternative to the economistic notions of resource management characteristic of conservationism (see, for early examples, Marsh [1965] and Leopold [1966]). In this view, environmental crises, such as the Dust Bowl, were not problems of poor planning and management, but rather symptoms of a greater imbalance between humans and nature, particularly as a consequence of industrial production. Preservationism, while politically an

American movement, also drew inspiration from nineteenth-century British romanticism (Worster 1994:1–25). Generally posing the environment as an ethical problem as opposed to an economic one, preservationists fell into three strands: ethical/aesthetic, scientific, and colonial.

The fundamental interdependence, relation, and holism of humanity and nature was an early theme of many who favored an ethical/aesthetic approach (Worster 1994:58). The naturalists' conception of nature found political expression in U.S. and British preservationist movements. This thrust of preservationism often came from amateur naturalists, as distinguished from professionally trained ecologists or managerial groups who advocated conservation. Preservationism at first implied a retreat, an essentially private and "direct personal relationship with the non-human" (Worster 1994:351). However, this relationship eventually was seen as one worth nurturing for the public good as well. The landscape visions of beauty, grandeur, and religious inspiration articulated by John Muir and exemplified by Yosemite National Park were the rallying points.

Another important thread, that of the scientific preservationists, arose from the geological and biological sciences, which early on had developed ideas of ecological balance that resisted a managerial/economistic logic. The science of ecology was elaborated in 1867 by Ernest Haeckel, and the concepts of "ecosystem" and "biosphere" date at least as early as 1935 in an article in the journal *Ecology* (Caldwell 1996:19).

In addition to the United States and the United Kingdom, preservation movements appeared in other parts of the globe, including Canada, New Zealand, and Australia (McCormick 1989:12; Boardman 1981).[5] The national parks movement also inspired interest in the preservation of flora and fauna in the "pristine" colonies, a concern that boosted the "acceptance [of the notion] that national conservation and protection movements ultimately had interests that transcended national frontiers" (McCormick 1989:24).

Internationalization/Globalization of the Political Problem

After the end of World War II, the conservationist-preservationist conflict set the terms through which the preceding global disasters could be (at least partially and potentially) explained, and on which a new global environmental order could be founded to deal with future instabilities. The vehicle for posing global environmental problems then became the (now familiar) international conference.

A managerial orientation to posing global environmental problems was evident in early efforts of the Food and Agriculture Organization (FAO), the World Health Organization (WHO), and UNESCO (Kay and Jacobson 1983:10; Boardman 1981; Caldwell 1996). A proposal for a conference on conservation and utilization of resources (the United Nations Scientific Conference on the Conservation and Utilization of Resources, or UNSCCUR), although only coming to fruition after Pinchot's death, was in form and content all but identical to Pinchot's proposal (Boardman 1981; Kay and Jacobson 1983; McCormick 1989:27; Caldwell 1996). Sponsored primarily by UNESCO, with the involvement of FAO, the International Labour Organization (ILO) and WHO, UNSCCUR took place in Lake Success, New York, 22 August to 1 September 1949, and had a decidedly economic and technological mandate. It focused primarily on the depletion of natural resources of minerals, fuel and energy, water, forests, land, wildlife, and fish (McCormick 1989:36; Caldwell 1996:51–52).[6]

The conference's main concern was the "practical application of science to resource management," with a secondary issue being "how techniques in use in specific climates and in specific levels of economic and technical development could be brought into wider use for the benefit of less-developed areas" (United Nations 1956:xii). As Caldwell writes: "Although the importance of ecological knowledge as a guide to action was mentioned in several papers and addresses at the UNSCCUR conference, at no point was a truly holistic view taken of the relation among population, resources, and environment" (Caldwell 1996:53).

Preservationism, on the other hand, was asserted through the initiatives of leaders of international organizations. Under the directorship of Julian Huxley (Boardman 1981:36,38), an avid naturalist who "was convinced of the relevance and urgency of nature protection" (McCormick 1989:32), UNESCO undertook to advance the preservationists' agenda by beginning deliberations to set up an international organization for environmental preservation. The new international nature protection body proposed by the Europeans was discussed at a meeting sponsored by the Swiss between 28 June and 3 July 1947 at Brunnen. The Europeans tended to support the idea of an independent body, while the Americans and the British favored incorporating preservationist efforts under the United Nations. They argued that without governmental support and the leadership of a UN agency, such a body would have little success (for more detailed analysis of these deliberations, see Boardman 1981:40–43).

Huxley did succeed, against U.S. opposition, in his proposal to convene a parallel conference to UNSCCUR that would explicitly address nature protection. The International Technical Conference on the Protection of Nature (ITC), also held at Lake Success, New York, 22 August to 1 September 1949, was organized jointly by UNESCO and the International Union for the Protection of Nature (IUPN), formed in 1948 (Boardman 1981:43). In contrast to the economistic language of UNSCCUR, this conference called for "respect of Beauty and appreciation of living things as well as moderation in exploiting and developing resources" (UNESCO 1950:vii). Thus, a different thrust from conservation found some expression in global environmental discourse and institutions.

Ethical arguments had slightly more success when they appealed to the humanistic sensibilities of liberal internationalism, rather than to a universal naturalism or ecological aesthetic. For example, many at the ITC conference connected protection of nature with UNESCO's project of fostering widespread acceptance of the Universal Declaration of the Rights of Man. An opening speech asked, "Is it not true that one of the most sacred of these rights is to be able to benefit from the invigorating outlet and aesthetic inspiration which only unspoiled Nature is likely to provide" (UNESCO 1950:15)? Nature preserves and parks would, therefore, form a spiritual resource that could provide opportunities for universal insights and knowledge into the essence of humanity as well as nature. National parks, then, stood not only as symbols of as-yet-unspoiled wilderness, but were also political and cultural symbols of national pride and the objects of social engineering.

While the scientific stream of preservation ecology asserted itself at the ITC, where resolutions focused on the need to exchange knowledge among scientific disciplines and foster environmental education (UNESCO 1950:ix), a managerial direction persisted. One contributor noted, for example, that "permanent use means conservation in the widest sense—preservation through wise use" (UNESCO 1950:167). Even though ecological science and the subversive and possibly revolutionary implications of ecological models were well known to the scientists participating, discussion of these was excluded by the narrow mandates of the conference, and efforts to articulate wider critiques failed. While this may have imbued the ITC initiative with impartiality and thus prestige, "too earnest a clinging to a belief in the separability of science and politics" (Boardman 1981:75) led to a narrowed scope for efforts to fundamentally change the way people and organizations make decisions.

Resolution of the Conflict: Institutionalization of Conservationist Management

Craig Murphy argues that, historically, one of the important purposes of international institutions in the global liberal order has been the management of potential conflicts with organized social forces (C. Murphy 1994:34). To the extent that the Dust Bowl era, the Depression, and World War II had revealed a crisis in world order that was at least partly environmental in nature, environmental politics focused on the management of potentially destabilizing social conflicts as much as on the need to protect and preserve nature.

Managing conflicts required the reformulation of the consensus that would secure the conditions for orderly global economic growth and development while containing potentially divisive political struggles and challenges. Growth in the core was a key component since, as the experience of World War II had revealed, duplication of political contests and struggles over natural resources could destabilize the system, particularly in the context of Cold War ideological divisions. Moreover, the necessity (made urgent by the ideological rivalry of the Cold War) of consolidating Western models of development in the third world made conservation an important component of U.S. foreign policy. These challenges militated in favor of a hands-on managerial approach rather than a laissez-faire approach.

These twin goals, growth and development, facilitated the extension of some of the political components of conservationism, but also the suppression of others. Pinchot's political program even included a reference to the United States' Manifest Destiny to "demonstrate that a democratic republic is the best form of government yet devised" and to act as "an influence for good among the nations of the world" (Nash and Pinchot 1967:121). Pinchot also argued that "the development of natural resources should be for the many, not the few" (McCormick 1989:12). Some activists in the 1940s and

1950s echoed Progressive-era critiques of the profit motive and free enterprise (e.g., Vogt 1947). However, these were not often accompanied by calls for economic democracy, accountability, and redistributive rights in natural resource policy. On the contrary, by the 1950s, debates were dominated by the Malthusian issue of whether technology would outstrip population needs (Gottlieb 1993:37).

Managing potential conflict also involved reducing environmental problems to a narrow range of choices. Where there had been some affinities between the conservationists and the preservationists in their political programs, as well as a complex intertwining of environmental visions among early environmentalists, there emerged a dichotomy between the landscape visions of beauty, grandeur, and religious inspiration articulated by John Muir and exemplified by Yosemite National Park, and the aesthetics of efficiency and wise use exemplified by the TVA.

It is important that this reduction of environmental ideas formed an *asymmetrical* opposition. The politics of nature *preservation* became narrowed to the agenda of setting aside wild areas rather than continuing the wider spiritual or systemic critiques of modernization and development projects of earlier days. While preservationism was marginalized to UNESCO, conservationist management was expanded until its principles engulfed even modest efforts to establish nature preserves. "From the late 1950s and early 1960s began a process of adaptation by conservation organizations to the imperatives of economic development" (Boardman 1981:67). Perhaps the defining moment of the shift was the 1956 decision to change the name of the IUPN to the International Union for the Conservation of Nature (IUCN).

As mentioned above, the preservationist movements had also inspired interest in colonial environments. However, the weaknesses of preservationism's limited focus on wilderness and wild species protection were recognized in debates over African development during the decolonization period following World War II. At the Third International Conference for the Protection of the Fauna and Flora of Africa in 1953, for instance, delegates agreed that "the vital problem of protecting the human environment of Africa could not be solved solely by the creation of nature reserves and the protection of certain species" (McCormick 1989:43).

Preservationism could, however, offer little resistance to the imperatives of conservationist management. Preservationism's focus on the periphery, for instance, led to a neglect of potentially subversive ideas about the sources of threats to nature from the industrialized core. Because it didn't focus on the core, colonial preservationism could be dismissed using the justification that preservation applied only to the pristine.

Despite early resolutions at the ITC, such as Resolution No. 7, which emphasized the necessity to promote detailed ecological surveys of the impact of large-scale development projects on natural systems (McCormick 1989:43), preservationist principles were increasingly linked to a managerial/economic logic. As noted earlier, even at the ITC it was argued that, while nature protection and preservation were the goals, they could often be justified in terms of the economic value of the preserved resources, presaging the rise to prominence of environmental economics in the 1980s and 1990s. One presenter argued that "the real chance of maintaining extensive and exclusive reservations for the protection of nature depends on (a) selecting areas that are no good for anything else and (b) improving productivity of the used lands so that nations can afford the luxury of withdrawing lands from economic use" (UNESCO 1950:168).

The third step in managing potential conflicts involved establishing and supporting forms of community and interest at the global level that would reinforce rather than undermine managerial conservationist conceptions of environmental order. The terms under which scientists convened and exchanged their knowledge at UNSCCUR and the ITC discouraged discussion of not only political issues of distribution and equity, but also the wider application of scientific principles of ecology. The purpose of UNSCCUR and other institutional initiatives was the "practical application of science to resource management" (United Nations 1956:xii). Robert Boardman (1981:71) points out that this kind of specialization was necessary "because the process of legitimization tended to put a premium on distinctiveness and the exclusive possession of special skills." The purpose of sponsoring scientific exchanges, then, was to construct what Peter Haas (1992:2) terms epistemic communities or networks of knowledge-based experts whose knowledge would serve to direct the control and management of nature and natural resources.

The U.S. conservationist-preservationist debate, partly reproduced in the different mandates of UNSCCUR and the ITC, set the terms of reference for posing global environmental problems. Ultimately, despite the efforts of the preservationists, global environmental politics would be about the essentially technical problems of natural resource management. This focus was illustrated by the overriding interest in data collection and classification (Boardman 1981:54).

However, this narrow global environmental agenda encountered contradictions. Global macromanagement implied a concentration of resources and knowledge in core countries. Conservationist management displaced social critique as a basis for decisionmaking, resulting in a technology-dependent rationalism that objectified the problems. Eventually, these contradictions led to calls for change that would have to be addressed once again.

The Weak Hegemony of Sustainable Development: From the 1960s to the Brundtland Report

Perceptions of the Crisis

In the 1960s and 1970s, extensive and intensive growth of the global economy resulted in increased attention to environmental problems and their restatement in broader ecological terms. New military and production technologies revolutionized the marketplace for products, labor, and services, accelerating the rate of exploitation of natural resources. In addition, the abrupt dislocations caused by the energy crisis suggested that environmental changes could occur suddenly and that these were not necessarily within the capacity of experts to predict or manage. However, this also sparked a greater concern with "a loss of control on the part of governments, which mirrored an immediate concern with the diminished position of the U.S.A." (Vogler and Imber 1996:5; Morse 1976).

The emergence and wide social penetration of image-based media was also a key influence in this preservationist resurgence. The "Earthrise" photograph, taken from the Apollo 11 spacecraft in 1969, illustrated both the awesome scale and the power of technology to facilitate ultimate control over natural forces, while simultaneously bringing home the fragility of earth's self-contained ecosystem. At the same time, images of destruction and degradation were more easily transmitted across the globe; international audiences were graphically informed of the 1959 outbreak of mercury poisoning near Minimata Bay in Japan, the 1967 grounding of the supertanker *Torrey Canyon*, and the 1968 PCB poisoning on Kyushu (Itai-Itai disease) (Haas 1992:2; Tolba et al. 1992:249–251). By the early 1970s, the groundwork for (re)creating the conditions for political action on environmental problems was laid.

The oil shocks of the 1970s also gave rise to the perception that it was imperative to include the South in any global environmental arrangements. The political potential of the South to disrupt international economic arrangements and to make demands based on their control of scarce natural resources became evident in the new activities of the Nonaligned Movement, the activities of the UN Conference on Trade and Development, the demands for a new international economic order (NIEO), and the Organization of Petroleum Exporting Countries (OPEC). Developmentalism shifted from a top-down to a bottom-up focus; however, this focus did not necessarily imply that the imperatives of the environment would take precedence.

Political Expression of the Problem

Thus, new lines of conflict would emerge between developmentalism and environmentalism. The lines of differentiation can be illustrated briefly by debates on global economic reform that took place during the early 1970s. One of the essential premises of the Group of 77's demands for a new international economic order was that globalized economic forces produced differential effects and development trajectories between the rich and poor countries, and therefore that the North and the South should be allowed to play by different rules. Ecologists, however, pointed out that pollution problems in the North and overpopulation and poverty in the South were symptoms of a common social process of development. The view of political ecologists, therefore, went beyond the idea that the South should be allowed to play by different rules to the more radical position that the chessboard should be redefined (Dryzek 1997:13).

Yet, environmentalism as a political movement should not be reduced to this formulation alone. One strand emanated from the (now more politicized) scientists, loosely following the diverse traditions of the scientific preservationists. Leaders here were Rachel Carson (1962), Barry Commoner (1971), Garrett Hardin (1968), Paul Ehrlich (1968), and William Ophuls (1974). As early as the 1960s, this critical scientific approach of ecological thought, which had been marginalized in post–World War II environmental discourse, reemerged, partly in response to increased awareness of environmental disasters. An important early vehicle for this resurgence was the Biosphere Conference of 1968 (discussed below).

A second more technocratic strand reinserted Malthusian ideas through the work of Hardin, the Ehrlichs, and the Limits to Growth group. Sponsored by the Club of Rome, Limits to Growth addressed itself to "the human predicament," including "poverty in the midst of plenty; degradation of the environment; loss of faith in institutions; uncontrolled urban spread; insecurity of employment; alienation of youth; rejection of traditional values and inflation and other monetary and economic disruptions" (Meadows et al. 1972:ix). In response, it favored a radical disciplinarian approach that "recommended, among other things, a 40 percent reduction in industrial investment, a 20 percent reduction in agricultural investment, a 40 percent reduction in the birth rate, and a massive transfer of wealth from rich to poor countries" (McCormick 1989:77).

Yet another strand included more grassroots political ecologists such as the Greens. These organized groups joined (if at times uneasily) other critical social movements in underlining the contradictions of the Western post–World War II world order, particularly the failure to question the social purposes of economic development.

Similarly, developmentalism also contained a series of strands: some procapitalist Southern elites sponsored a kind of predatory developmentalism that used sovereignty as a barrier against environmental arguments. Others in both the North and South opted for a reformist approach. Finally, the persistence and resurgence of conservationist management (to some extent reflected even in the Club of Rome and Global 2000 reports) were challenged in the early 1980s by resurgent hyperliberalism with the goal of reconstructing the global economy.

It is in this context that some important historical contrasts emerged. The globalism of the scientific and political ecologists of the 1960s had been a call to action to achieve a balance between human society and nature. The calls for a renewal of development by the Southern countries had (at least implicitly) been a call for the need for social justice. The starting premise of global environmental politics during the 1960s had been that the trajectory of orthodox development was unsustainable. This was displaced in the early 1970s by the idea that development could be reconstructed as a (newly sustainable) common social project between North and South. Thus, neither managerial conservationism nor politically based ecology would dominate global environmental problem posing during this period. Instead, developmentalist management promised to cope with the many conflicting demands of North and South, environment and development.

While the Northern conservationists had *assumed* that economic forces would produce development, the new environmental critiques suggested that this assumption was inadequate. Development could no longer be considered a technical, self-reproducing process, but rather one requiring conscious political direction from state governments and international institutions. While the debate now centered on a more active role for governments beyond investment to include strategies for welfare and environmental regulation, this was not so much a departure from the management approach as a reproduction of it.

Politically, the potential conflicts arising from the "development and geographical extension of the industrial system" (C. Murphy 1994:18)[7] included (most significantly for environmental politics) the tension between the industrialized and less industrialized world (C. Murphy 1994:22). The need to manage this tension made development issues, rather than pollution or toxic wastes or oil spills, the primary engine of *global* action on the environment. Environmental problems were *re*posed in the language of developmentalism (Sachs 1993).

Robert Sutcliffe (1995:232) writes that "it was during the period roughly between the first Indian Five Year Plan and the first oil shock that the time came for the idea that the whole world, including the poorer countries, should be developed." What did "development" mean? Arturo Escobar (1995:4) describes development as a "growing will to transform drastically two-thirds of the world in the pursuit of the goal of material prosperity and economic progress" (see also Peet and Watts 1996:16–27; Sachs 1993). Sutcliffe argues that all sides (including critics) in the development debate of the 1960s and early 1970s agreed on the general parameters of development. In summary, there was a consensus that development was a basically objective process that would result ultimately in an endpoint where equalization among countries would lead to enhanced human welfare.[8]

North-South positions would tentatively converge around

rejection of the idea that obstacles to development were natural rather than social, political, and economic (Sutcliffe 1995:236). Liberal development economists such as Wassily Leontief argued that "no insurmountable physical barriers exist within the Twentieth Century to the accelerated development of the developing regions" (Leontief et al. 1977:10–11).

For the most part, third world radical development economists shared this view, even if only implicitly. By the time of the Stockholm Conference, Southern developmentalists accepted the environment as an important but clearly subordinate dimension of development (McCormick 1989:92). Many of the representatives of a third world perspective, including dependency theorists and Marxists, chose to articulate a basic needs approach that, while offering a potentially more environmentally sustainable model based on self-sufficiency and local development needs, failed to "attack the issue of transforming world economic structures . . . and become a strategy for structural change with an alternative pattern of development" (Cox 1996a:398).

The dissemination of ideas on the nature of the environmental problem and the maintenance of an uneasy consensus on the need to link environment with development was an incomplete and somewhat ambivalent process throughout the late 1970s and early 1980s. The second oil shock, accompanied by global recession and renewed militaristic politics in the North, proved hostile to environmentalism. Economically, this period was a disaster in the South. Rising interest rates and energy costs accelerated debt loads, while Northern protectionism cut export earnings. Development thinking entered a period of "retrenchment and restructuring in which recession and the debt crisis focused attention on short-term management ('disequilibria')" (Peet and Watts 1996:24).

During the early 1980s, global IGOs were again oriented toward a renewal of developmentalist management in the South. The stock of Western knowledge developed by engineers and economists continued to provide the terms of reference for defining the problems to be solved, and increasingly so for third world elites. The "destination of development," as Sutcliffe (1995) describes it, was still imagined by Southern elites as the unsustainable vision of developed or industrialized countries, whether East or West. Bruce Rich, in his book *Mortgaging the Earth,* describes many examples of a philosophy of natural and social engineering in which large-scale industrial/

technological infrastructure projects dominated (1994:25–47). He writes that these projects, which incurred large-scale environmental and human costs, viewed nature as the "physical playing fields for economic development . . . a world of a ceaseless quest for more intensive economic use of the earth's space and time, a world conceived as an abstract expanse which through the correct method can be controlled and manipulated" (Rich 1994:47). Although development institutions began to change their approaches by the end of the 1980s, a development philosophy based on management persisted for a surprisingly long time.

Globalization/Internationalization of the Political Problem

The globalization of environmental views during this period reflected the shifting balance between the various expressions of developmentalism and environmentalism. The major steps in this process included the 1968 Biosphere Conference, the Stockholm Conference and its preparatory meetings, the World Conservation Strategy (WCS), Reaganite hyperliberalism, and the Brundtland Report.

In September 1968, UNESCO sponsored the Intergovernmental Conference of Experts on a Scientific Basis for a Rational Use and Conservation of the Resources of the Biosphere. The Biosphere Conference marked the reemergence of a naturalist (in the tradition of scientific/ecological preservationism) approach to the environment. The conference reflected renewed activism within the scientific community, adopting twenty recommendations for future action on the part of governments and international institutions, particularly UNESCO (Caldwell 1996:54).

Planning for the Stockholm Conference took up where the recommendations of the Biosphere Conference had left off, articulating the need to address these political and social problems. In response, development-interested Southern countries and Northern nongovernmental organizations (NGOs) formed alliances to counter environmental alarmists who advocated a no growth philosophy. This tended to blunt the destabilizing implications of environmental critiques that argued that the post–World War II project of global development needed radical restructuring (McCormick 1989:92; Sachs 1993).

The official deliberations at Stockholm in fact only reinforced the agreement that had been articulated at two preparatory meetings held during 1971: the Panel of Experts on Development and

Environment (Founex, Switzerland, 4–12 June) and the Scientific Committee on Problems of the Environment/UN Conference on the Human Environment (SCOPE/UNCHE) working party on environmental problems in less developed countries (Canberra, Australia, 24 August–3 September) (McCormick 1989:92). This agreement stressed that "the kind of environmental problems that are of importance in developing countries are those than can be overcome by the process of development itself" (United Nations 1972:par. 4–5).

The suspicion and skepticism with which the Stockholm process was greeted by the more preservationist institutions such as the IUCN also suggested that the basis of the Stockholm consensus integrating environment into development was not entirely complete. Despite the enthusiastic claims that environmental issues had broken through, the IUCN criticized Stockholm for not paying enough attention to "the theme of wilderness and the need to maintain and enhance diversity" (McCormick 1989:98).[9]

By 1980, the IUCN began its own initiative, the World Conservation Strategy, to bring together the large multilateral banks, the UN Development Programme, the UN Environment Programme, and the Organization of American States. The WCS argued that three priorities should be included in development programs: "maintenance of ecological processes, the sustainable use of resources, and the maintenance of genetic diversity" (Pickering and Owen 1994:301). While offering badly needed suggestions for reforming existing development philosophies, the WCS displaced issues of pollution prevalent at Stockholm. The main objective of the WCS was "to ensure the sustainable use of species and ecosystems" (Sanger 1993:156). Substantively, then, it represented a renewed conservation program under the banner of development. The WCS contributed to the synthesis evidenced in the Brundtland Commission Report of 1987, which became the preferred vehicle for the institutionalization of sustainable development.

The chair of the United Nations Commission on Environment and Development, Gro Harlem Brundtland, had expressed publicly her conviction that free market principles were inappropriate and prejudicial to effective environmental management in the South (Redclift 1987:13). In this way, the impetus for the commission was a reaction to Reaganite and Thatcherite hyperliberalism. The synthesis of environment and development was achieved by identifying the primary problems as poverty, population, and scarcity—problems optimistically understood as manageable through higher levels of global cooperation.

Sustainable development seemingly resolved many of the key differences between developmentalism and environmentalism through the modification and extension of the time horizons of development,[10] clearly an important step. However, the concept of sustainability ultimately suffered from its status as a modifier of development (Dalby 1992:121).

Resolution of the Conflict: Institutionalization of Sustainable Development

The sustainable development consensus claimed to ensure the sustainability of the global economy without the need to recognize the limits to growth. Development was no longer automatically considered a feature of economic growth; yet, the focus on distribution of benefits and absorption of costs left the fundamental problematic of development intact (Escobar 1995:5).

Domestically, Northern states could address environmentalism by introducing environmental and pollution control legislation, as was done in the United States, Japan, and Western Europe (Brenton 1994:30). The regulatory approach offered a means of incorporating environmentalist critiques while externalizing the costs of adjustment through freer trade and investment regimes. This approach was less tenable in the South, however, where vulnerability to global economic changes meant such efforts would jeopardize development strategies.

Managing conflicts meant narrowing environmental issues. Important to this was the pessimistic Malthusian premonition of global disaster, famine, and conflict, given a high-technology gloss through the newly developed science of computer modeling (Meadows et al. 1972; Council on Environmental Quality 1980). The Club of Rome, for instance, concluded its analysis of the relationship between food, nonrenewable resources, and pollution absorption with the warning words, "The short doubling times of many of man's activities, combined with the immense quantities being doubled, will bring us close to the limits to growth of those activities surprisingly soon" (Meadows et al. 1972:97).

These apocalyptic visions of disaster were explicitly rejected in the official deliberations at Stockholm and were implicitly rejected by the Brundtland Commission and other conservationists in the 1980s. Paradoxically, the findings of Brundtland ultimately rested on the dire warnings of the doomsayers by reinserting these themes with an antipoverty twist. The Brundtland Commission stated forcefully that "the Earth is one but the world is not" (WCED 1987:27), suggesting that humanity's political and social divisions were the primary problem, rather than the increasingly integrative forces of centralized economic development. Where *Limits to Growth* warned of the environmental dangers of boundless economic growth, the commission sounded a very different warning about the threats of "recession, austerity, and falling living standards" (WCED 1987:70), particularly in the debt-ridden developing countries of Africa and Latin America. Economic *successes*, on the other hand, were clearly linked with the potential for "greater attention to the long-term questions of environmental management and appropriate technology" (WCED 1987:71). Thus, the case for social welfare and ecological sustainability again rested ultimately on development.

As a result, the global environmental problem was more often posed in terms of order rather than ecological balance or social justice. As Chatterjee and Finger (1994:14) argue with respect to the Brundtland Report, "The environment was actually more of a rallying point to foster cooperation among nation-states than the real common challenge." However, this order was not that of the elite managerialists of earlier years, but rather an organic, integrative order of "coordinated and collective efforts" at many different levels (Dryzek 1997:125). This integrative impulse and a managerialist shadow cast by development theory made the commission's concept of sustainable development both universalized (see Chatterjee and Finger 1994:27) and vulnerable. It easily could be used to justify orthodox rather than innovative applications (for example, regulatory initiatives, market-based solutions, and end-of-pipe environmental cleanup (see Chapters 3, 8, and 9).[11] Michael Redclift (1987:2) argues, in addition, that "the constant reference to 'sustainability' as a desirable objective . . . obscure[d] the contradictions that 'development' implies for the environment."

Interestingly, any calls for greater equity and justice in the Brundtland Report tended to fall away in later debates, as ultimately did sustainability itself. Brundtland's successor, UNCED, "did not start by asking questions about equity" (Kirkby et al. 1995:8). Furthermore, the weaknesses of the sustainable development paradigm for dealing with environmental problems were apparent from the very beginning. The Reagan administration was hostile to further efforts at global macromanagement projects that contained any hints of redistribution. The critics of the disaster scenarios further refined and restated their views that human ingenuity and technological innovation would likely lead to solutions for environmental problems before natural limits to growth were reached (Simon and Kahn 1984; Lewis 1992). With respect to questions of redistribution, these critics argued that, in fact, gaps between rich and poor were not likely to widen, and that the world's people had "increasingly higher incomes, better housing, mobility, better roads, and more vehicles" (McCormick 1989:174).

Political ecologists, on the other hand, viewed sustainability as participatory rather than managerial (de Campos Mello in Chapter 7; Sachs 1993; Shiva 1993). According to this perspective, sustainability was not understood in terms of the resource base but in terms of society, culture, and people in sustainable communities (Chatterjee and Finger 1994:168). As Chatterjee and Finger (1994:67–73) argue, there has been a transformation of ecology into global environmental management accompanied by the fading away of the political ecologists in the North. This is in contrast to the more promising emergence of "third generation NGOs" (for example, the Third World Network) in the South (Chatterjee and Finger 1994:73–78). Globally, however, it is clear that structurally oriented ecological critiques of the development model that imply the necessity of both ecological balance and social justice have not found an institutional vehicle comparable even to the admittedly flawed new international economic order (NIEO) movement.

Ecological challenges to the mainstream can, however, be found at peripheral levels and locations in the global political economy, from European green parties to Southern NGOs and protest movements. One example is the effort by NGOs to hold parallel consultations (as was done at Stockholm and Rio) and draft treaty proposals that embody alternative programs of action (as at Rio). At the latter conference, these efforts featured issues given scant attention in the official deliberations: trade, debt reduction, and consumption patterns in the North (Sanger 1993:166).

The achievements of Stockholm and Brundtland in heightening awareness and creating urgency for global action should not be dismissed. These successes were not inevitable but rather were the outcomes of hard-fought struggles. The concept of sustainable development as outlined by the Brundtland Commission Report thus represents a compromise on the most urgent and divisive questions of growth, development, equity, and ecology. Institutional changes, environmental agreements, and regulatory actions have, consequently, proceeded to grow in quantity but not necessarily in quality. Sustainable development could be *assumed* in these deliberations, in ways that facilitated the marginalization of political ecological critiques. As John Dryzek (1997:46) states, "It is at the discursive level that dilemmas are dissolved by sustainable development, not at the level of policies and accomplishments."

Conclusion

This chapter has explored processes of global environmental problem posing from the era of conservation to the development debates of the 1970s and 1980s. As stated in the introduction, analyzing the ways in which problems are posed contributes to understanding the specific ways in which dominant environmental paradigms have been legitimated and disseminated through global institutions while competing views have been coopted or marginalized.

This analysis has several implications for global environmental politics. One is that solving environmental problems can be easily reduced to the problem of managing resource scarcity. This can be seen most clearly in the case of conservationist management. However, there are echoes of this orientation in the developmentalist discourses of the 1970s and 1980s as well. The construction of this social purpose favors forms of knowledge that are quantitative, objective, differentiated, and directional, as opposed to experiential, qualitative, holistic, or historical. This resource orientation reinforces the idea that nature is manageable. The paradigms and discourses of scientific and political ecology (as opposed to technology) and those of social ethics and justice consequently are delegitimized.

Another implication is that environmental issues, while new items on the global agenda, can easily become routine problems for conventional international relations (Pirages 1978:263). Politically, this means that environmentalism becomes vulnerable to displacement by other issues and approaches as powerful actors narrow the available choices or selectively apply concepts such as sustainable development. Like peace, sustainability is a fragile priority, and when conditions dictate, the urgency of environmental action can be denied or diminished as public interest declines.

Finally, a third focus of this chapter has been that environmental paradigms have supported or subverted historical configurations of order and power. This account begins with the idea that global environmental order is constituted through historical and political struggle rather than through a progressive and smooth evolution and integration around growing environmental consciousness. In other words, "these matters are subject to continuing dispute between people who think about environmental affairs in sharply different ways" (Dryzek 1997:5). Thus, the transformative potential of environmental politics has existed across different time periods, even if it has yet to be realized.

In addition, debates over problem posing have tended to focus on the potential of environmental issues to disrupt prevailing configurations of order and power. Arguably, the purposes and processes of innovative social learning, which involves not just accommodation but full exploration of differences in environmental ideas, can be supplanted by a project of conditioning and containment. Political institutions that reflect this project are likely either to be marginalized as struggles continue in more relevant (perhaps local) sites or supplanted by purposes more explicitly directed to social control and enforcement.

Ronnie Lipschutz and Ken Conca (1993b:7) argue that "if global environmental change has consequences on a more fundamental level—if it calls into question not just the distribution of power but also the meaning of power, the legitimacy of rules, and the nature of authority," then moving multilateral institutions toward more ecologically sustainable paradigms ultimately involves asking questions that are subversive of modern industrial forms of states and markets (Dalby 1992). Qualitatively, this suggests either reinvesting environmental paradigms and concepts with new meaning or searching for more innovative and inclusive paradigms.

Notes

1. Institutions are defined by Oran Young as "arrangements designed to resolve social conflicts, promote sustained cooperation in mixed-motive

relationships, and more generally, alleviate collective-action problems in a world of interdependent actors" (Young 1997:4).

2. The latter was spearheaded in early years by two major bureaucracies: the Reclamation Service (later Bureau of Reclamation) and the Forest Service (for more, see Gottlieb 1993:22).

3. It was not inevitable that the TVA would reflect an engineering or management orientation; this was a result of the "intense interest of Senator George W. Norris in electric hydro power and in public power policy generally" (Wengert 1972:39).

4. The TVA exemplified notions of environmental management that held considerable cultural power and appeal by virtue of its identification with development, progress, and the aesthetics of efficiency, sophisticated and coordinated management through rationalized methods, and technological accomplishment.

5. For more on the Canadian debates, see Woodrow (1980:28–29).

6. The 28 March 1947 Resolution 32(IV) of the Economic and Social Council convened the UNSCCUR "for the purpose of exchanging information on techniques in this field, their economic costs and benefits, and their inter-relations." The UNSCCUR "Conference [would] be devoted solely to the exchange of ideas and experience on these matters among engineers, resource technicians, economists and other experts" (United Nations 1956:ix). As a scientific and educational exchange, however, this conference came under the primary sponsorship of UNESCO.

7. One may also add here the intensification of production, consumption, and exchange processes over time through technology.

8. For more on development theory, see the review of the literature by W. Adams (1990:66–86).

9. While these environmental critiques would have grown in power as the Cold War ground to a halt and the world moved toward UNCED, their association with the rear-guard actions of preservationism also blunted their potential to radically critique development.

10. Sustainable development is that which "meets the needs of the present without compromising the ability of future generations to meet their own needs" (WCED 1987:8).

11. Having said this, Brundtland should be distinguished from the conservationist and developmentalist management prevalent in the United States during most of the post–World War II era, as well as acknowledged as a progressive concept in an age of hyperliberalism that permeated the United States and the United Kingdom and, increasingly, the erstwhile leaders of the NIEO.

Marc Williams 3

In Search of Global Standards: The Political Economy of Trade and the Environment

The latent conflict between trade liberalization and the environment erupted in the 1990s as the result of two events. The U.S. decision to enter into negotiations with Canada and Mexico on a free trade pact in late 1990 generated intense opposition from many U.S. environmental groups. A subsequent ruling by a General Agreement on Tariffs and Trade (GATT) dispute panel in 1991 on the tuna-dolphin dispute between the United States and Mexico that upheld Mexican sovereignty and thereby rejected the extraterritorial expansion of U.S. law appeared to many environmentalists to be fundamentally flawed. The ensuing conflict between advocates of trade liberalization and environmentalists led to a policy process that sought to reconcile competing interests in the trade-environment debate. Through an examination of this debate in the World Trade Organization (WTO), this chapter explores the construction of the trade and environment relationship and the search for new global standards. Avoiding the state-centric and unreflective approach of orthodox international political economy, I argue that the formation of global standards is better understood through attention to the discursive field of knowledge construction, material change in the global economy, the institutional venue for negotiation, and the array of actors involved.

The first part of this argument posits that the relationship between trade and the environment is the result of a specific discursive process that privileges environmental economics at the expense of ecological and social approaches to sustainable development. The second part assesses the implications of the globalization project and the WTO as a system of global governance for the consolidation of liberal environmentalism. This is followed by an examination of the uneven influences of firms and nongovernmental organizations (NGOs) on the introduction of environmental concerns into the WTO, and the subsequent evolution of the debate. The conclusion reflects on the debate on trade and the environment and the search for regulatory mechanisms by various actors.

The basic premise of this chapter is that it is inadequate to begin a study of policy with the already given preferences of the actors. Rather, such a study should recognize the mutually constitutive interaction of agents and material and ideational structures. Thus, I show how the positions of two key sets of actors, firms, and NGOs are shaped by material change in the global economy, the decisionmaking forum of the WTO, and the language, norms, and values implicit in dominant conceptions of sustainability. For reasons of space, less attention is given to transformations in the global economy in shaping the terms of engagement.

Constructing Trade and the Environment

The trade-environment debate has been constructed at the confluence of two previously separate discourses: neoclassical economics and sustainable development. The final result denuded sustainable development discourse of its political and social dimensions, allowing the emergence of weak environmental sustainability and environmental management as dominant principles in the international political economy of the environment.

The Language of Economics: The Dominance of Neoclassical Economics

The dominance of neoclassical economics reproduces a set of core values and preserves certain interests. Proponents of free trade assume that in the absence of politically inspired and state-imposed barriers, trade functions freely and to the common good. The theory of comparative advantage and its modern variant, the Hecksher-Ohlin-Samuelson model of factor endowments, urge countries to specialize based on differences in production costs and then to engage in trade. From this perspective, free trade is beneficial to all participants. That this construction of free trade is itself a historically specific normative proposition is rarely acknowledged.

Neoclassical economics assumes and reproduces the separation of society and nature. Within this paradigm, the economic system is the space wherein individuals interact to satisfy human needs and wants through the rational use of resources (for a critique see Daly and Cobb 1990). The model also assumes that efficiency, rational exploitation of resources, productivity gains, economies of scale, and other goals can be satisfied without reference to environmental degradation.

Not unexpectedly, the eruption of environmental issues onto the multilateral trade agenda caught trade theorists and policymakers by surprise. One response of the trade community was to conceptualize the issue in a manner familiar to trade theory—that is, it was immediately couched in terms of the ongoing debate between free trade and protectionism. While these strategies sought to weaken and delegitimate environmental concerns, a second response sought to incorporate the environment within the parameters of liberal economics.

From this view, the problem is not increased trade but the exclusion of the environment from economic analysis. The solution to trade-environment problems, therefore, is not to tamper with the trading system but rather to assign economic value to the environment. Proponents argue that unless the environment is internalized through cost-benefit analysis, it will be taken for granted and its value ignored, leading to its depletion. On the other hand, adopting an economic approach allows the use of a powerful array of economic techniques that can be used to protect the environment (Turner et al. 1994:vii). It is assumed that once natural resources are subject to the laws of the market they will be used efficiently and in a sustainable manner. Thus, environmental economics, which engages in the valuation of the environment, is an extension, not a critique, of neoclassical economics (Williams 1996:56).

There are, of course, differences among variants of environmental economics (Jacobs 1995). But recent intellectual and political developments have given greater weight to neoclassical analysis. The eruption of environmental issues onto the trade agenda occurred simultaneously with the end of socialism and the triumph of neoliberal capitalism. In this context, advocates of environmental protection have been swimming against the tide of increasing liberalization. The intellectual choices open to policymakers have been constricted as liberalization, deregulation, and increased competition have been presented as the correct responses to structural changes in the global economy.

Sustainable Development

The conventional interpretation of sustainable development derives from the Brundtland Commission and from attempts to integrate multiple dimensions of development and sustainability within its analysis. The economic concept of discounting is given a key role, but the debate about sustainability also covers noneconomic factors. The emphasis is on sustainable development for essential human needs rather than on the trade-offs between economic and biological systems. The Brundtland Commission's definition of sustainable development as "development that meets the needs of the present without compromising the ability of future generations to meet their own needs" (WCED 1987:3) has become the focal point from which other contestations flow. This definition recognizes that effective transition to sustainable development is a political process with wide-ranging social and political changes. Nevertheless, the report remained within the language of consensus sufficiently to be accepted in principle by many governments.

Increasingly, however, the discourse of sustainable development has been colonized by environmental economics. As a result, sustainable development has been transformed from a sociopolitical into a principally economic concept. It thus becomes incorporated into environmental management.

A number of writers distinguish between advocates of strong sustainability and proponents of weak sustainability (for example, Dobson 1990; Pepper 1996). Strong sustainability approaches reject the dominant discourse of modernization and are opposed to increases in economic growth. Such theories adopt an ecological perspective.[1] The current fashion for sustainable development is based on theories of weak sustainability. Here it is assumed that the current development trajectory can be maintained in an environmentally safe manner through relatively minor modifications. These models favor market-based approaches, private ownership of natural resources, and technical solutions to environmental problems. Weak sustainability theorists assume that far from being incompatible with environmental protection, economic growth is a precondition for the achievement of sustainable development. A decoupling of growth and adverse environmental impacts is possible in this view. The key concept of weak sustainability is substitutability. There is no need to distinguish between physical and natural capital; sustainability is simply achieved by the transfer of an "aggregate capital stock" at least equal to that currently existing—for example, more forests can be offset by fewer roads and vice versa, as long as they have the same or higher value (Turner et al. 1994:56). Thus, the orthodox approach to sustainable development endorses environmental management as a key strategy toward weak sustainable development.

Two consequences follow from this neutralization of sustainable development. First, instead of posing a threat to dominant political and economic interests, the merger of environmental concerns and economic growth ensures that existent economic and political structures can be preserved with minor modifications. Second, this approach has constrained efforts to develop an alternative paradigm partly by its incorporating the goals of environmentalists and developmentalists and partly by adjusting the language of the environmental and developmental movements to other purposes.[2] This has further contributed to the weakening of the environmental movement, exacerbating divisions between moderate, reformist, and radical environmentalists. The sharpening of these divisions, in turn, facilitates the formation of alliances around the principles of environmental economics and environmental management that include state agencies, corporate groups, and environmentalists.

In Search of Global Standards

The international policy process moved one step further toward integrating environmental issues into the world trading system with the creation of the WTO's Committee on Trade and the Environment (CTE). Although it was created against much opposition and given a restricted mandate, it nevertheless heralded a shift in the controversy over trade and the environment. While not a central concern of governments and industries, the debate moved from rhetoric to a policy arena where norms and guidelines for action could possibly be negotiated.

Globalization and the World Trading System

The conflict between trade and the environment surfaced at a moment of profound change in the global political economy. Globalization is an uneven process whereby essential elements of social organization and control have been gradually, and at a generally accelerating pace, displaced from conventionally understood spaces. Social relations, formerly conducted in local, national, and international arenas, now inhabit an additional "global" space. Globalization exhibits a number of key features. Among these are the changing role of the state, the increased mobility and velocity of capital, the deregulation of the economy, and the absence of social protection.

Two prominent issues on the trade and environment agenda were growth in world trade and reform of the world trading system. The massive expansion of trade across frontiers, greatly exceeding the growth of world output, has been a powerful globalizing force in the world economy. Trade liberalization in the postwar era was uneven and limited largely to the successful reduction of tariffs on manufactured goods. The rise of the new protectionism in the 1970s and the weakness of the GATT dispute settlement mechanism, combined with the extension of the multilateral trade regime to include services, intellectual property rights, and investment, heralded a new phase in the global regulation of trade. In this changing environment, the Tokyo Round began the process of extending traditional trade negotiations to include trade agreements on standards. The Uruguay Round further extended the scope of global governance. For environmentalists, this expanded agenda is virtually synonymous with the loss of national control over environmental policy. It was during the Uruguay Round negotiations that ushered in the WTO, an organization with an expanded scope and domain, that the debate on trade and environment developed, redefining the trading relationship between national governments. Insofar as globalization is driven by the interests of transnational corporations (TNCs) that will benefit from increased deregulation and the liberalization of international standards prohibiting the use of national instruments, the outcome of the Uruguay Round could easily be seen as detrimental to the environment. Ever since, the increased scope, permanence, and rule-making authority of the WTO have alarmed those who fear that environmental decisions gradually and irretrievably have been displaced from the national realm, where environmentalists can exercise some influence, to a supranational organization shrouded in secrecy.

David Levy and Daniel Egan (1998:338) distinguish between enabling and regulatory institutions, with the former providing a framework for a neoliberal world order and the latter a forum for the negotiation of specific policies (see also Chapter 4). Applying this distinction to the WTO provides an insight into contestations over the future of the organization itself. In these terms, the WTO is primarily an enabling institution. However, the incursion of some so-called new issues, such as labor and environmental standards, provides an opportunity for constructing the agenda in regulatory terms.

The Relevance of Institutional Venue

The WTO, of course, cannot be understood solely as part of the evolving structures of globalization and global governance. It also has to be examined within its own highly specific terms of reference. From the perspective of critical analysis, the WTO serves to organize and legitimate particular concatenations of trade and the environment. On the one hand, its formal rules directly limit the impact of environmentalist and other societal forces while privileging trade liberalization over social regulation; on the other hand, its operational secrecy allows some stakeholders greater access than others.

The sole formal agents in the negotiation and operation of the WTO are the member states. States and their governments, however, are not monolithic organizations. Trade policy is the subject of bargaining and debate among domestic groups representing multiple interests—for example, importers, exporters, and consumers. Thus, even though trade negotiations involve the interests of a wide range of actors, policy formulation in multilateral trade negotiations is formally restricted to government delegations. But the culture of secrecy that permeates international negotiations on trade policy effectively excludes some actors and grants privileged access to others. Within this context, industry groups and their representatives occupy an important place, not only because of their structural power but also instrumentally, through their contacts with political leaders and their inclusion in national trade policy delegations. For example, the issue of intellectual property rights was placed on the agenda of the

Uruguay Round largely through intensive lobbying by those TNCs that stood to benefit most from a more liberal regime (Watkins 1992:91–92). Furthermore, agreements in the Uruguay Round concerning trade in services and agriculture were heavily influenced by transnational commercial interests.

The limited access or exclusion of environmental and other social movement organizations from international trade negotiations and the WTO restricts their ability to shape its principles and affect its operations. The earlier closure of the WTO process to noncorporate actors has been tempered, but the venue still privileges those who possess structural power, granting them superior instrumental access. While the WTO has progressively expanded access to nongovernmental organizations, the fact that the organization includes business groups in the NGO category reinforces the influence of the corporate sector in the policy process.[3]

The new institutional arrangement is central to the framing of connections between trade, sustainable development, and environmental protection. The current dominance of weak sustainable development is written into the WTO's constitution. The preamble to the 1994 agreement establishing the WTO commits member states to raising standards of living and expanding production and trade in accordance with the objective of sustainable development, seeking both to protect and preserve the environment.[4]

The implementation of this commitment depends on the integration of environmental considerations into the workings of the WTO. The key site for environmental issues is the CTE, established at Marrakesh as part of the WTO to "identify the relationship between trade measures and environmental measures in order to promote sustainable development" and to "make appropriate recommendations on whether any modifications of the provisions of the multilateral trading system are required."[5] Initially, the CTE adopted a ten-point agenda of issues linking trade and the environment and was given a two-year mandate. Although directed to explore whether modifications to the multilateral trading system were required, the CTE in fact restricted its recommendations to a number of technical issues relating to the impact of environmental policies on trade, such as the creation of databases relating to trade-environment measures. Subsequent to the December 1996 Singapore Ministerial Conference, the CTE's work program has been based on a thematic or issue-cluster approach. Two clusters were identified: market access and linkages between the multilateral environmental and trade agendas. Meeting three times a year, the CTE has made little progress since the Singapore Ministerial Conference.

At the same time, environmental issues have arisen in other contexts within the WTO, notably through the work of its dispute settlement procedures. The case with the farthest-reaching implications to date is the so-called shrimp/turtle case. This dispute arose from a challenge by India, Malaysia, Pakistan, and Thailand against a U.S. measure prohibiting the importing of shrimp from countries that do not require the use of turtle-exclusion devices on shrimp fishing nets in areas where sea turtles are found. The Dispute Panel decision, upheld by the Appellate Body, found that the U.S. measure could not be justified under the environmental exceptions to Article XX of GATT. But the Appellate Body also declared that the use of environmental exceptions in GATT was important, saying that they have to be interpreted in the light of current conceptions of sustainable development, thus opening the way for higher priority to be given to environmental protection in the trading system.[6] Moreover, the Appellate Body also opened the door to NGOs, allowing them to submit briefs to panels and appellate bodies. The implications of the ruling are still unclear but appear to give greater salience to environmental considerations, opening a new avenue of access to the WTO for business and environmental NGOs (ENGOs). On balance, however, the record of the WTO to date shows that it has marginalized environmental regulation both at the level of its constitutional principles and its actual operation.

So far, I have outlined the dominant discourse and the institutional parameters within which the trade-environment nexus is developing. Next, I examine how business and environmentalists have conceived of their interests and sought to affect these parameters. The engagement of corporate interests and environmentalists in the context of the WTO is, as I have argued in the previous two sections, shaped by the dominance of environmental economics. This ensures that access to key decisionmakers is based on sharing the same analytical framework (or at least being in possession of the same tools and ready to speak the same language). At the same time, advocates of regulatory approaches are less likely to prevail given the commitment of the WTO to maintaining an open trading system.

Constructing Actors' Interests:
Nonstate Actors and the Trade and Environment Debates

Undeniably the state remains a crucial actor in the formation of international environmental and trade regimes. States, after all, officially negotiate and ratify multilateral treaties. States still formally control territorial space and make and enforce national laws. This formalistic picture, however, conceals profound changes in world politics and the nonunitary nature of states. Such perspectives allow little scope for the impact of structural conditions on policymaking and for the autonomous role played by social forces in world politics.

Quite clearly, globalization disrupts traditional conceptions of the state (Levy and Egan 1998:337–342). The issue is not simply one of the erosion of sovereignty versus the continued relevance of the state; it is rather more complex, especially concerning the conditions under which authority patterns are created and maintained. The state plays a central role in international relations in a number of ways and for varied reasons, and major states retain the capacity to initiate international norms and agreements. State behavior, however, varies in different institutional contexts, requiring that the focus on states be supplemented not only by attention to the role of nonstate actors but also by increased focus on the derivation of state interests.

In the trade-environment debate, states are positioned in ways that have crucial consequences. In the first place, states maintain— through trade, finance, environmental, and other ministries—the ability to create legislation. States thereby become arenas for contestation between business, social movement groups, and state agencies concerning standard setting on trade and environment. One strategic response to the environmental critique is what can be termed the greening of government, involving an array of environmental policies and institutions. It is arguable to what extent these policies and institutions have reduced environmental degradation. What is indisputable, however, is that there has been a shift in priorities and actions (rhetorical or not). Accompanying these largely domestic interventions is an internationalization of state activities relating to the environment. This is a reciprocal process. It involves the partial transfer of policymaking from the domestic to the international levels, which, in turn, reshapes domestic policy and internationalizes the environment. Central to both strategies is the recognition of the role that intergovernmental organizations (IGOs) can play in this process. The Organization for Economic Cooperation and Development (OECD), for instance, has played a critical role in defining the trade-environment agenda for the industrialized countries through reports and meetings (see, for example, OECD 1993a, 1993b). Furthermore, states have exhibited a willingness to engage with a vast array of nonstate actors—including national and transnational firms, coalitions of business groups, environmental NGOs, agricultural associations, trade unions, and consumer associations—in the search for solutions to environmental problems.

Such entities, in this case business and ENGOs, are not simply pressure groups acting within the domestic constituencies of states. They are political actors in their own right able to supplement, replace, bypass, and sometimes supplant traditional interstate politics. NGOs, TNCs, and their networks are likely to perform an increasingly important role in concert with the state, sometimes in competition and sometimes as an alternative organizing principle for world politics based on new constitutive rules and institutional forms (Conca 1993). Nonstate actors are crucial catalysts for state action in global environmental politics. Through the mobilization of opinion, the development of new international norms, and the scrutiny of state practices, these actors exert significant influence on the construction of the interests of states. It is not, however, the case that nonstate actors enjoy equal influence within or on the neoliberal state and interstate institutions. The structural power of capital, linked to dominant modes of thought, privileges private firms and those individuals and groups sharing the dominant frameworks of knowledge.

In an era when deregulation, liberalization, and privatization are central goals of public authorities, policies that promote these goals, such as the Multilateral Agreement of Investment (MAI),[7] are favored over social regulation. In addition, in this context of shifting public-private demarcations, the pressure to privatize international regulation is growing (see Cutler 1995; Clapp 1998).

Business and the Environment

From a business perspective, the key to ameliorating environmental ills or halting, if not reversing, degradation rests with the business community. While various sectors and elites may differ in their responses, most agree that although acute environmental problems are a product of industrial processes, the continuation of the industrial capitalist system is also the best solution to these problems.

Historically, business has viewed the environment as a source of resources and as a depository for wastes. Until the 1950s, the environment was not really seen as an issue. Early suggestions that this was not the case, such as Rachel Carson's *Silent Spring* (1962), were met with vehement denials before their claims were accepted (Murphy and Bendell 1997:15). As environmental concerns grew through the 1970s and 1980s, business reactions continued to be hostile. Research revealing negative environmental impacts, such as acid rain, was claimed to be unreliable and largely ignored. By the early 1990s, however, an environmental trend had surfaced within business, articulated around environmental economics and legitimated by the increasing involvement of certain business groups with domestic and international environmental politics and with ENGOs.[8]

Four factors caused the advent of this new era of business environmentalism: a public concern with environmental issues, the growth of green consumerism, the diffusion of ecological values, and the intensification of state regulation of environmental matters (McGrew 1991:17). It is within this context that some business leaders recognized the inevitability of coordinated international responses and the need for positive business strategies.

The practical manifestations of corporate environmentalism could be seen, for example, in the effective lobbying by industry groups during negotiations for the Montreal Protocol on the Ozone Layer and at the United Nations Conference on Environment and Development (UNCED) (see Benedick 1991; Rowlands 1992). Corporate influence in UNCED decisively shaped the outcome of the negotiations, most notably with regard to ensuring that no regulatory standards were imposed on business. Ever since, business coalitions express their awareness of environmental concerns, assert their willingness to be involved in environmental monitoring and protection, and stress the positive role that business can play for the environment. In the post-UNCED period, the business community has devised a number of strategies to further its trade and environment agenda. These strategies may be divided into two categories: those that seek to shape and influence state and interstate policies and institutions, and those that involve private arrangements with or without ENGOs.

From the outset, corporations perceived the WTO as a key instrument in the system of global governance. One prominent business view of the WTO was expressed by Stephan Schmidheiny of the World Business Council for Sustainable Development (WBCSD). In a 1995 speech, he declared, "I would . . . urge business people and organizations to engage in the development of the WTO, helping to keep it sane, sensible and businesslike" (Schmidheiny 1995:1). As a result, corporations have sought to influence the WTO—indirectly at the national level and directly through delegations to the WTO and access to its secretariat in Geneva. Business coalitions have consistently expressed support for the WTO's liberal agenda. In the context of the trade and environment debate, for example, the International Federation of Agricultural Producers (IFAP) and the International Council on Metals and the Environment (ICME) have responded positively to its free market agenda (IFAP 1996; ICME 1996). In preparation for the Singapore Ministerial Conference, an ICME spokesperson warned of the potential for conflict between the WTO and environmental legislation (Smith 1996:4), and the IFAP noted the need for trade and environment policies to be integrated (IFAP 1996:20) to protect the liberal trading order.

The central business message articulated by individual corporations and influential umbrella organizations such as the International Chamber of Commerce (ICC) and WBCSD is that there is no inherent conflict between trade and the environment (ICC 1996:1). Indeed, trade and environment are seen as in harmony rather than in conflict: an open, vigorous, and healthy trading system is not incompatible with the objectives of sustainable development (WBCSD 1998:1), but "sound environmental policies can contribute to avoiding trade frictions" (ICC 1996:2). The WBCSD, the premier umbrella organization for the corporate sector on sustainable development, champions greater engagement by firms with national and international policymaking processes. It argues that an open trading system improves efficiency and therefore sustainability. From this perspective, increased trade creates wealth, thereby ensuring technological (and sustainable) change. Moreover, the diffusion of appropriate technology is advanced through open markets (WBCSD 1998:3). In turn, economic growth can be used to develop improved technological solutions to environmental degradation.[9]

Corporate access to the WTO is enhanced by the organization's approach to civil society. The WTO uses an inclusive classification of NGOs that makes no distinction between the nonprofit sector and business groups. It includes consumer groups, development and environmental NGOs, industry groups, and trade unions in the same category. Private sector groups support demands for greater participation by nonstate actors in the WTO and have been active participants in meetings open to nonstate actors. The U.S. government, under pressure from private sector interests and environmental and development NGOs, has been instrumental in opening the WTO. The U.S. position is evident, for example, in President Bill Clinton's optimistic assertion at the Geneva Ministerial Conference that the WTO provides the first forum where business, labor, environmental, and consumer groups can speak out and help guide the further evolution of the organization and the international trade regime (*Bridges Weekly Trade Digest* 1998).

Business organizations have been well represented at the three Ministerial Conferences (Singapore, Geneva, and Seattle) held to date. Indeed, business representation outstrips that of environmental NGOs. The first Ministerial Conference, in Singapore in 1996, attracted 108 NGOs, forty-eight from the business world; of the 128 NGOs represented at the second Ministerial Conference, in Geneva in 1998, forty-six were business groups. In contrast, only eight environmental NGOs were present in Singapore, and twenty-two attended the second Ministerial Conference.[10] Corporate interests have been represented by national and international sectoral interest (e.g., agriculture, mining, manufacturing) and general interest (e.g., chambers of commerce) umbrella organizations. The pattern of attendance shifted at the Seattle Ministerial Conference in 1999. The number of NGOs attending exploded to a staggering 737. This rise in NGO attendance is partly explained by the venue, attracting large numbers of U.S. and Canadian NGOs, and partly by the fact that a new round of trade talks were scheduled to be launched at Seattle. Once again ENGOs were less well represented than the corporate sector. However, no meaningful comparison of their respective strengths can be made given the diversity of NGO representation in Seattle. Business organizations have also been well represented at the trade and environment symposia convened by the WTO in 1997, 1998, and 1999.

The WBCSD and the ICC are in the forefront of the corporate approach to the WTO. Both organizations recognize the WTO as an important site for the trade and environment debate. The slow progress of reform in the WTO has disappointed both organizations. But while the ICC has expressed concern, it remains supportive of the work of the CTE (ICC 1998:5). The WBCSD recently suggested that changing international trade law may be too cumbersome a process for corporations seeking to enhance competitive advantage (WBCSD 1998:21) It argues that efforts may be better focused on developing ecolabeling, implementing the International Organization for Standardization (ISO) 14000 series of standards, and supporting multilateral environmental agreements. The difference between the two organizations does not represent fundamental disagreement. Whereas the ICC's perspective emphasizes a way out of the impasse, the WBCSD, in this instance, emphasizes seizing the opportunity to preempt future environmental legislation.

Three issues—the use of trade restrictions in multilateral environmental agreements (MEAs), the salience of process and production methods (PPMs), and ecolabeling—command attention from business groups. From the corporate perspective, MEAs are a preferred method for addressing environmental issues of international interest because they maximize consensus and prevent states from taking unilateral action.[11] Trade-related environmental measures (TREMs) may regulate trade that is directly harmful to the environment or generate "carrots" and "sticks" to influence other states to change their behavior toward the environment (Ewing and Tarasofsky 1996:6). Such restrictions contravene the basic principles of the multilateral trading system and are allowed only if they can be justified as general exceptions to the rules. Thus, the private sector is keen to limit the use of trade policy measures in enforcing MEAs (Erlam and Plass 1996:34–41; ICC 1996:2). For business, the use of trade measures in MEAs should be a matter of last resort. Opposition has also been expressed regarding the extension of environmental concerns to PPMs (Erlam and Plass 1996:33; WCBSD 1998) and the applicability of WTO rules to national and regional ecolabeling schemes (ICC 1999).

While business has sought to shape public policy, it has also sought to avoid, and in fact preempt, mandatory regulations by adopting voluntary self-regulation arrangements. One example of lobbying against regulation is provided by business opposition to the proposed European Community carbon tax. In 1994, the original proposal was abandoned. Measures in this area are to be drawn up by individual member states and harmonized at a later stage (see Ikwue and Skea 1996 for an extended discussion).

The preferred business alternative to mandatory legislation has been the promotion of voluntary standards that are part of a broad strategy by firms to counter governmental regulation. Recent attention to corporate responsibility, of which voluntary codes are a result, arises from fear of impending legislation. The ISO 14000 series[12] has been the most noticeable of these developments at the intersection of trade and the environment (see Clapp 1998 for an extended discussion). However, these codes do not entail specific performance or emissions targets. The WBCSD has stated that "applying the same environmental criteria to all investment decisions, whether at home or abroad, and adopting ISO or equivalent environmental management standards, ecoefficiency, cleaner production or other related approaches, would be the most effective way for business to improve environmental practice and reverse negative presumptions" (Erlam and Plass 1996:6). As can be seen from the above quotation, the WBCSD argues that conforming to voluntary standards is one method whereby business can "reverse negative presumptions" (Erlam and Plass 1996:6). Another strategy is to coopt and enlist the help of environmental NGOs through various ad hoc and private and voluntary arrangements.[13] Such partnership projects are increasingly common.

ENGOs, Trade, and the Environment

The involvement of ENGOS in the trade-environment debate has been receiving more attention recently (Audley 1997; Williams and Ford 1999). What follows concentrates on ENGO involvement in the debate over the WTO. This account demonstrates both the limited impact of ENGOs on the WTO and the divisions among them. ENGOs identify the WTO as a key factor in trade and the environment because the WTO is the legal and institutional foundation of the global trading system. Moreover, intense debate on trade and environment developed when the GATT was in the process of being superseded by the WTO; hence, the scope for institutional reform in the world trading system presented an opportunity to reshape the agenda.

Not surprisingly, ENGOs cover a wide range of opinion on this issue. Two strategies—accommodationist and rejectionist—are most clearly delineated (Audley 1997; Williams and Ford 1999; Ford 1999). By accommodationist, I mean those groups engaged in lobbying the WTO directly. Some groups attempt to effect transformation in the world trading system through constructive engagement with trade officials. As I show below, accommodationists can be further divided into moderate engagers, such as the World Wide Fund for Nature (WWF), and critical engagers, such as Friends of the Earth (FOE). ENGOs with offices in Geneva engaging in lobbying and advocacy activities are more likely to adopt a moderate stance. While mutual mistrust resulted in limited real dialogue at first, increasing contact with the trade community has lessened the degree of polarization between these environmental groups and representatives of trading interests. For example, accommodationist ENGOs and trade officials now accept that one crucial obstacle to meaningful progress in the negotiating process arises from the limited nature of existing knowledge on trade-environment linkages.

The term "rejectionist" is applied to the less institutionalized grassroots movements that have adopted a confrontational position and reject any form of engagement and accommodation with national and international bureaucracies. Groups such as the People's Global Action attempt to mobilize direct action against the WTO (Williams and Ford 1999:282–286; Ford 1999:71–72). This brief overview focuses on those civil society actors engaging in dialogue with the WTO.

Polarization among ENGOs engaging the WTO was evident before and during the Singapore Ministerial Conference in December 1996. A number of ENGOs rejected the underlying trade liberalization ethos of the WTO, contending that no resolution is possible between environmental degradation and the trading system if the starting point is one of free trade. For example, the Institute for Agriculture and Trade Policy rejected free trade as a positive tool, especially in relation to food security, arguing that developing countries would be better served by state protection of domestic agriculture (Dawkins and Suppan 1996:2). This is a fundamental rejection of the WTO's philosophy and operating methods. Also, the *Joint NGO Statement on Issues and Proposals for the WTO Ministerial Conference* (1996), issued by thirty-two NGOs based mostly in developing countries, highlighted the negative effects of trade liberalization, arguing that the GATT agreements lead to marginalization and increased disparities of poverty and wealth between and within countries.

Friends of the Earth also expressed dissatisfaction with the slow pace of reform. Its briefing document for the Ministerial Conference was forthrightly entitled *A Call to Close the Committee on Trade and Environment*. FOE claimed that the CTE had made very little progress and had failed to fulfill its mandate, and that its work could be better carried out by a panel with more commitment to the environment (FOE 1996:2). FOE's position is not outwardly rejectionist. It starts from a general concurrence with the aims of the WTO and CTE, but takes issue with the lack of progress made toward them and the way the CTE is attempting to achieve such progress.

Among ENGOs seeking to influence WTO policy through constructive dialogue, the WWF has been the most active. Although extremely critical in its report *The CTE: Is it Serious?* WWF International maintained support for the continued operation of the CTE despite the fact that some parts of the environmental community are likely to call for its abolition (Arden-Clarke 1996a:7). WWF International argued that CTE performance to date has been unsatisfactory and that the committee must take meaningful action on its mandate in order to provide input on sustainable development for future WTO trade negotiations. In an effort to stimulate the international decisionmaking process, the WWF established an Expert Panel on Trade and Sustainable Development to generate policy recommendations that could be circulated and publicized among WTO members (Gonzales 1996).

Another NGO interested in maintaining a dialogue with the CTE is the International Institute for Sustainable Development (IISD), which criticized the CTE for narrowing its agenda "away from sustainable development towards environmental management" (IISD 1996a:24, 1996b). According to the IISD, this resulted in "an approach that is increasingly detailed and technical and risks losing sight of the ultimate goal of sustainable development. And it permits the WTO to continue to pursue solutions on its own to issues that demand cooperative approaches" (IISD 1996a:25).

Accommodationist ENGOs begin from the assumption that trade is a necessary source of finance for sustainable development (IISD 1996a:15) but cannot by itself guarantee such development. They advocate policies to ensure that trade-generated resources are used in a sustainable manner and also that trade activities take sustainable forms (see IISD 1996a:15; WWF 1996; Gonzales 1996:4). Such organizations maintain that it is vital that trade and environmental policies be integrated so that they are mutually reinforcing.

Linkages between environmental protection and development policies constitute another focus of conflict. Perhaps because it has pitted Northern and Southern NGOs against each other, the trade–environment–sustainable development debate is often seen as an area of conflict between developed and developing countries (Runnalls 1996:5; Dawkins and Suppan 1996). Developed countries are accused of imposing environmental regulations that developing countries cannot afford and that hamper opportunities for development. This view was trenchantly expressed at the Singapore Ministerial Conference by an NGO coalition. On the one hand, the trade community must recognize that where trade patterns contribute to economic practices that produce environmental problems, adjustments in trade are required. On the other hand, the environment should not be used as a pretext for protectionism by the powerful, for that would unfairly shift adjustment costs to the weaker countries and peoples (*Joint NGO Statement* 1996:7).[14]

NGOs engaged in active lobbying at the WTO have focused on two substantive issues: the use of trade restrictions in MEAs and the salience of PPMs. As noted above, corporations support MEAs because they prevent unilateral action and ensure that all countries are faced with the same constraints. Yet, ENGOs, which also support the increased use of MEAs, are concerned that current uncertainty over the consequent status of such trade restrictions undermines the authority of MEAs and discourages the incorporation of trade measures into MEAs in the future (Arden-Clarke 1996a:2; FOE 1996:3). This concern and uncertainty arises from the disputed status of trade-related environmental measures. The aim of TREMs is to protect the environment through the use of trade instruments. For example, the Montreal Protocol, which deals with the elimination of CFCs, prohibits trade in controlled substances between parties and nonparties to the protocol. But TREMs can be seen as discriminatory and hence in contravention of the basic principles of the multilateral trading system—that is, of not restricting trade or discriminating between trading partners. It thus becomes unclear whether these trade restrictions can be justified as general exceptions to the rules (Ewing and Tarasofsky 1996:8). There are proposals to modify Article XX of the GATT to incorporate MEAs explicitly, but no particular conclusions have been reached (Ewing and Tarasofsky 1996:16; Reiterer n.d.:3).

Attention has also focused on GATT and WTO rulings and their possible impact on national legislation designed to protect the environment. Most involve trade restrictions on commodities produced through environmentally damaging production processes. WTO rules permit the regulation of products but prohibit discrimination against imports on the basis of their PPMs. For environmentalists, PPMs are a key element in the move toward sustainable development. Some argue that the WTO stance, inherited from the GATT, is unhelpful in that it does not accept the need to take production methods into account (Arden-Clarke 1996b:2–3).

In addition, "the issue of PPMs has unfortunately tended to be polarized along North-South lines" in the WTO (Arden-Clarke 1996b:2). One of many reasons is that those from the South fear the imposition of a new kind of protectionism cloaked in environmental or social concerns. Imports from developing countries could be discriminated against on the real or imagined basis that the PPMs in that country were environmentally damaging or socially unjust (Arden-Clarke 1996b:3). ENGOs recognize these fears and the possibilities that protectionism lies behind calls to regulate PPMs. However, they argue that this is not a justification for neglecting the environment and that these issues should be addressed by the WTO together with other relevant bodies (IISD 1996a:32).

In this examination of the positions of business groups and environmentalists, my primary intention was not to assess the relative influence of firms and ENGOs. However, this review of the trade and environment debate reveals the importance of structural power in shaping outcomes. The discursive dynamics of environmental management discourage radical environmental groups from participating at this level of the trade and environment debate. They also privilege the understanding of sustainable development held by the business community and incorporate moderate and critical engagers into the language of environmental economics.

Conclusions: Environmental Management
and Competing Representations of Trade and Environment

It may be correct that the creation of the CTE reflects the recognition by governments that the trade-environment relationship is a priority issue (Hopkinson 1995:5). But the history of the WTO's engagement with environmental issues does not support the claim that a serious attempt has been made to reconcile the objectives of sustainable development with those of an open trading system. The efforts of some environmentalists to engage with the trading community met with some success in placing environmental issues on the agenda. However, there have been no policy developments in that direction. In terms of the arguments advanced in this chapter, the reasons for this failure are twofold. First, the dominant discourse of sustainable development articulated by international organizations is based on weak sustainability principles. Couched in terms of environmental economics, it represents an accommodation to the pressures to take account of environmental issues without proposing solutions to the underlying problems. Second, the dominant values within the debate on trade and the environment support the preservation of a liberal multilateral trading system. Consequently, environmentalism was inscribed at the outset as a protectionist challenge to the prevailing order rather than conceptualized as a different order.

In defining sustainable development to mean environmental management, the dominant conception privileges a particular set of values. The search for a reconciliation of competing perspectives on trade and the environment is part of the broader terrain of environmental management. P. Rikhardsson and R. Welford (1997:43–45) argue that such management strategies arise from a positivist approach to the environment based on scientific evidence and a belief in technological solutions. Such policies also preserve the status quo by providing a framework for analysis that is too narrow to address environmental problems adequately.

Environmental management is based on a number of ideological assumptions. One is that the environment can and should be managed, a positivist approach that avoids countenancing any major change in the system of production and consumption. Another is that corporate managers are the right people to undertake this task. This implies that managers have an appreciation of the environment and its best interests, and also assumes that business has the technical resources necessary to tackle environmental problems. A third assumption is that environmental management is a win-win strategy designed not only to protect the environment but also to enhance business opportunities. This dispenses with the need for compulsory regulation, as it implies that business will naturally take up environmental management. Finally, traditional management tools are assumed to be both appropriate and adequate to the task of caring for the environment. This reinforces the status quo by discouraging external involvement in business affairs (Levy 1997:137–140).

Environmental management is the business approach to environmentalism. It involves developing and instituting private environmental codes, reducing pollution, and developing, identifying, and promoting environmentally friendly products. Environmental management's promotion of private environmental practices deflects more radical challenges. In doing so, however, business has given ground to environmental interests, which could serve as a basis for new attacks (Levy 1997:141–142). In urging a redefined agenda, ENGOs face powerful vested interests as they engage in competing constructions of knowledge and power. At this juncture, however, the activities of the WBCSD and other proponents of neoliberal ideology appear to have been successful in capturing the debate on trade and the environment, influencing its terms and directions.

Notes

I would like to thank the editors for their constructive comments and suggestions. I would also like to thank Felix Jones, Heike Fabig, Lucy Ford, David Levy, and the anonymous reviewers for their comments and suggestions.

1. See Kütting's discussion of environmental effectiveness in Chapter 9.

2. See the critiques of Irwin (Chapter 2) and Laferrière (Chapter 10), and the latter's exploration of a radical approach.

3. Crucial decisions have been taken with respect to the derestriction of documents (WTO 1996a) and the expansion of secretariat contact with NGOs (WTO 1996b, 1998c). In July 1998, further access for NGOs was initiated by Renato Ruggiero (the first director-general of the WTO). See "Ruggiero Announces Enhanced WTO Plan For Co-operation with NGOs" (WTO 1998a). The WTO now distributes all position papers submitted by NGOs/civil society to WTO delegations, maintains an NGO section on the WTO website, and holds regular briefing sessions.

4. For the agreement, see General Agreement on Tariffs and Trade (GATT 1994), which contains the Marrakesh Agreement Establishing the World Trade Organization.

5. For this decision, see GATT (1994), which contains the Decision on Trade and Environment at Marrakesh.

6. For the text of the ruling, see WTO (1998b).

7. For an extended discussion of the MAI in this context, see Chapter 4.

8. One must keep in mind that related and parallel to these

environmental efforts, business has also led an assault against environmentalism. For analysis of "greenwash" and the "green backlash," see Rowell (1996) and Beder (1997).

9. This issue is explored in different ways in Chapters 8, 9, and 10.

10. These figures were obtained from the WTO (1998c).

11. This does not mean that MEAs always include trade measures. Of the 180 MEAs in existence in 1996, only eighteen included trade provisions, of which few are significantly trade restrictive (IFAP 1996:15).

12. The ISO 14000 series of standards were first developed in 1991 by the ISO. They consist of a set of documents that define the key elements of a management system that will help an organization address the environmental issues it faces (IISD 1996b:1). The standards developed by the ISO are strictly voluntary. The ISO process seeks to establish a comprehensive private tripartite system that includes government officials, albeit not as authoritative policymakers. On the other hand, the strategies that Newell discusses in Chapter 5 are ad hoc, bipartite arrangements that are even more private and voluntary.

13. See Chapter 5 for an extended discussion of this issue.

14. The absence of a Southern NGO presence in Geneva constrains their input into the policy process. The activities of the International Centre for Trade and Sustainable Development and the participation of representatives from the developing world in WTO symposia ensure that these voices are not completely silent.

Daniel Egan
David Levy **4**

International Environmental Politics and the Internationalization of the State: The Cases of Climate Change and the Multilateral Agreement on Investment

By now, the term "globalization" has been so overused in mainstream discourse that it has become a cliché. In response, a veritable industry of academic inquiry has attempted to analyze and disaggregate the constituent elements of globalization. There is significant debate over the extent to which we have, in fact, entered a new era in which multinational corporations (MNCs) have become footloose, stateless entities able to evade and erode the power of territorially organized states and domestic social forces. If the nation-state has historically been a site where the power of business was at least contested and constrained, the increased mobility of capital and interdependence of national economies coupled with a system of international institutions short on democratic process has, it is argued, eroded the autonomy and power of states and outmaneuvered domestic social forces such as labor and environmental groups (Barnet and Cavanagh 1994; Held and McGrew 1994; Appelbaum and Henderson 1995; Korten 1995; Teeple 1995; Castells 1997). Other commentators have questioned the extent to which markets and production have been integrated on a global basis and have pointed to the national character of even the largest MNCs (Gordon 1988; Carnoy 1993; Hirst and Thompson 1996; Storper 1997). More fundamentally, globalization has been seen more as an ideological weapon deployed by capital and states committed to the project of neoliberalism than as a fundamentally new economic system (Ruigrok and

63

van Tulder 1995; Hirst and Thompson 1996; Piven and Cloward 1997).

We take a position between these poles. While there *have* been important developments in the internationalization of production and finance and new constraints placed on national states, it is wrong to see these as a monolithic juggernaut driven by global capital or technological development. Also, while globalization *is* a potent tool for disciplining subordinate social forces, seeing globalization as a purely ideological construction runs the risk of downplaying important trends that signify ongoing structural changes in the political economy. Globalization is both an ongoing, if uneven and incomplete, process of rationalizing and integrating markets and production geographically, and also a discursive framework for legitimizing this process. Indeed, it could not be otherwise, as the stabilization of social structures requires that relations of meaning and relations of production mutually constitute, or coproduce, each other (Callon 1998; Clegg 1989).

In this chapter, we examine a major element of globalization: the internationalization of the state. We argue that the internationalization of the state can be characterized by two ideal types: market-enabling regimes and regulatory regimes. Market-enabling regimes, such as the World Trade Organization (WTO) and the now stalled Multilateral Agreement on Investment (MAI), provide the infrastructure for the global neoliberal system and facilitate capital accumulation. Regulatory regimes, such as the Kyoto Protocol to limit emissions on greenhouse gases, place limits on capital accumulation through regulation of labor, social, and environmental policies. These ideal types are analytically distinct, but in any particular case representing one type, there will be elements of the other—for example, as the cases below demonstrate, the United States wants the Kyoto Protocol to employ market principles to reduce greenhouse gas emissions, while the proposed MAI was forced to incorporate regulatory components as a concession to opposition movements.

As ideal types, however, these categories reflect the essential conflict over the nature of internationalization. As Wolfgang Streeck (1998:429) argues, "Internationalization is not necessarily denationalization" and is better understood as a multilevel system providing structural opportunities and resources to social actors. Social actors can then be expected to prefer arenas where the existing balance of power provides them with particular advantages. For market-enabling regimes, capital is generally supportive of the construction of supranational institutions in which states and nongovernmental organizations (NGOs) representing labor, environment, women, or other social interests have limited influence. NGOs, by contrast, tend to oppose the creation of international market-enabling regimes precisely because of the constraints imposed on their bargaining position. For regulatory regimes, these positions are usually reversed. Capital tends to prefer the national level for regulation and implementation of environmental and social issues because of the state's historical support for business interests. NGOs, recognizing their relative weakness at the national level in confronting globally mobile capital, prefer multilateral international arenas, such as the United Nations, in which capital has less developed channels of influence. Market-enabling and regulatory regimes are thus new terrains of contestation for national states, capital, and social forces. Rather than merely reflecting a unilateral extension of corporate power, this perspective recognizes that internationalization can also create new arenas for resistance.

Internationalization as a Contested Process: The Neo-Gramscian Perspective

Our analysis of internationalization makes critical use of transnational historical materialism (Cox 1987, 1996b; van der Pijl 1984, 1998; Gill 1990; Gill and Law 1993; Robinson 1996a, 1996b, 1998), which offers a theory of international relations based on the Gramscian theory of hegemony (Gramsci 1971). Hegemony refers to the cultural, moral, and economic dominance of the ruling class; it is an integrated system of values and beliefs that is supportive of the established social order and projects a particular set of class interests as the general interest. Transnational historical materialism points to organizations such as the Organization for Economic Cooperation and Development (OECD), the World Economic Forum, and the Trilateral Commission as reflecting the emergence of a transnational hegemonic bloc. This coalition of capitalists, state managers, and intellectuals transcends any one class and is bound together through common identities and interests by material and ideological structures. This new bloc, with a conscious internationalist perspective, supersedes systems of national hegemony and the global power of particular countries.

Although transnational historical materialism emphasizes the role of capital in constructing this hegemonic bloc, it also sees the national state playing a major mediating role. The dominance of the transnational hegemonic bloc is founded on the national state adopting the fiscal and monetary policy necessary to maintain economic stability, creating the basic infrastructure for global economic activity, and providing social control and stability (Robinson 1996a). At the same time, however, transnational historical materialists see the national state as playing a subordinate role in the process of internationalization. Cox (1987:254), for example, defines the internationalization of the state thus:

> *First*, there is a process of interstate consensus formation regarding the needs or requirements of the world economy that takes place within a common ideological framework. . . . *Second*, participation in this consensus formation is hierarchically structured. *Third*, the internal structures of states are adjusted so that each can best transform the global consensus into national policy and practice.

From this perspective, the national state appears as a derivative institution that translates the global economic consensus into nationally specific forms.

William Robinson (1996a:19) likewise argues that the transnational hegemonic bloc exercises class power through a "dense network of supranational institutions and relationships that increasingly bypass formal states" and conversion of national states "into transmission belts and filtering devices for the imposition of the transnational agenda." He goes even further, suggesting that "with the rise of the global economy and globalization processes, the nation-state is increasingly becoming obsolete as the unit of analysis" (Robinson 1996b:366). While transnational historical materialists acknowledge the possibilities for challenges to this emerging transnational hegemony (Cox 1993; Gill and Law 1993), they still produce a relatively monolithic and deterministic understanding of the internationalization of the state.

Transnational historical materialists have used Gramsci's framework to challenge more conventional definitions of hegemony that focus on military or economic domination by one state, but at the same time they have underemphasized the negotiated nature of hegemony. Both within the dominant hegemonic bloc and in its relations with subordinate social forces, dominant groups must negotiate, within historically specific conditions, with subordinate groups to secure the latter's consent to the rule of the former. Dominant groups attempt to accommodate challenges without fundamental changes in social relations in a process that typically entails making material concessions, coopting the discourse of challengers, and bringing moderate groups into the coalition while marginalizing more radical elements.

The negotiated nature of hegemony means that domination is never seamless or completely stable. The stability of the hegemonic bloc rests on a historically specific alignment of material, ideological, and organizational structures that sustain the social order. Changes in markets, technologies, relative power positions, or ideologies can lead to moments of crisis in which the existing alliances and arrangements are challenged and become unstable. If the subordinate classes are unprepared or organizationally underdeveloped, the hegemonic bloc will be able to restore hegemony through passive revolution, a realignment of forces that grants some concessions but that leaves underlying social relations untouched. On the other hand, Gramsci sees hegemonic instability as providing opportunities for more thorough social change from below through a "war of position," a strategy in which subordinate groups create new cultural expressions and social institutions that gradually undermine the hegemonic bloc. Political struggles are seen as Machiavellian games of strategy and maneuver in which more powerful opponents may be outflanked.

A reading of Gramsci that emphasizes the *process* of hegemony provides a more indeterminate interpretation of internationalization than that currently associated with transnational historical materialism. In this alternative reading, internationalization is a highly contested process in which national states, capital, and social forces negotiate and struggle over the form and content of the new international structures of governance. Although transnational historical materialism acknowledges the role of social forces, they are seen as secondary to capital and the state; Robert Cox (1996b), for example, sees the state and civil society, the space where social forces are capable of organizing (Shaw 1994), as so interpenetrated that any distinction between the two is not very useful. When the contested nature of hegemony is emphasized, however, it is a mistake to pre-sume that capital necessarily seeks the internationalization of the state or that the state is becoming a mere transmission belt for capi-tal. National states, capital, and social forces are strategic actors that have different interests and capacities and whose preferences for forms of governance may vary from issue to issue. International institutions created for one purpose as the outcome of a particular historical conflict become active agents with some degree of auton-omy that change the course of future negotiations. As a result of this complex, dynamic, and somewhat indeterminate process, the evolu-tion of international institutions will necessarily produce uneven and often contradictory results. Thus, the international arena, rather than displacing the state, is better seen as a new forum for contestation alongside, and interdependent with, the national arena.

We seek to build on the work of transnational historical material-ism by developing a framework in which internationalization is understood as the outcome of strategic behavior among social actors engaged in conflict over defining the general interest. Here we pay particular attention to hegemonic conflicts over the environment, first in the Kyoto Protocol to limit greenhouse gases and then in the proposed MAI.

International Climate Change Negotiations

The climate change negotiations, held under the auspices of the United Nations and the World Meteorological Organization, present an important example of an emerging regulatory regime with the potential to cause dramatic disruption in markets for fossil fuels and related industries. Carbon dioxide, the single most important green-house gas, is released through the combustion of fossil fuels. Peter Newell and Matthew Paterson (1998:682) conclude that "when the centrality of fossil fuels in producing global warming is combined with the centrality of fossil energy in industrial economies, it becomes clear that the fundamental interests of major sectors of those economies are threatened by proposals to limit greenhouse gas emissions."

Faced with this challenge, companies need to decide whether the national or the international arena is more favorable for political con-testation. Companies will prefer the international arena only if they enjoy a balance of power more favorable there than at the national level and if it is not too costly to participate. If, however, international economic integration increases the political leverage of business *within* the nation-state and erodes the access of nonbusiness social interests to decisionmaking at the national level (Schmidt 1995), companies may prefer the well-charted waters of domestic politics. Moreover, efforts to coordinate social or environmental policies in international forums could be seen by business as leading to a costly upward harmonization of standards. It is not surprising, in this context, that some companies fear the emergence of an international environmental bureaucracy with the mandate to set emission-reduction targets to which individual countries will be bound. Thus, when business does exert its power in international negotiations, it is often to keep regulation at the national level.

As for considerations of cost and competitive strategy, only the largest companies are able to participate directly in international negotiations (Getz 1993). Given the consensual norms of decision-making in international environmental negotiations, companies might choose to focus their efforts on a single state in a hegemonic bloc that is predisposed against strong mandatory emission controls. Rather than negotiate the issue on a country-by-country basis, MNCs would need fewer resources to resolve an issue in one international forum, especially if they can share costs through participation in industry associations. Moreover, an international forum offers MNCs the opportunity to share the costs of political activity with foreign companies. A harmonized set of international standards would usually preempt a patchwork of national standards that would be stricter in some cases; multiple standards also impose significant costs on companies in terms of product adaptation, loss of economies of scale, and administrative compliance costs.

In the case of climate change, David Levy and Daniel Egan (1998) demonstrate that fossil fuel industries focused their political efforts at the national level where they appear to enjoy greater access and influence, at least in the United States. Large U.S. corporations benefit from revolving door connections with government agencies, the leverage afforded by political campaign contributions, and a well-organized lobbying effort. U.S. industry recognized the climate issue as a potential threat relatively early and, in an effort to form a broad-based coalition representing multiple sectors, formed the Global Climate Coalition (GCC) in 1989. The GCC represented about forty companies and industry associations, primarily major users of fossil fuels such as the oil, automobile, and electric utility sectors, but also other energy-intense sectors. Recognizing the importance of civil society in policy struggles, one industry tactic has been to establish "astroturf" organizations ostensibly representing private citizens (Stauber and Rampton 1995) but staffed and funded by industry associations.

The organizational capacity of business in the international negotiations on climate change is somewhat more circumscribed. The negotiations involve more than 100 countries with which U.S. companies share few ties and whose politicians are generally beyond the reach of political action committee (PAC) money. The major industry associations have had only limited success in extending their membership to non-U.S. companies. The International Chamber of Commerce (ICC), whose membership is drawn primarily from OECD countries, has tried to coordinate international business responses to the climate change negotiations through a very active working party on climate change. Intersectoral and regional differences, however, have hindered its efforts. Despite these divisions among industry sectors, international industry groups were much more successful at coordinating their positions on detailed implementation mechanisms by the UN Framework Convention on Climate Change (FCCC) Bonn meetings in June 1999. Even companies that still belonged to the GCC and were publicly opposed to Kyoto were willing to work on specific proposals for emissions trading, emissions inventorying, and the Clean Development Mechanism. Industry associations previously in competition established a more cooperative relationship for this meeting and were more willing to share information. The ICC was particularly effective in facilitating daily information exchanges and in organizing delegations for meetings with FCCC officials for which common themes and strategies were developed.

The international institutions guiding the negotiations, although formally accountable to country delegates through the Conferences of the Parties, have developed a degree of autonomy and legitimacy that provides some insulation from the interests of particular countries or industry sectors. For example, the GCC's attempt to undermine the credibility and legitimacy of the Intergovernmental Panel on Climate Change (IPCC), the body of scientists charged with providing periodic assessments of the impact of greenhouse gas emissions and mitigation options, ultimately fell short and forced the U.S. delegation to distance itself from the industry challenge (Edwards and Lahsen 1999). Industry efforts at the international negotiations were also constrained by the effective organization of national environmental NGOs into an international umbrella organization called the Climate Action Network (CAN), which coordinated positions, lobbied, and published a newsletter that was widely read in climate policy circles.

Business has also engaged in major efforts to influence the science and policy discourse by stressing the scientific uncertainties and the high economic costs of curtailing carbon emissions (Gelbspan 1997). Advertising and education are two channels through which industry associations have tried to influence public opinion. The best known among these are the publications by Western Fuels, a U.S. utility association and member of the GCC, which claim that carbon dioxide emissions will have a net beneficial effect on agriculture, plants, and wildlife. More recently, the GCC organized a $13 million advertising campaign in the preliminaries to the Kyoto conference in December 1997, emphasizing the cost of controls on greenhouse gases and the lack of developing country participation. Astroturf groups have also played an important role in discursive politics, demonstrating the link between organizational and discursive strategies. Coal, oil, and utility interests in the United States established a group called the Information Council for the Environment in 1991, whose purpose, as stated in internal documents, was to "reposition global warming as theory, not fact" (Ozone Action 1996).

The GCC and its member organizations have also attempted to convince U.S. business leaders and policymakers that measures to curb greenhouse gas emissions "are premature and are not justified by the state of scientific knowledge or the economic risks they create" (GCC 1995). The GCC commissioned a series of economic studies suggesting the United States might suffer economic losses approaching 3 to 5 percent of GDP annually if it follows proposals to cut emissions 20 percent below 1990 levels by 2005 (Montgomery and Charles River Associates 1995; WEFA Group 1996). The magnitude of such economic costs has been a central and hotly contested issue in the climate debate (Repetto and Austin 1997). Discursive strategies to emphasize these costs can be interpreted as an effort to translate the structural economic position of the fossil fuel industry into policy influence.

Fossil fuel interests have also attempted to convince opinion leaders and policymakers that the science of climate change is dubious at best. The GCC has actively promoted the views of "climate skeptics" in its literature, press releases, and congressional testimony and directs press inquiries to these people (Gelbspan 1997). It sponsored a number of reports, such as Accu-Weather (1994) and Davis (1996), and also used reports from other sympathetic organizations, notably the Marshall Institute. The theme of scientific uncertainty is developed in GCC publications that critique general circulation models (GCMs), pointing to their well-known limitations in modeling complex phenomena such as cloud cover, regional processes, and ocean circulation (Shackley 1999). This skeptical approach to GCMs stands in ironic contrast to the credibility the GCC has bestowed on general equilibrium economic models such as that used by the WEFA Group (1996), even though these models are just as complex and rest on less secure theoretical foundations than GCMs. Despite the resources invested in influencing scientific and policy debates, industry's point of view has not achieved hegemonic status even within the United States. Nevertheless, the "climate skeptics" have succeeded in turning climate change into an apparently balanced media debate, and they have provided cover for politicians who want to delay any action on greenhouse gas emissions (Gelbspan 1997).

Although these strategies achieved some limited success, particularly in the United States, in delaying regulatory controls, the hegemonic position of the fossil fuel industry has been undermined in a series of economic, discursive, and organizational changes. In a process of "passive revolution," companies have moved toward strategies of accommodation and compromise, generating a new hegemonic configuration based on the emerging "win-win" discourse of "ecological modernization" (Hajer 1995). The obvious appeal of this paradigm is the assertion that being "green" can also be good for business, a discourse that has rapidly gained currency among a number of industry associations, NGOs, and government agencies forming the core of a realigned hegemonic bloc. This discursive framework facilitated a political compromise on climate, demonstrated when U.S. delegate Tim Wirth, at the Second Conference of the Parties, in Geneva in July 1996, declared that the United States would support an internationally binding agreement on greenhouse gases (Wirth 1996). Wirth went on to promise the business community that the United States would pursue "market-based solutions that are flexible and cost-effective," and that "meeting this challenge requires that the genius of the private sector be brought to bear on the challenge of developing the technologies that are necessary to ensure our long term environmental and economic prosperity."

The shifting discourse on climate began to undermine the fossil fuel industry alliance. In May 1997, British Petroleum's (BP's) group chief executive, John Browne, publicly stated that "there is now an effective consensus among the world's leading scientists and serious and well informed people outside the scientific community that there is a discernible human influence on the climate" (Browne 1997). A broader fissure in industry's position was revealed the following month, when the U.S. Business Roundtable sponsored full-page advertisements in the U.S. press signed by 130 CEOs arguing against mandatory emissions limitations. A dissenting group of eighty Business Roundtable members, however, did not endorse the advertisements, and the views of this dissenting bloc were brought to President Clinton's attention, creating some political room for action.

The GCC was further weakened by a series of defections in the post-Kyoto period and by the growth of organizational vehicles representing more accommodating sectors of industry. The Pew Center on Global Climate Change was formed in April 1998 and includes companies such as BP, Toyota, Boeing, Lockheed, Enron, United Technologies, American Electric Power, Whirlpool, Maytag, and 3M. These companies endorsed newspaper advertisements stating that they "accept the views of most scientists that enough is known about the science and environmental impacts of climate change for us to take actions to address its consequences" (Cushman 1998). According to Eileen Claussen, founder of the Pew Center, "Joining Pew gives companies credibility, and credibility means political access and influence" (personal interview, 3 February 1999). In this case, once the policy train was seen as leaving the station, companies felt the pressure to get on board.

These organizational and discursive changes have been accompanied by a dramatic increase in investment in low-emission technologies. BP-Amoco is now the world's largest producer of solar photovoltaic (PV) panels, with plans to reach $1 billion in sales by 2010. Shell has also announced its intention to invest $500 million in PV over five years as part of a new International Renewable Energy Division (Boyle 1998). Ford and Daimler-Chrysler have each invested several hundred million dollars in a fuel-cell joint venture with the Canadian company Ballard, while General Motors has formed an alliance with Toyota to invest in a range of technologies.

This analysis of the emerging climate regime demonstrates that MNCs have focused on national channels in their opposition to emission controls. The contours of the regime reflect not just bargaining among states but also broader political struggles between industry sectors, national states, and social forces. In keeping with Tim Wirth's 1996 promise to business in Geneva, the United States has been the major advocate for an international regime based on flexible, market mechanisms for controlling greenhouse gases, and it has been successful in this effort. Although emission cuts are negotiated at the international level, each country is responsible for implementation, and the United States has opposed any coordination of policies and measures. The United States has also insisted on a few key points: the basket approach to greenhouse gases, which allows reductions to be averaged over a range of gases; emissions trading, which enables countries with high mitigation costs to buy carbon credits from other countries where costs might be lower; the Clean Development Mechanism, which provides funding for emission-reducing projects in developing countries while awarding the carbon credits to the industrialized countries and firms investing in the project; and five-year budget periods, possibly with banking among periods, allowing flexibility over emission-reduction trajectories. These measures not only reduce the adjustment burden on industry but also create profit opportunities for firms selling relatively low-emission technologies and products. This is the essence of the emerging grand compromise that will enable the climate regime to move forward.

Negotiations for the
Multilateral Agreement on Investment

The now stalled MAI presents an important example of a proposed market enabling regime that would further institutionalize the power of global capital; in addition, the collapse of negotiations for MAI illustrates the contested nature of internationalization. Secret negotiations began in September 1995 within the relatively narrow confines of the OECD, and it was only after a draft treaty was leaked in February 1997 that public awareness of MAI emerged. The draft MAI (OECD 1998a) called for the extension of national treatment and most-favored-nation treatment by member states to foreign capital. To ensure that member states would uphold these standards of nondiscrimination, the agreement required transparency in all laws and regulations that could affect investment. MAI also prohibited member states from imposing requirements on foreign capital mandating performance-related criteria (such as domestic content requirements and requirements mandating levels of local employment or the use of locally provided goods and services) as conditions for investment, although it did permit member states to impose such requirements in return for a specific advantage granted an investor. While member states were allowed to lodge country-specific exceptions to the agreement, these were subject to the principles of standstill and rollback. "Standstill" prohibited new exceptions from being made after the member state ratified the agreement, while "rollback" reduced and eventually eliminated those exceptions that were made prior to ratification; country-specific exceptions were thus meant to be very precise and short-term, ensuring a steady movement toward maximum liberalization. Finally, MAI sought to create a new, transnational form of economic citizenship (see Sassen 1996) that applied only to global economic actors. Among nonstate actors, only investors were recognized as global citizens possessing the legal standing to seek relief for breaches of MAI. Indeed, since there were no obligations for foreign capital in MAI, the agreement's dispute resolution mechanisms were not available to member states for redressing conflicts with foreign capital.

The OECD, largely in response to NGO opposition to MAI, sought to include some recognition of the need for foreign capital to act responsibly toward the environment, but this concern clearly remained secondary. Since 1976, the OECD has had a set of voluntary standards for the behavior of MNCs in host countries (OECD 1997c); standards for environmental protection were added to the guidelines in 1991. The section on environmental protection states that

> enterprises should, within the framework of laws, regulations and administrative practices in the countries in which they operate take due account of the need to protect the environment and avoid creating environmentally related health problems. (OECD 1997c:34)

Multinationals are encouraged to take into account the potential environmental consequences of investments, provide "adequate and timely information" (OECD 1997c:34) to host country authorities regarding the potential environmental consequences of their activities, and take appropriate measures to "minimize the risk of accidents and damage to health and the environment"(OECD 1997c:35). Negotiators concluded that the OECD Guidelines on Multinational Enterprises could be associated with MAI without changing their status as nonbinding recommendations (OECD 1997e), and this is reflected in the preamble of the MAI, which pointed to the guidelines as a model for investor behavior. In addition, although there was some disagreement as to the precise language, the preamble did refer to the importance of "appropriate environmental policies"(OECD 1998a:7–8) for sustainable economic growth.

This preambular language, however, is not reinforced by strong language in the body of the MAI. As the guidelines are voluntary standards, their inclusion in the agreement meant that MAI's statements on environmental protection lacked enforcement mechanisms. Environmental standards were not subject to MAI's dispute resolution procedures. In addition, policies targeting investors for violations of environmental standards in other countries were seen as a form of discriminatory treatment, in violation of the MAI, for which investors could seek compensation. Finally, no agreement was reached on language addressing the lowering of environmental standards to attract investment. The question whether this point referred to universal or domestic standards as a benchmark seemed to have been resolved in favor of the latter: "Most delegations preferred 'domestic' which was recognized as wider in scope" (OECD 1998b:54). The question of whether member states "should" or "shall" avoid weakening regulation to attract capital was also unresolved. "Should" made this provision an advisory one and allowed authorities to grant specific waivers under domestic law. "Shall," while making this provision a stronger, mandatory standard, was conditioned by its limitation to regulatory reductions designed to encourage specific investments; such a standard ignored the more significant case of a general lowering of standards to provide a more favorable business climate for capital.

Thus, unlike the strong and enforceable provisions in the MAI for liberalizing global movements of capital, the social regulation of capital remained voluntary, unenforceable, and *national*. Language protecting environmental policies from the prohibition on performance requirements (as long as those policies are nondiscriminatory and "not applied in an arbitrary or unjustifiable manner" [OECD 1998a:23]) remained unresolved, but it is clear from the significance given to the OECD guidelines as a model for social responsibility that MAI saw these policies as remaining national in scope. The state was, therefore, an essential feature of MAI, but only insofar as it contributed to the power of global capital. By keeping the social regulation of capital national within the context of the broader transnationalization of capital, MAI sought to institutionalize the market discipline that would ensure that state policy be constrained along neoliberal lines. In addition to providing a degree of ideological rationalization suggesting that economic growth and environmental protection are not incompatible (see Levy 1997), the agreement's respect for national environmental standards meant that capital would encounter a fragmented system of social regulation, one that would significantly increase capital's power relative to the state.

This hegemonic project has not been successful to date. A combination of conflicts between member states and opposition from social forces led the OECD to halt negotiations for MAI in October 1998. While this does not mean that MAI is dead, it does illustrate the contested nature of internationalization in this arena.

Conflicts over the MAI emerged at the very beginning of negotiations in choosing the appropriate forum for an agreement. European Union countries, many of which face the political constraint of established left-wing parties with representation in both national parliaments and the European Parliament, initially argued that MAI be negotiated in the WTO, which has a much broader membership than the OECD. While the WTO would have provided greater legitimacy for an agreement, it would also have provided a venue for opposition from poorer countries to increased liberalization, or at least for the inclusion of some concessions to their interests in the final agreement. Indeed, poorer WTO members, including India, Malaysia, and Egypt, successfully derailed attempts to create an investment agreement within that organization. The United States, which does not face the same level of political opposition to liberalization, argued forcefully and successfully for using the OECD, which consists of twenty-nine of the wealthiest countries, as the proper forum for MAI. Although the OECD organized a number of conferences for nonmember countries and invited Argentina, Brazil, Chile, and Slovakia to become observers in the MAI Negotiating Group, only OECD member states were granted formal rights in the development of the agreement.

While MAI negotiators and OECD documents offered a number of justifications for developing MAI within the OECD, particularly the need for a free-standing agreement that could complement existing international bodies on trade (WTO) and finance (IMF) and the concentration of foreign direct investment flows among OECD member states (OECD 1997d), it is clear that the narrow membership base of the OECD provided opportunities for the wealthiest countries to control the process of internationalization. An OECD-constructed MAI would offer poorer countries the choice of joining MAI in the hope of attracting foreign capital or putting themselves at a competitive disadvantage by rejecting the protections the MAI accords to capital. As William Witherell, the OECD's director for Financial, Fiscal and Enterprise Affairs, stated at the October 1997 symposium on MAI in Cairo:

> Less advanced developing countries will also have reasons for looking closely at the MAI. These countries probably have the greatest need for additional foreign capital, technology and know-how. Their governments need to do everything in their power to provide an attractive climate that can be harnessed durably for development purposes and to promote integration into the global economy. Even if less developed economies find they are not ready to accept the international commitments of the MAI, they should study its provisions as a reference tool for domestic policy reform. (OECD 1997f:13–14)

Thus, the OECD provided the opportunity for the wealthiest countries to construct an agreement that could then be presented as a fait accompli to nonmember states, one that they could ignore only at their peril.

With the negotiations currently stalled in the OECD (in part because of France's withdrawal from MAI negotiations prior to the October 1998 OECD meeting), there are calls from European negotiators to try again in the WTO (European Commission 1998). The United States continues to resist such a move and instead has suggested the possibility of changing the IMF's Articles of Agreement to create a de facto MAI (see Fischer 1997). With voting power in the IMF based on monetary contributions, the United States would have sufficient power to ensure an agreement in line with its commitment to maximum liberalization. However, given long-standing criticism of the IMF for the social and environmental consequences of its structural adjustment program (see Brecher and Costello 1998), it is unlikely that such an agreement would win sufficient legitimacy to be successful. With the suspension of negotiations within the OECD, this conflict remains unresolved, a fact that reflects the continued significance of specific levels of national political organization and commitment to political-economic values in the process of internationalization.

This is also reflected in the efforts of OECD negotiators to shield member states from the core elements of MAI. For example, Australia (OECD 1997a) reserved the right to reject foreign takeovers of Australian businesses and the establishment of new businesses by foreign interests that are contrary to the national interest, to place limits on foreign ownership of media, and to maintain or adopt any performance requirement in any sector. Canada (OECD 1997b) likewise reserved the right to protect cultural industries and to place limits on the acquisition of Canadian businesses by non-Canadians. Among other things, the United States sought to reserve the right to exempt subsidies given by U.S. states and localities (Dougherty 1998). In all, more than 400 specific reservations were made, suggesting that nationally specific levels of organization and instrumental power among economic sectors contributed to preventing the conclusion of a strong, inclusive agreement. Subordinate social forces also played a major role in the fate of MAI. Although the OECD negotiations were conducted in secret and excluded popular participation, and although the draft agreement did not recognize popular forces as a legitimate global actor, negotiations stimulated considerable international opposition by labor and environmental groups. National and international campaigns by NGOs such as Friends of the Earth, Public Citizen, the Council of Canadians, and the Third World Network were of sufficient strength to compel the OECD to informally recognize them. The MAI's language on the environment, however weak and tentative, reflected an (unsuccessful) attempt to grant concessions that did not challenge the core elements of the agreement.

When MAI negotiators met with representatives of NGOs for an "informal consultation" in Paris in October 1997, the latter called for an immediate suspension of negotiations (*Joint NGO Statement* 1997). More substantively, the NGOs rejected MAI's combination of strong, enforceable, supranational provisions for liberalizing global movements of capital and voluntary, unenforceable, national regulations on capital. Such a fragmented system of regulations, it was feared, would lead to a downward spiral in which states relax standards so as to encourage inward investment. Instead, in the *Joint NGO Statement* they called for binding supranational agreements on environmental, labor, health, safety, and human rights standards and replacing investor-state dispute resolution mechanisms with "democratic and transparent mechanisms which ensure that civil society . . . gain new powers to hold investors to account." NGOs appear, then, to prefer strong supranational regulatory regimes that ensure an upward harmonization of standards in the interest of the environment.

Finally, the MAI negotiations stalled because those forces that would most directly benefit from its creation—global capital—began to question whether this particular agreement could deliver what they sought. The major corporate lobbying groups pushing for MAI included the U.S. Council for International Business (USCIB), the Union of Industrial and Employers' Confederation of Europe, the International Chamber of Commerce (ICC), and Keidanren (the Japan Federation of Economic Organizations). For example, the USCIB provided technical advice to U.S. negotiators and briefings to state officials and business leaders in major U.S. corporate centers to build support for MAI. It opposed the inclusion of any language referring to environmental protection. As OECD negotiators granted concessions on the environment in the hope of winning the consent of subordinate social forces, they progressively alienated the USCIB to the point where continued business support for the Clinton administration's efforts to continue the process was "not even an inch deep—it's skin deep" (*Inside U.S. Trade* 1998). Likewise, Helmut Maucher, president of the ICC, stated that he was "not that supportive of MAI, because they added social wording in at the very last moment" (*Corporate Europe Observer* 1998). At the same time, the volume of country-specific exceptions so restricted (from capital's perspective) the applicability of MAI that the chair of ICC Netherlands, Herman van Karnebeek, was led to say, "What then, we are beginning to ask ourselves, is in the MAI for us?" (*ICC Business World* 1998). At a January 1998 meeting between a delegation of business representatives brought together by the OECD's Business and Industry Advisory Committee and MAI negotiators, "business expressed concern that negotiators' attempts to respond to conflicting pressures by various interest groups would undermine prospects for a meaningful agreement"(*ICC Business World* 1998). For capital, the combination of significant country-specific exceptions and the inclusion of language on the environment rendered MAI so problematic that no agreement was preferred to a watered-down agreement that did not deliver maximum liberalization.

This combination of internal conflict among state interests and external conflict between forces in favor of liberalization (capital and state) and social forces opposed to it has, at least temporarily, put on hold efforts to create an agreement. Despite their commitment to a neoliberal global economic order, OECD state managers are still dependent on national political and economic interests for legitimacy and material resources, and both transnational capital and national states are not so powerful that they can ride roughshod over social forces opposed to economic liberalization. The case of MAI suggests that rather than following an inexorable path of development, the internationalization of the state will be a dynamic process emerging out of struggles and alliances between capital, state, and social forces.

Conclusion

Our case studies suggest that internationalization is not a uniform process but is instead characterized by conflict and indeterminacy. MAI is an example of an effort to create a market-enabling regime through which capital is attempting to institutionalize its global power at the expense of national states and social forces, but the current suspension of negotiations suggests that transnational capital may not be the all-powerful juggernaut claimed by proponents of the globalization thesis. Conflicts among OECD member states over protection of national political and economic interests, and the opposition of social forces making effective use of new communications technology to organize a global movement against the agreement (Drohan 1998) have, at least for the moment, derailed MAI and set the stage for new conflicts—for example, WTO versus IMF. Likewise, efforts to create a regulatory regime limiting greenhouse gas emissions illustrate a strategic choice by sectors of capital to place constraints on a new international regime primarily by acting at the level of the national state. This reflects the substantial degree of influence that NGOs have in the United Nations as well as capital's preferences for national regulation both in terms of well-established national channels of influence and the advantages of a globally fragmented regulatory system. Both cases reveal that internationalization contains sufficient contradictions to provide movements from below, including environmental movements, with considerable opportunities to resist and affect its boundaries.

Our comparison of MAI and the Kyoto Protocol leads us to take a sympathetic yet critical position toward transnational historical materialism. While neo-Gramscians have acknowledged the significance of conflict between capital, the national state, and social forces, they also tend to have a relatively monolithic conception of the internationalized state. We argue that while transnational historical materialism has much to offer for understanding the internationalization of the state, it must be more sensitive to the uneven and contradictory nature of this process. Capital, the national state, and social forces engage in struggles over the nature of market-enabling and regulatory regimes and make strategic choices concerning where and how to engage in these struggles. These choices and the outcomes of these struggles will be the result of a historically specific balance of economic and political forces. As a result, the internationalization of the state is not something that is *happening to* national states, but a process in which national states are active participants (Panitch 1996; Sassen 1996). Rather than reflecting a decline in the significance of the national state, we argue that internationalization reflects an extension of the contested nature of the state, which critical state theorists (Carnoy 1984; Barrow 1993) have to date located only at the national level, to the international level.

In its emphasis on internationalization as a process of the state becoming a transmission belt for transnational capital, transnational historical materialism offers a relatively structuralist reading of Gramsci, one that has totalized hegemony by seeing it "largely as a one-directional power relationship" (Germain and Kenny 1998:18). Our interpretation of transnational historical materialism, on the other hand, is grounded in a reading of Gramsci that is antideterminist, emphasizing instead the role of political agency in defining internationalization. We believe that such a reading is closer to the spirit of what Sassoon (1987: xvii) calls "a *Gramscian* materialism."

This less determinist reading of Gramsci has much to offer the study of international environmental politics. Although historical materialist interpretations of ecology have emerged in recent years (see Foster 1994; Harvey 1996; O'Connor 1998), to date transnational historical materialism has largely ignored the environment. While this may be due to its relatively recent emergence, we believe that the overly structuralist, totalizing reading of Gramsci that characterizes transnational historical materialism has contributed to this silence. While ecological movements have tended to be movements from below, transnational historical materialism, with its examination of how the state is being transformed by transnational capital, is likely to miss the significance of these movements (but see Mittelman 1998b; also Laferrière in Chapter 10, for another interpretation). Although our cases are centered on environmental movements, our version of transnational historical materialism allows for a greater sensitivity to the role of those movements in contesting internationalization by bringing contradiction and the indeterminacy of political conflict to the fore. The questioning of capitalism's degradation of the environment is precisely the kind of counterhegemonic praxis that is at the core of Gramsci's theory of social change; to the extent that transnational historical materialism emphasizes the creation of transnational hegemony and undervalues the possibilities for resistance and counterhegemony, it will undervalue environmental issues. There is thus nothing inherent in a neo-Gramscian perspective that prevents it from being used as a tool for understanding international environmental issues. Rather, it must more completely recognize how Gramsci's dialectic of structure and agency is relevant for understanding, shaping, and resisting internationalization.

Peter Newell 5

Environmental NGOs, TNCs, and the Question of Governance

> Those standing up against globalism or its effects are not governments (who mostly approve, having given the corporations the authority) but non-governmental groups, which are being pushed into the role of social justice watchdogs, moral arbiters and spokespeople for those without a voice.
>
> —Vidal 1996:260

Many claims have been made with regard to the phenomenon of globalization. One of the most prominent claims pertains to the effect of global economic processes on traditional structures of authority, particularly the nation-state (Cerny 1990; Ohmae 1990; Sassen 1996), leading to assertions about the retreat of the state (Strange 1996). The starting point for this chapter is the state's withdrawal from certain regulatory functions with regard to transnational corporations (TNCs), particularly in relation to the environment (Clapp 1997). It can be argued that this creates a crisis of governance because new forms of state regulation and oversight are not replacing them.

Given the perceived unwillingness or inability of national governments to impose adequate environmental safeguards and the failure of internationally orchestrated attempts to regulate TNCs, environmental nongovernmental organizations (ENGOs) have increasingly been adopting nontraditional means to impose accountability upon TNCs through a variety of strategies. This chapter aims, first, to explore this emerging trend toward the informal regulation of the environmental impacts of TNCs. Second, it seeks to account for the significance of this phenomenon and to identify some of its implications, particularly whether these ENGO strategies constitute

85

an effective and legitimate alternative source of regulation to that of the state. It examines their limits as strategies of social control in this light.

The point is not that all of these strategies are novel but that there has been a resurgence in their use and that they are increasingly important in a contemporary context. Their use at a time of heightened globalization, coinciding (not incidentally) with a perception within the environmental movement of the shortcomings of existing regulation of TNCs, offers an interesting example of the ways in which ENGOs adapt their strategies to changing political and economic circumstances.

Such an analysis of the role of ENGOs in the global economy contributes simultaneously to a less state-centered understanding of the importance of NGOs in global affairs and to the development of an international political economy (IPE) of the environment. The course of global economic development is affected by nongovernmental organization (NGO) strategies that seek to embed the economic activities of private actors within social priorities, a central issue for scholars of IPE. James Mittelman (1998b) and Dominic Glover (1999) have both described resistance to globalization in these Polanyian terms. Also, the ways in which economic change shapes the practice of environmental politics suggest the need to integrate perspectives from IPE with those on the environment.

This chapter proceeds in three parts. First, I outline a number of academic debates within global environmental politics and global political economy that suggest the relevance of these NGO practices at this juncture in global politics. Second, I discuss a range of strategies employed by environmental groups targeted at TNCs; finally, I address the limits of these mechanisms as a system of governance.

Environmentalism in an Age of Globalization

The background to the growth of the relationships between ENGOs and TNCs is informed by twin developments in global environmental politics and the global political economy. First, the effectiveness of traditional mechanisms for achieving environmental protection has come under critical scrutiny. International environmental institutions have been criticized as a result of the disappointment felt by many at the outcome of the 1992 United Nations Conference on Environment and Development (UNCED) in Rio. This disillusionment was heightened by the Rio+5 evaluations of 1997, which demonstrated a lack of progress in implementing the goals of the conference (Dodds 1997). Often international agreements are arduous to negotiate, vaguely worded, and difficult to enforce. The greatest indictment of all is that despite the proliferation of interstate accords relating to the environment, the rate of environmental degradation in most areas proceeds unabated (Conca 1993). Existing mechanisms for environmental governance currently amount to little more than an institutional bandage applied to a structural hemorrhage (Vogler 1996).

Of particular concern has been the failure of international environmental agreements to regulate the companies that are responsible for ecological degradation. This is explained both by the political influence of industry lobbies and the reluctance of states to impose restrictions on the companies they depend on for investment (Newell and Paterson 1998). This reluctance is heightened by the process of globalization, which allows companies greater freedom to choose where to locate their business, because of enhanced capital mobility and the internationalization of production. The structural power of capital over states, therefore, also becomes a disciplinary power that penalizes, through the threat of relocation, governments that propose market interventions to protect the environment. This makes it costly for states to adopt unilateral and regional environmental measures in the absence of similar measures by rival states and firms. At the same time, during the UNCED negotiations, TNCs successfully presented themselves as part of the solution, arguing that only they can deliver the necessary capital, technology, and expertise to promote positive environmental change (Chatterjee and Finger 1994).

An international code of conduct to regulate the activities of TNCs has been on the international agenda since the 1970s (Muchlinski 1999). The United Nations Center for Transnational Corporations was set up in 1973 to perform this task, but after two decades of failed negotiations, it was closed in 1993 and replaced by the Division on Transnational Corporations and Investment located within the United Nations Conference on Trade and Development (UNCTAD). In place of binding commitments at the international level, there has been a proliferation of voluntary agreements, self-monitoring, and sustainability audits of corporations by external consultants. The best-known voluntary guidelines on the environment are those endorsed by the International Chamber of Commerce (ICC) and known as the *Business Charter for Sustainable Development*, a document of sixteen principles produced prior to UNCED (Schmidheiny 1992).

The failure of states and interstate organizations to regulate TNCs also coincides with a changed context of ENGO-TNC relations, informed by organizational and perceptual changes within both the business and NGO communities. The opportunity for more cooperative solutions has been occasioned by a more solutions-oriented approach adopted by many NGOs that have sought to move beyond raising awareness to engage directly in reform, sometimes by collaborating with TNCs (*SustainAbility* 1996; Murphy and Bendell 1997).

The growth in the size of many ENGOs (particularly during the mid- to late 1980s) also means that they cannot afford the risk of litigation. They now have sizable assets that would be threatened by successful court action against them. Hence, despite the ongoing role of Brent Spar–style confrontations,[1] cooperative approaches have become more important for some groups aiming to develop credibility among those able to generate reform and to avoid financial loss.

Businesses have also become more proactive in their responses to environmental issues since the late 1980s (Fischer and Schot 1993; Hoffman 1996). As Virginia Haufler (1997:7) notes, in order to preempt government regulation, firms may decide it is in their interest to construct their own regulatory framework. In so doing they make it more difficult for governments to impose regulations and easier for them simply to endorse the company's own framework and incorporate it into law.

The challenge for ENGOs monitoring the global activities of TNCs is made more difficult by the fact that, as Julian Saurin (1996) argues, globalization permits increased distance between the source and site of consumption. However, technological advances in transportation and communications have also compressed time and space such that flashpoints can spread rapidly around the world; instead of having to deal with a single and more manageable source of opposition, corporations today have to deal with simultaneous, coordinated actions of an international nature. Contemporary communications technologies thus enable ENGOs to organize more quickly and effectively and to extend the reach of their surveillance of TNCs, so that, ironically, TNCs have also provided the means for their own monitoring. Public relations disasters can be ignited easily and with global ramifications.

The New Governance

In the context of this crisis of governance, altered global circumstances, and shifting patterns of business-ENGO relations, a number of strategies have been employed by ENGOs in recent years to target TNCs. Many are not new strategies as such; for example, there is a long history of the use of consumer boycotts (Smith 1990). Other mechanisms of restraint, such as exposure of corporate misconduct and noncompliance, also have a (relatively) long history. Shareholder activism and the emergence of stewardship councils, as they are applied in the environmental area, do seem to be largely new phenomena, however. The point, though, is that all these strategies, whether new or not, now appear to be applied more frequently than was the case even ten years ago.

These strategies may be proactive, reactive, confrontational, or collaborative in nature. NGOs often employ different strategies alongside one another to supplement the strengths and limits of other tactics. Consumer boycotts may be used alongside shareholder activism, and propaganda wars can be waged in conjunction with a project collaboration. Nevertheless, while there is overlap in which some groups are willing and able to use cooperative (liberal) and confrontational (critical) strategies at the same time, others tend to engage in one *or* the other.

Before distinguishing between liberal and critical strategies, it is important to ask whether the strategies described below can legitimately be considered a form of governance. There can be little doubt that pressures on TNCs to subscribe to principles or sign up to codes of conduct, for instance, do create checks and balances in a system in which the pressure of competition often results in the removal of conditions on investment. They have the effect of encouraging TNCs as private actors to justify their actions to broader public constituencies of shareholders, consumers, and civil society at large. Such practices introduce, therefore, new dialogues and forms of authority. In this sense, the politics that the groups practice contribute toward a new code of ethics and a (limited) framework of norms about how companies should view their impact on the environment. Insofar as governance describes the way in which social activity is rule bound and socially regulated, the interactions between NGOs and TNCs—which these new strategies of engagement describe—can be couched in the language of governance. This is consistent with James

Rosenau's (1992:5) broad definition of governance as "a set of regulation mechanisms in a sphere of activity which function effectively even though they are not endowed with formal authority." It includes therefore "informal, non-governmental mechanisms," (Rosenau 1992:5) where systems of rules (at any level) within which goals are pursued through the exercise of control have transnational repercussions (Rosenau 1995:13–14).

It is in this broad sense that the term "governance" is used in this chapter, and thus it differs from more traditional applications in international relations (IR). The key concern for a number of post-realists is how to maintain order and manage complex interdependencies amid the alleged breakdown of traditional structures of authority (Smouts 1998). Liberal institutionalists such as Oran Young (1997) explore the role of international regimes in contributing to global governance. Even within these narrow conceptions of governance as institutions, however, there is room to ascribe governance functions to the forms of regulation created by relations between NGOs and TNCs. For example, Young (1994:3) considers institutions to be "sets of rules of the game or codes of conduct that serve to define social practices, assign roles to the participants in these practices, and guide the interactions among the participants of these roles." Paul Wapner (1997b:81) argues on this basis that "to the degree that NGOs successfully shift the standards of good conduct, the economic incentives of certain actions, or fundamental understandings that animate particular widespread activities, it represents an important strategy for establishing institutions to govern widespread behavior."

The social regulation that NGO strategies help to produce does not often derive from consensus-building politics, however. It is often "minilateral" rather than global in scope (Hirst and Thompson 1996) and is not principally aimed at the reform of international organizations (conventionally understood). The sources of power used to produce sites of social control in this context are markedly different from more formal and institution-bound concepts of regulation that pervade traditional IR thinking.

Nevertheless, the governance literature in general provides a useful starting point because of its twin emphases on governing mechanisms that do not rest on recourse to the authority and sanctions of government, and on the shifting negotiation of responsibilities between the state and civil society (Stoker 1998). To reduce the concept of governance to a framework of formal law enforced by institutions with coercive capacity is to uphold as legitimate only those social relations that rest upon an ability to mobilize overpowering force in order to be effective.

In terms of environmental governance more specifically, governance is thought of in statist terms (as regulatory control), in market terms (as a price mechanism), and in social terms (as the role of civil society in creating social ties) (Glasbergen 1998). The use of "governance" to describe relations between ENGOS and TNCs is a departure from this literature. It transgresses these categories by showing how civil society can use the market to effect new forms of regulation. This is important in the environmental area because of the limited capacity or willingness of governments to orient the market toward sustainable practices of consumption and production. The focus here is also on less cooperative modes of engagement. It considers the ability of oppositional tactics to promote company regulation, albeit through nontraditional means. Thus, two types of governance are discussed below: liberal and critical governance.

Liberal Governance

Liberal governance refers to a range of strategies that aim at rewarding good business practice. These strategies work within the current economic system to improve the way in which it functions and to offset its worst ecological excesses. In short, the preference is for responsible management rather than ideological confrontation.[2] There has been significant growth in the adoption of liberal governance strategies since the 1980s. Below is an elaboration of some of the prominent strategies of liberal governance.

Ecoconsumerism. The trend toward purchasing products considered to have a less damaging impact on the environment (or "green consumerism") exploded first in the 1980s in the United States. In promoting ecoconsumerism, groups such as Greenpeace have tried to provide companies with financial incentives to pursue markets for environmentally sound products by showing that such markets exist. Greenpeace's promotion of a "greenfreeze" refrigerator, which runs without the use of ozone-depleting chemicals, is a prominent example. Attempts to promote social reform through purchasing power have a long history (Smith 1990). The ethical consumerism that appeared in the late 1980s, however, responded to different impulses and issues. The magazine *Ethical Consumer* captures its contemporary form:

> We argue that the rise of ethical consumerism is closely connected to globalisation and the pressures this puts on democratic governments to avoid corporate regulation. . . . With few ideas on the horizon which so directly address the social and environmental consequences of globalisation, most evidence points to increasing levels of activity in this field. (*Ethical Consumer* 1997/1998:25)

Under the heading "Democratising the Market," the magazine declares that

> in a world where people feel politically disempowered and where governments are becoming less powerful than corporations, citizens are beginning to realize that their economic vote may have as much influence as their political vote. This is true both for individuals and institutional purchasers. This enables purchasers to assert their ethical values *through* the market by providing information. (*Ethical Consumer* 1997/1998:inside cover, 3)

What makes this a liberal governance strategy is the use of the market to express political will and the harnessing of consumer power to the goal of corporate reform. Hence, while the impact of consumption is an issue, the strategy for reform is different consumption, not necessarily less consumption.

Project collaboration.   There has been a substantial growth in recent years in environmental partnerships between businesses and environmental groups. These partnerships have taken a number of forms. Often the goal is joint research output, the preemption of political conflict, or the desire to implement a mutually beneficial project (Long and Arnold 1995). One of the most famous examples of ENGO-TNC cooperation is the project undertaken by the Environmental Defense Fund (EDF) and McDonald's Corporation, often held up as a model of NGO-TNC collaboration. The focus of concern was the company's "clamshell" polystyrene container for hamburgers. In August 1990, representatives of McDonald's and the EDF signed an agreement to establish a joint task force to address the company's solid waste issues. The agreement allows the EDF to criticize the company and permits both parties to produce separate statements if they disagree on research findings. Broader issues relating to the company's role in accelerating rainforest destruction, for example, were strictly off limits, however. The mandate was deliberately defined narrowly to avoid broader conflicts of interest.

The payoff for the company was obvious. By January 1991, a Gallup poll found that McDonald's was regarded as the most environmentally responsible food chain. McDonald's also gained access to the waste management expertise of EDF (Long and Arnold 1995). For EDF, the partnership is seen as a model for other environmental groups to pursue, though involvement with the task force did divert attention from some of EDF's ongoing projects.[3] The strategy of this project collaboration is liberal in its emphasis on pooling expertise and avoiding conflict, and in its belief in the reformability of a company that, due to the nature of its operations, has an enormous ecological impact.

Codes of conduct. One increasingly popular form of liberal governance is the negotiation of a code of conduct between environmental NGOs and businesses, often in a particular sector. This code is recognized by both parties as a commitment to fulfill stated environmental goals.

In 1989, a coalition of environmental, investor, and church interests known as the Coalition for Environmentally Responsible Economies (CERES), met in New York to introduce a ten-point environmental code of conduct for corporations. One month later, CERES, along with the Green Alliance, launched a similar effort in the UK. The aim was to provide criteria for auditing the environmental performance of large domestic and multinational industries. The code called on companies to minimize the release of pollutants, conserve nonrenewable resources, use sustainable energy sources, and consider environmental commitment as a factor in appointing members to the board of directors. The principles are known as the Valdez Principles (named after the *Exxon Valdez* disaster in 1989) and have been used by groups such as Friends of the Earth (FOE) to encourage corporations to pledge compliance. Companies endorsing the CERES principles are required to report annually on their implementation of the principles.

Wapner (1997b:82) argues that "the CERES Principles represent a new set of institutional constraints on companies and thus another instance of going outside the state system to institutionalize guidelines for widespread and transnational behavior." Accepting the principles enables companies to legitimize their activities by representing them as ecologically responsible.[4] While the principles also provide a useful lobbying tool that environmental groups can use to pressure companies to remain faithful to their promises, companies have been able to use them as a way of avoiding government regulation.[5]

Private regimes.   Stewardship regimes that bring together environmental groups, companies, and other interested parties to formulate accreditation procedures for good corporate conduct have also developed in recent years.[6] These are more formalized and institutionalized than codes of conduct. They provide an ongoing arena in which dialogue and review take place. The Forestry Stewardship Council (FSC) provides an interesting example of this form of governance.

In response to the "lack of commitment and progress being observed at the international policy level" (Murphy and Bendell 1997:105), World Wide Fund for Nature (WWF)–UK decided to pursue a campaign aimed at ensuring that, by the end of 1995, all tropical wood and wood products traded in the United Kingdom would come from well-managed forests. Manufacturers' misuse of claims about forestry management led to pressure for the establishment of a standard-setting body with a system for verifying product claims. As a result, the FSC was established in 1993. The founding group consisted of environmental NGOs, forest industry representatives, community forest groups, and forest product certification organizations. Members of the FSC agreed to nine principles of forestry management. The council set up an independent forest accreditation program to alleviate consumer confusion about sustainable timber by issuing FSC logos to products from forests independently certified according to the established principles.

There has been a proliferation in similar schemes elsewhere in the world, with NGOs initiating buyer groups and FSC working groups. In each case "a lack of effective government action was a significant factor in making environmental groups turn to the industry itself" (Murphy and Bendell 1997:130). The success of the scheme is based, in part, on the exchange of the perceived legitimacy of ENGOs as the appropriate arbiters of what constitutes sustainable practice for company concessions on forestry reform. The strategy also plays on the power of the consumer to alter corporate practice and upholds the market as the appropriate mechanism by which to pursue change.

Critical Governance

Alongside the proliferation of liberal governance strategies, there has developed another, and altogether different, range of strategies. What sets them apart from liberal strategies is the goals they adopt and the forms they take. They are more oppositional than liberal governance strategies without being transformative in the way the term is used in critical theory (Cox 1996b:87–91). Critical governance defines a broad set of strategies designed to bring about immediate changes even if they are driven by larger transformational ambitions. Hence, while they may ultimately have systemic implications, it is the short-term impacts that are of interest here. Evaluating the contemporary role of critical strategies in producing informal governance in the global economy requires such a short-term focus.

The growth in consumer boycotts and campaigns specifically targeted against TNCs, and the proliferation of groups whose principal aim is to document and expose corporate malpractice, provide evidence of a countercorporate culture. These strategies allow less scope for compromise and dialogue than liberal strategies. Unlike liberal governance strategies, the aim of ENGOs engaged in critical governance actions is primarily to punish and expose what they consider to be irresponsible corporate conduct. Insofar as the company responds to ENGO criticisms, reforms its behavior in light of the confrontation, or adopts new working practices, informal regulation has taken place, albeit not through open discussion.

Critical governance campaigns often constitute a refutation of the practices and goals of transnational corporate activity. In this instance, the term "resistance" rather than "governance" may be more apt. However, where social regulation is achieved and new working practices are put in place in response to normative pressures, a framework of governance can be said to be in operation. Therefore, even if the intention behind a particular strategy is not to create new forms of regulation, strategies of resistance, such as those pursued by the McLibel group (see below), do have the effect of producing social control.

Critical governance strategies demonstrate a greater diversity in tactics and goals than liberal governance strategies. They range from consumer boycotts that are closely associated with the liberal strategy of ethical consumerism to strongly anticonsumerist campaigns of groups like AdBusters, which targets the advertising industry. Despite this breadth, the term "critical" is useful in distinguishing the strategies described below that seek to confront and challenge aspects of corporate power from those that pursue reform, often through liberal devices of dialogue and accommodation. The following examples help to illustrate the forms that this type of governance takes.

Consumer boycotts.   Often a reaction to the unwillingness of states to address allegations of corporate misconduct, consumer boycotts have been used to effect change across a range of issues and tend to follow a similar path. ENGO efforts are geared toward ensuring that individuals and institutions (churches, universities) boycott goods from the firm in question (Rodman 1997). Sometimes the very threat of a boycott is sufficient to bring about change in the behavior of a TNC. The company has only to anticipate the commercial and political damage that a successful boycott may inflict on its profit margins and public reputation to change its behavior.

One of the most internationalized boycotts in recent times was directed at the Shell Oil Company. Allegations about the company's destruction of the Ogoni people's land in Nigeria and complicity with state suppression of Ogoni human rights led to a boycott campaign that arose in response to the absence of government pressure.[7] The campaigns of ENGOs and other groups failed to induce governments to impose an oil embargo or mandate disinvestment (Rodman 1998). The call for sanctions encountered corporate opposition, and asset freezes and investment bans were not forthcoming. Given the unwillingness of states to support sanctions, ENGOs applied direct pressure on the company. The groups sought to stigmatize the company's Nigerian operations through Europe-wide demonstrations at its service stations. Shell was forced to suspend operations in Ogoniland in January 1993 after protests by the Movement for the Survival of the Ogoni People (MOSOP) against the company's environmental practices had successfully drawn overwhelming international condemnation of the company's activities.

However, while Shell was forced to acknowledge that it had responsibilities in the regions in which it invests, boycotts of Shell, Chevron, Mobil, and others investing in Nigeria did not succeed in bringing about the withdrawal of those companies. Nigeria was Shell's second largest source of crude oil after the North Sea, so compliance with the boycotters' demands would have been costly. Shell did, however, retreat from its initial position that it was not responsible for environmental damages caused by its operations. In 1996, it hired Integrity Works, a business ethics consulting firm, to use the media to defend the company's presence in Nigeria on moral and commercial grounds. The company also accepted some financial responsibility for repairing the damage it had caused, committing itself to a five-year, $100 million per year program to clean up oil spills and underwrite community investments in Ogoniland (Rodman 1997:33).

There has also been some long-term sensitization by the company to NGO concerns in the light of the Ogoni affair. Recent Shell investments in forest areas of Peru, for instance, have followed careful guidelines to ensure that the scrutiny of NGOs does not uncover grounds for complaint (Chatterjee 1997).

The aim of consumer boycotts is the abandonment of activities rather than dialogue about limiting the impact of operations. The issue is not worked out in closed-door meetings between business and NGOs, as is often the case in liberal collaborations, but in the public arena (through the media and at service stations) with the explicit intention of exposing and punishing environmental (and other) abuses.

Counterinformation.   Advertising is key to the ability of TNCs to project themselves globally. Building a transnational base of customers who associate a company's product with quality requires good public relations. Acknowledgment of the importance of this aspect of corporate power has led some ENGOs to engage in what is loosely termed counterinformation, or perhaps more appropriately, propaganda wars. This strategy centers on attacking a company on the basis of the claims it makes about itself and encouraging customers to boycott the company. Such campaigns are intended to expose perceived corporate misconduct, force the company to defend its reputation in public, and dent its political and economic power.

The most recent and prominent example of such a campaign was the McLibel case between the McDonald's corporation and London Greenpeace.[8] The case against McDonald's, orchestrated initially by London Greenpeace and delivered through the distribution of leaflets within the United Kingdom under the title *What's Wrong with McDonald's*? was that the corporation was exploiting its workforce, treating animals cruelly, and engaging in practices destructive to the environment (including excessive packaging, generation of litter, and clearing of tropical forests for use as ranchland). The leaflet led to prosecution of the McLibel Two, who were pinpointed for their involvement in the authorship of the leaflet alleged to be libelous by the corporation; the result was the longest libel trial in British legal history. McDonald's had enormous financial muscle, good political contacts, and access to the best libel lawyer in the country. The McLibel Two relied on portraying themselves as victims of corporate suppression of the right to express their opinions, successfully manipulating "David and Goliath" parallels.

The corporation felt that the verdict of the trial cleared its name. While finding that there was no basis for the leaflet's claim that McDonald's directly contributed to the destruction of the rainforests, the judge ruled in favor of the defendants' claims that the company was investing in practices considered to be cruel to animals, targeting children with misleading claims about the nutritional content of its foods, and to some degree exploiting its workforce. The campaign currently continues through the distribution of materials (including the libelous leaflet) aimed at exposing the alleged malpractices of the company, and the McLibel Two are appealing the verdict to attract further public scrutiny of McDonald's activities. The attempt by the company to silence its critics provoked a strong backlash against what many considered to be suppression of dissent and an act of corporate bullying. The publication of the leaflet served to engage McDonald's in an acrimonious dialogue in which it was forced to respond to critics and defend its reputation. The McLibel case, however, was as much about resisting the culture of globalization, which the activists felt McDonald's was propagating, as it was about controlling the environmental impact of the company. It was an attack on the "McDonaldization of society" (Ritzer 1993).[9]

TNC monitors. Another trend within the environmental movement has been the growth in organizations solely devoted to the surveillance of the activities of TNCs. These organizations are at the front line of action against TNCs, implicating them in acts of environmental degradation and disseminating this knowledge to a broader community of activists who then employ the sorts of strategies described above to effect change in the company's behavior. Examples of groups that fit into this category are CorporateWatch in the United Kingdom, The Multinationals Resource Center in the United States, the Centre for Research on Multinational Corporations in the Netherlands, and the People's Action Network to Monitor Japanese Transnationals in Japan; also active are sector-specific monitors such as OilWatch, which has offices in a number of developing countries in which oil companies operate. Based on the premise that what companies say about their own activities is not to be trusted and that government surveillance of TNC operations is limited, TNC monitors seek to deter companies from violating their legal and social obligations by threatening exposure and the activation of campaigns against them. Such criticism and exposure helps to pave the way for confrontational campaigns, including demonstrations and company boycotts.

Shareholder activism.   In recent years, particularly in the United States and the United Kingdom, there has been growth in shareholder activism, whereby environmental and other groups buy a small number of shares in a company and encourage their supporters to do the same as a way of obtaining access to the company's annual general meeting, a forum in which they can influence company decisionmaking. Oil and road-building companies have been the principal targets of this strategy to date. The sponsorship of resolutions at company meetings is aimed at overturning management decisions or forcing the adoption of a social responsibility measure (Vogel 1978). The tactic is to play on the "hassle factor," forcing corporations to devote a disproportionate share of their resources to defend a small part of their global operations where the alleged offense is taking place (Rodman 1997, 1998).

Shell Transport and Trading, the United Kingdom arm of Shell International, had an embarrassing confrontation with institutional shareholders in April-May 1997 over its environmental (and human rights) record in Nigeria (see above). A group of shareholders holding just 1 percent of company shares called upon the company to improve accountability by establishing new procedures for dealing with environmental and human rights issues (Lewis 1997).[10] The resolution called for a designated member of Shell's committee of managing directors to take charge of environmental and corporate responsibility policies and for an external audit of those policies. The resolution, supported by groups such as WWF and Amnesty International, called on Shell to publish before the end of the year a report on its controversial activities in Nigeria. In an effort to "ward off further trouble" (Caulkin 1997), Shell attempted to preempt the shareholder motion prior to the meeting by revamping the corporation's Statement on General Business Principles to include human rights and sustainable development and by publishing its first report on worldwide health and safety and environmental activities.[11]

Limits of Nonstate Governance

It is apparent, then, that the difference between liberal and critical governance amounts to more than a distinction between insider and outsider strategies. The same strategy can serve different purposes for different groups. There are also areas of overlap between the strategies, and they are often used to complement one another. Ethical consumerism is the positive, reforming side of the more punitive consumer boycott, for instance. The same group can simultaneously pursue liberal and critical strategies across different issues, so that while Greenpeace is encouraging consumers to boycott Shell, it is also working with companies to develop ozone-friendly refrigerators. Critical and liberal strategies can even be used by the same group at the same time with the same company. Greenpeace mounted a hostile public relations campaign against the Monsanto food company for promoting genetically modified organisms but has simultaneously engaged in dialogue with the company about developing a PVC–free credit card for its supporters (Fabig and Boele 1999). In lobbying for sustainable forestry, FOE has both participated in the liberal FSC and encouraged members to use a critical boycott strategy against products not produced from sustainable forest sources. The two strategies complement each other such that critical strategies may, in some cases, clear the path for the pursuit of more liberal forms of engagement. Groups therefore tend to employ a package of tactics on particular issues to maximize the potential for reform. Clearly, then, it is particular campaigns or strategies that are liberal or critical and not the groups themselves, which often seem to transcend such categories.

If such strategies are to be regarded more widely as mechanisms that can help to reinforce existing state regulation of corporate activity as it relates to the environment, the ENGOs pursuing them will have to address a number of issues. First, although ENGOs themselves undoubtedly consider what they are doing to be in the public interest, there are thorny issues regarding representation and accountability that arise from ENGOs assuming these functions. In order to legitimately act in the public interest, ENGOs will have to respond to a broad base within society. Yet there are few mechanisms for channeling public concerns into ENGO campaigns. Even mass membership organizations represent only a fragment of the broader population who may not share ENGO's concerns about TNCs and who may perceive themselves to be benefiting from TNC activities even where they impose environmental costs. There is a danger here not only of paternalism in terms of NGOs' presumption of an enlightened understanding of what is in the public interest, but also of elitism, where the agenda of international politics is driven by the concerns of a small, often white middle-class Western segment of society.

This is clearly less the case with governance strategies that depend on large-scale consumer cooperation to make an impact. Boycotts in particular, if they are to be successful, have to be undertaken by a significant number of people in different markets if TNCs are to take them seriously. Similarly, for shareholder activism to be effective, there has to be a large constituency of shareholders willing to back proposals for reform. If these campaigns amounted to nothing more than Western ENGOs acting in their own interests, it is plausible to argue that TNCs would not feel the need to respond. It is when issues of broader public credibility are at stake, when potential shareholder revolts loom, or popular boycotts appear imminent, that TNCs are drawn into dialogue or change their behavior.

At the moment, these strategies are also ad hoc, limited in geographical scope, and focused on particular TNCs. Boycotts have to be adopted in those markets of greatest importance to the TNC. Fortunately for the environmental movement, many of those TNCs that have been the target of consumer action depend on success in Western markets for their profit margins, where environmental concern is strongest. Although there is evidence of ENGOs employing some of these strategies in developing world contexts, at the moment they serve principally as a mechanism to embed TNC activity in a framework of Western norms and expectations about environmental conduct that may not be appropriate elsewhere.

It is apparent, moreover, that different TNCs are more or less vulnerable to such strategies, a factor that further underscores the currently parochial nature of these models of governance. Kenneth Rodman, in his discussion of ENGO pressure on TNCs investing in Burma, shows that the oil companies have been "the most impervious to non-governmental pressures" (Rodman 1997:29) because their access to technology, expertise, and distribution networks cannot easily be replicated by companies from other regions. This encourages the host governments to provide extra inducements for the company to continue investing in their countries. Thus, where ENGO strategies directly conflict with key state interests, it will always be more difficult to change TNC behavior.

Campaigns likely to be most successful are those targeted against particular projects that are of negligible value to the overall operation of the company, so that fear of loss of profits and damage to reputation in other—more profitable—markets may be enough to make the targeted operation a liability. Only those TNCs vulnerable to ENGO pressure where consumer preference really matters are likely to be affected by such initiatives. In this sense, the scope of the surveillance is restricted to easy targets.

As a set of mechanisms for regulating environmental impacts, the strategies are highly discriminatory. It is difficult to be sure of ENGOs' motivations for targeting TNCs. There is some suggestion, for instance, that part of the incentive for Greenpeace to target Shell over the disposal of the Brent Spar oil rig derived from membership pressure to reestablish its credentials as a direct action organization (Dickson and McCulloch 1996).

In terms of enhancing the governability of corporations, the shifting and unpredictable terrain of confrontations with different ENGOs may be considered a poor substitute for government interventions. Businesses find it hard to anticipate what degree of responsibility is expected of them and what sort of programs, measures, and actions they need to take to pacify their critics, particularly when traditional tools of engagement, such as the use of science and economic studies, cannot be used to rationalize their position in a debate. The only reference point is the past experience of other companies faced with similar situations and a moral discourse that in many ways is subversive of their core beliefs and assumptions. This makes it difficult for TNCs to establish, in a proactive manner, the type of environmental protection measures ENGOs demand of them.

In general, the problem is that rather than constituting a consistent tier of governance, the pockets of restraint are just that—a patchwork of often unorchestrated activities and campaigns aimed at regulating and resisting selected environmental impacts of TNCs. It is perhaps unreasonable, or even undesirable, for them to be more than this, but the impact of these strategies is curtailed as a result.

The issues raised above about the scope of these strategies, about the right of ENGOs to act as a mouthpiece for the public interest, as well as problems of internal organization as they relate to transparency, all center on the question of legitimacy. This is important in terms of the future applicability and viability of the governance practices ENGOs are creating as alternative sites of regulatory authority. It is also necessary to question what impact these strategies really have in order to assess whether they can produce forms of social regulation adequate to the task of substituting for government regulation of the environmental impact of TNC activities. It is very difficult to assess the effect of a particular campaign in political or economic terms because of the closed nature of boardroom decisionmaking, and because TNCs rarely concede that ENGO pressure led them to change their behavior for fear of further encouraging such actions. The process is often invisible. It centers on corporations anticipating the reactions of ENGOs, preempting a backlash by not pursuing a particular course of action, and therefore engaging in nondecisionmaking (Bachrach and Baratz 1963). Despite the unpredictability and malleability of the governance framework produced by ENGO strategies, companies can anticipate that certain forms of behavior will be considered unacceptable, sometimes based on the experience of another company's battle with an ENGO, but more often than not by being aware that tacit boundaries exist that it is costly to transgress.

Clearly, in many cases, business has continued more or less as usual in spite of these activities. It is questionable whether companies really learn from their encounters with ENGOs or whether, in all but the most extreme cases, they are insulated from these pressures. The likelihood of success appears to be greater where ENGO pressures coincide with pressure from governments or international institutions. ENGO action against TNCs is therefore likely to make a bigger impact where the threat of governmental regulation looms on the horizon or where NGO campaigns are backed by governments. For example, in the Brent Spar case, the campaign led by Greenpeace against Shell coincided with pressure on the British government from various governments, led by Germany. This combination of "inside" and "outside" pressures had a mutually reinforcing effect, leading to the British decision to abandon the option of disposing of the oil rig at sea. Similarly, the experience to date of codes of conduct and other forms of cooperative environmental management suggests that businesses often promote self-regulation in response to demands for more stringent government action and to undermine the need for binding government interventions (Glasbergen 1998; Murphy and Bendell 1997; Muchlinski 1999).

Conclusion

The theoretical implications of the relationships described here are significant and contribute to a more comprehensive global political economy of the environment. They offer a less state-centered reading of the important dynamics in global environmental politics by focusing on the interaction of economic agents with nonstate environmental actors. They highlight the need to transcend narrow and restrictive definitions of international environmental politics that reify interstate accords as the only appropriate and legitimate mechanism for addressing environmental problems.

This is especially problematic given the repeated failure of states and international regimes to confront the environmental impact of TNC activity. We should recognize that there are very real constraints on the ability of these institutions to deliver effective environmental protection when they have such close ties to the industries they are supposed to regulate. At the same time, however, a note of caution has been struck about reifying the ability of nonstate actors to deliver effective and lasting environmental protection (Lipschutz with Mayer 1996:254) without addressing issues such as transparency, consistency, and accountability in the way they organize their activities.

This exploration of the relations between ENGOs and TNCs provides a useful way of understanding power shifts in the global economy, the way ENGOs perceive and react to them, and the contribution of noneconomic actors to the governance of the global economy. The activities of ENGOs described in this chapter are contributing to the reconfiguration of the landscape of global economic affairs by creating new social norms and changing the practice of transnational firms, as well as by highlighting, as others have done, pockets of resistance to globalization (Gills 1997).

In terms of broader changes within the global political economy, the odds are not good for these informal patterns of governance. Globalization strengthens TNCs in many ways by allowing them unprecedented freedoms. The World Trade Organization (WTO) and the Multilateral Agreement on Investment (MAI) seek to enshrine the rights of capital at the global level (Gill 1995; see also Chapters 3, 4, 6, and 7). It should also not be overlooked that governments are driving the globalization process forward. They protect and defend the interests of TNCs as well as seek to extend them in new directions. In a wider sense, TNCs still have legal backing for their activities, even though social norms may be outstripping the legal requirements imposed on firms (Mitchell 1997). Corporations argue that only governments can determine what is legitimate and illegitimate behavior (see Chapter 4). Companies prefer regulations that come from governments dependent on them for investment, because they can shape their content or resist their development. In contrast, the power they exercise over ENGOs is much reduced and the rules of engagement less familiar or predictable.

The fact that states will continue to be the primary source of environmental regulation of TNCs should not be grounds for dismissing the importance of ENGO governance forms. While there are areas of overlap, complementarity, and resemblance between state-based and ENGO-centered regulation, they operate differently and in pursuit of distinct goals. The analogy drawn between ENGO strategies and the tools of statecraft makes sense only inasmuch as boycotts are a form of economic sanction, insofar as codes of conduct are a form of legal regulation, and to the extent that stewardship councils count as a regime that ENGOs negotiate and help to police.

What is notable, however, is that ENGOs may be exercising a different form of power over corporations. These organizations use information and images to expose and educate the corporate sector. Theirs is a less coercive power than state-based regulation because it aims at changing consciousness and creating mechanisms of accountability. They employ informal channels of political engagement, such as norms, moral codes, and knowledge, rather than law and forced compliance, tools that the state has at its disposal

(Wapner 1996). To dismiss the importance of NGOs because they are not powerful in the way states are is to understate the complexity of their contribution to global affairs.

As was suggested at the start of this chapter, many of these ENGO strategies result from frustration with the formal political process and the incapacity or unwillingness of the state to act in defense of the environment. They seek to re-embed the activities of global economic actors within a political and social framework supportive of environmental protection. They may also, however, prompt government intervention to provide an element of uniformity, consistency, and public authority to these informal practices of regulation that may evolve into a broader attempt at reregulating the corporate sector.

Notes

I would like to thank the following people for useful comments made on earlier drafts of this chapter: Matthew Paterson, John MacMillan, David Levy, two anonymous referees, the editors of the book, and my colleagues from the Governance Group at IDS.

1. Shell was involved in a standoff with Greenpeace over its decision to dispose of the Brent Spar oil rig at sea. The rig was occupied by Greenpeace activists, and a boycott of the company was launched (cf., Dickson and McCulloch 1996).

2. This emphasis on cooperation should not be confused with work on cooperative environmental governance or cooperative management that refers to public-private partnerships between government and business in which NGOs play a mediating role (Glasbergen 1998).

3. For more details on project collaborations, see Dubash and Oppenheimer (1992), SustainAbility (1996), and Long and Arnold (1995).

4. See Humphreys (1997), Murphy and Bendell (1997), and Wapner (1996, 1997b) for more on codes of conduct.

5. Humphreys (1997) highlights the case of the Sun company (a petroleum refining company), which used its endorsement of the Valdez principles to gain credibility when lobbying against environmental legislation in Congress.

6. It should be noted here that the use of the term by Haufler (1995) to describe regimes in which exclusively private sector agents participate is different from my use of the term to imply a nongovernmental arena for the regulation of the activities of private sector actors by NGOs. Other ecolabeling schemes and international standard-setting authorities such as the ISO have not been mentioned here because they are primarily state-based initiatives.

7. For a disparaging account of the environmental impact of Shell's investment in Nigeria, see *Greenline* magazine (1997:13).

8. For more on this case, see Murphy and Bendell (1997), Gorelick (1997), *The Economist* (1996:77–78), and Vidal (1997b).

9. Ritzer (1993:1) uses the term "McDonaldization" to describe a "wide-ranging process . . . by which the principles of the fast-food restaurant are coming to dominate more and more sectors of American society as well as the rest of the world."

10. The Shell resolution was said to be the first of its kind in the UK.

11. See also Marinetto (1998) and Vidal (1997a).

Part 2

Policy and Politics in the South

Marian A. L. Miller 6

Tragedy for the Commons: The Enclosure and Commodification of Knowledge

The task of enclosing and commodifying material resources such as land and water is almost complete. Now the focus has shifted to the enclosure and commodification of knowledge. Knowledge and information have always been seen as crucial commodities in the capitalist enterprise, and in the era of biotechnology, their control and manipulation are of growing importance.

This chapter focuses on the increasing enclosure of knowledge about natural resources and processes, and it assesses the consequences of that enclosure for communities and the natural environment. Because of the profitability of biotechnology applications for agriculture and pharmaceuticals, corporations are rushing to commodify knowledge about biological processes. As a result, they are enclosing systems of knowledge associated with the local stewardship of nature, as well as information about the genetic blueprint. To facilitate the process, regulatory changes have been made within global and regional trade institutions.

The European enclosure movement predated the sixteenth century, but that century, which saw the emergence of the capitalist world economy (Wallerstein 1974:67), also saw the beginning of the first major wave of enclosure. This marked the start of a worldwide process of privatization and commodification of land, ocean, and atmosphere. It fundamentally restructured the way people perceived themselves, each other, and the land. Land and people were more likely to be treated as means rather than as ends. This enclosure movement helped create the conditions for the emergence of integrated national economies, and it became international in scope as the social and environmental externalities of enclosure were transferred to colonies. The process of enclosure continues, although there are changes in its scope and nature. It is now a transnational project that includes the commodification and enclosure of intellectual property.

Hence, I argue that the commodification and privatization of knowledge—like the commodification and privatization of land—inexorably lead to tragedy for the commons. The term "commons" can be used to refer to any of a varied group of resources, including land, forests, atmosphere, oceans, seeds, and knowledge. The common factor is joint use. For commons such as oceans and atmosphere, exclusion is difficult. But commons can also include resources such as land and forests, where exclusion is possible. In addition, although one person's use of exhaustible commons resources may subtract from the welfare of others, this is not the case with all commons resources. An inexhaustible commons resource such as knowledge is not subtractable in this fashion.

The commons discussed here do not reflect Garrett Hardin's (1968) limited use of the term. He focused on commons in an open access regime, and his problem could have been more appropriately described as a "tragedy of open access" (Stevenson 1991:3). Despite Hardin's assessment of the commons, they do not have to be despoiled by the drive for individual gain. For example, the commons can be held in a common property regime. Many scholars who have studied the commons issue have found that common property regimes work when the resources are used by a community with formal or informal rules regarding resource use and management.[1] The emphasis is on furthering community welfare rather than promoting accumulation.

Because of his generalization of commons issues within an open access framework, Hardin (1968) suggests enclosure as an appropriate policy recommendation. I disagree, suggesting that in the context of the structured inequality that is a consequence of unrestrained capitalism, enclosure sets in motion a chain of events that result in tragedy for the commons. This tragedy is inevitable given the remorseless logic[2] of the capitalist marketplace. Although land and knowledge are materially different, their enclosures have similar distributional impacts, exacerbating existing inequities. Those who are already privileged benefit disproportionately, and these distributional consequences can be seen among as well as within countries. The result is societal and environmental degradation.

An examination of two cases of enclosure of local commons illustrates the process. The first is the British enclosure of land in Kenya at the beginning of the twentieth century, and the second is the attempt by corporations to enclose knowledge about the neem tree in India. The results of the Kenyan enclosure case are indicative of the likely consequences of the ongoing enclosure of knowledge exemplified by the neem case. An overview of the English enclosure movement establishes the benchmark for the examination of these two, more recent, cases of enclosure.

Enclosure and the Dynamics of Capitalism

Integral to the logic of capitalism is the need for repetitive expansion, involving a continuous reinvestment of profits to create more profits.[3] This relentless, insatiable appetite fuels the drive to incorporate more raw material resources, processes, and markets. Enclosure is a part of the incorporation that occurs as the capitalist world economy expands its borders or as capitalist penetration deepens. For centuries, incorporation meant the expansion of capitalism to include areas outside of the capitalist orbit. But there is limited scope for that today. For the most part, incorporation today describes the deepening of capitalism rather than its expansion.

Capitalism is marked by waves of growth and stagnation. Periodic incorporations are used to address stagnation or other crises. Incorporations may refuel capitalism by reducing the cost of production, creating new products, or increasing consumer demand. Yet, incorporation and enclosure have negative social consequences for some groups, which often react by resisting the associated changes.

Enclosure is integral to the survival of capitalism because capitalism depends both on the institution of private property and on continued expansion of investment, markets, and profits. Private property allows the owners of capital the right of exclusion (Heilbroner 1985:38). Because they can legally refuse to allow their property to be used by others, they have the exclusive right to use particular resources to create more capital and therefore to extract profit from the system. This is the incentive to undo or enclose commons and other noncapitalist arrangements to commodify them.

Increasingly, capitalism has penetrated previously noncommodified areas of daily life and social relations. Much of what is called "growth" in capitalist societies consists of this commodification of life. One consequence of this deepening of capitalism has been the commodification of intellectual property. Science and technology have been enlisted in the deepening of capitalism, allowing owners of capital with access to scientific and technological resources to gain an advantage in the ongoing struggle of economic competition. So, knowledge of nature and natural processes are being enclosed. This enclosure is not limited to new knowledge. In their quest for differential profits, the owners of this kind of capital use patents to prevent others from using common knowledge (Nitzan 1998:192). The imposition of intellectual property rights provides owners of this kind of capital with the ability to enjoy monopoly rents for extended periods.

By redistributing advantages to the strong and from the weak, the continued exercise of the power of capital continues to weaken communities and degrade the commons. The enclosure of the English commons describes this process in the early phase of capitalism.

The English Enclosure Movement

The dismantling of the European commons began more than 700 years ago (Curtler 1920:82).[4] Feudal landlords leased land to peasant farmers under various tenancy arrangements (Curtler 1920:33–44). Some farmers were freeholders with perpetual tenancy; others were leaseholders with a limited multiyear tenancy that could be renewed or withheld; still others were customary tenants who had no legal rights and could lose their tenancy at any time. In return for their right to cultivate the land, tenant farmers had to hand over a portion of their harvest to their landlord or spend time farming the landlord's fields. In some cases, they also paid rents in currency (Curtler 1920:34–35, 41).[5] Peasants combined their individual holdings into open fields that were jointly cultivated, and their animals grazed on common pastures. This open-field system guaranteed access to land for most of the population, but it did not adapt readily to change (*The Ecologist* 1992:131–147). Some analysts conclude that it was a wasteful system that discouraged individual initiative and enterprise and led to the degradation of land and to poor-quality livestock (Curtler 1920:63–64). Yet, for the most part, the commons were self-sufficient. They were administered by peasant councils, and joint decisions were made on issues such as crop rotation, planting and harvesting time, the number of animals that could graze on the commons, and the cutting of forests (Rifkin 1991:38–39). They remained highly resilient to climatological and other environmental assaults as long as they continued to be organized communally for subsistence purposes.

The enclosure movement accelerated in the 1500s, when powerful political and economic forces undermined the village commons. In his 1516 book *Utopia,* Thomas More complained about the noblemen and gentlemen who enclosed all the pasture, removed houses, and destroyed towns (Curtler 1920:88). The enclosure movement was carried out by several means, including acts of Parliament, royal license, purchase of rights by one owner, and common agreement of the collective owners, usually under pressure (Curtler 1920:82). It essentially altered the economic relationship among people as well as between people and the natural environment. This economic, political, and social change paved the way for industrialization and urbanization. It moved millions of former peasants into the new industrial cities where employers in the new factories were eager to take advantage of their desperate circumstances (Rifkin 1991:39–40).

The English enclosure movement predated enclosures in the rest of Europe and illustrates the consequences of the privatization of commonly held land for the individual, the community, and the course of the global economy. England underwent two major waves of enclosure. The first occurred in the 1500s under the Tudor monarchy and the second in the late 1700s and early 1800s during King George III's reign (Slater 1968:6, 110). In the first case, two forces conspired to drive enclosure: inflation increased the cost to landlords whose land rents had been fixed at preinflationary rates; and an expanding textile industry was demanding more wool, making sheep grazing an increasingly lucrative prospect. With the assistance of merchants and bankers, landlords began to buy up the common lands, turning them to pastureland for sheep (Rifkin 1991:40).

An acre of arable land on the commons could produce grain for 670 pounds of bread, whereas the same acre, enclosed, could support only a handful of sheep producing less than 176 pounds of mutton (Slater 1968:264). Many people went hungry while sheep were fattened and fleeced to supply the new textile factories (Rifkin 1991:41). The peasants protested the first wave of enclosures. But many became resigned to their new status as landless people, with their existence marginalized and their worth measured strictly by their labor value. By the mid–eighteenth century almost half of agricultural land in Britain had been transferred to private possession (Rifkin 1991:42–43).

The second wave of enclosures was decisive in terms of the extent to which it reordered economic and social life. It began around 1760 and lasted into the 1840s, as England and the continent were industrializing. Trade routes expanded farther afield, a growing urban population required more food, and the emerging bourgeoisie wanted a greater variety of foodstuffs. To meet these new demands, landlords began their final drive to enclose the remaining English countryside, transforming it into a new, market-oriented agriculture (Gonner 1966:343–358). Under George III, at least 3,554 Acts of Enclosure were passed (Curtler 1920:148).

The enclosure movement affected the conception of time as well as space. A life oriented to the commons adhered closely to the rhythms of nature. But the incipient market economy disrupted this pattern, and natural rhythms and capacities were ignored. These changes had environmental consequences. Established practices of soil conservation were compromised or abandoned to accelerate production. Agricultural land, which had remained fertile for hundreds of years under the stewardship of village communes, was exhausted in the effort to meet the time demands of the market. Capitalists ploughed up ancient meadows to take advantage of high corn prices, and when the prices fell, the meadows were allowed to become degraded pasture (Cobbett 1912:285). Forests were enclosed because they were regarded as nests of sloth and idleness (Rackham 1986:296–297).

The English enclosure movement set the stage for the modern age with its privatization and commodification of land and people. The legions of the dispossessed provided surplus labor for the new industrial factories (Chambers 1953). The pattern of enclosure that was so integral to the success of the Industrial Revolution became a part of the colonial project as land was seized in the New World to feed the mills and mouths of England. This is exemplified in the Kenyan case. And, as the Indian case illustrates, the process continues in the postcolonial period as enclosers target knowledge and nature.

Enclosing the Commons in Kenya

Enclosure was an integral part of the process of colonization. Cecil Rhodes summarized Britain's colonial objectives when he described the new lands as sources of raw materials and cheap labor and as dumping grounds for surplus goods (*The Ecologist* 1992:134). Enclosing common land in the colonies helped Britain achieve three objectives. It provided immediate access to the available natural resources; it forced native peoples into labor at low wage levels; and it developed a colonial class with access to cash. This was done by dispossessing indigenous communities of the greater part of their traditional territories. Throughout the colonies, it became standard practice to declare all "uncultivated" land to be the property of the colonial administration. Local communities were denied legal title to lands set aside as fallow and to the forests, grazing lands, and streams they depended on for hunting, gathering, fishing, and herding. Where colonial authorities found that the lands they sought to exploit were already "cultivated," they solved the problem by restricting the indigenous population to tracts of low quality land (*The Ecologist* 1992:134).

Kenya became a British protectorate in 1895, when Britain began to build a railway from the port of Mombasa to Lake Victoria. The major purpose of the railway was strategic, but Britain needed to find a means of making the railway viable economically. Colonial officials offered settlers the best land in Kenya at attractive lease rates to entice them to set up plantations producing export crops. By 1903, settlers began to arrive from Britain and South Africa. During this process many Africans lost their land and as a consequence were forced onto inferior land or into the labor market. By 1915, the majority of the fertile highlands were held by the British, and Africans and Asians were effectively excluded from owning properties there. Europeans, who accounted for less than 1 percent of the population, controlled the fertile uplands that constituted 20 percent of the country's territory (Bodley 1982:97).

Before the British intrusion, there was no individual land ownership in Kenya.[6] However, there was an individual right to occupy a particular holding as long as it was used beneficially (Dilley 1966:249). In the 1880s, the inland areas of Kenya contained a web of domestic economies of complementary nomadic and sedentary pastoral forms of production. Both the nomadic and the sedentary groups accumulated livestock. The sedentary pastoralists, located primarily in the hillier areas of the eastern and western highlands flanking the Great Rift Valley, also grew cereal crops (Berman 1990:49–50). Both groups protected their resources and their environment. Farmers practiced irrigation, manuring, intercropping, and crop rotation to protect the fragile forest soils. Herders moved their stock regularly to balance their needs for pasturage and water, and they spread their herds over a wide area to avoid or minimize environmental degradation (Spear 1981:114). Conflicts between economic zones were not significant, but conflicts within the economic zones were a larger problem, as neighboring groups competed for the same resources. The Maasai wars of the nineteenth century are examples of this kind of conflict among the nomads. Because land was relatively abundant, it did not become a major source of conflict among the sedentary societies. When the need arose, household heads left to pioneer new territory. In this way, settlement spread across the area (Berman 1990:49–50).

In the Kenyan uplands, by the end of the nineteenth century, Maasai power was waning because of internal conflict and the rinderpest epidemic that was destroying livestock.[7] At the same time, the influence of such groups as the Kikuyu and the Kamba to the east and the Nandi to the west was beginning to grow. The area was also penetrated by Arab and Swahili caravans and, beginning in 1888, the Imperial British East Africa Company (IBEAC). These groups were primarily interested in the export of ivory. For the IBEAC, the uplands of Kenya were a costly route to the interior regions of Uganda and the equatorial zone. The efforts by IBEAC's European agents to control the local population along the route often resulted in violent clashes (Mungeam 1966:9–13, 18). Within three decades, the uplands region became the core of the White Highlands, and the region's economic and political structures were profoundly transformed by the colonial apparatus, linking it to the metropole and the wider capitalist world economy (Berman 1990:50–51).

One major change was the establishment of wage labor. Formerly, African peasants controlled the means of production in an essentially noncapitalist agricultural process where the bulk of production was for subsistence rather than for the market, and where land and labor were not exchanged for money. As a consequence, they produced for themselves and were unlikely to provide labor power as a commodity.[8] The settlers needed to transform this system since their success depended on African wage labor. After the more fertile land was taken from the indigenous population and given to European settlers, many peasants lost their economic independence. As a result, some became wage laborers.

By means of Crown Lands Ordinances in 1902 and 1915, Kenyan land was declared the property of the British Crown and was allotted to settlers on long-term leases (Lipscomb 1974:17). Large tracts of land were declared vacant (Tignor 1976:179). Individual settlers were given hundreds of acres, and concessionaires were offered tens of thousands of acres. In 1903, there were eighty-nine holdings totaling less than 5,000 acres; by 1905, the number of holdings allocated jumped to 263, totaling 368,125 acres. Increasingly, there was an emphasis on large landowners; by 1912, about 20 percent of the land alienated to Europeans in the colony was held by just five individuals and consortia. By the time of the 1915 Crown Lands Ordinance there was a virtual free market in land in the White Highlands, but it was subject to a prohibition on transfers of land from whites to people of other races. Leases were extended to 999 years, and development conditions intended to discourage speculation were abandoned (Berman 1990:56).

The process of expropriation and control was assisted by the colonial tax policy. The Africans had to pay hut and poll taxes in money. This forced some people to accept wage labor (Brett 1973:191–193). The British could depend on the collaboration of local chiefs and other notables who received material rewards for assisting the colonial system in areas such as tax collection and the mobilization of labor. The chiefs were clients of the colonial system. Chiefs who would not cooperate were replaced by more compliant locals. This cooptation of traditional leadership forms effectively undermined the moral authority of the commons regime. With each colonial edict they enforced, local leaders became estranged from their fellow villagers. At the same time, the colonial administrators treated them as representatives and spokespersons for their people (Berman 1990:60–61, 208–209).

Reserves were established for the African population, but this did not provide land security because the size of the reserves decreased as arable land continued to be shifted to settler control. In addition, in the Kikuyu areas, chiefs who had collaborated with the colonial regime gained control of large tracts of land, leaving less for use by the remainder of the population (Berman 1990:62).

Consequently, population pressure on the reserves drove some Africans to become wage laborers in spite of terrible labor conditions (Tignor 1976:179).

Some Africans tried to ameliorate their circumstances by squatting. This involved African families and their livestock gaining access to land on settler estates for cultivation and grazing. In return, they would work for a stipulated period on the settler's fields at minimum wage. For a time, this arrangement suited those Europeans who were land-rich and capital-poor, as well as Africans, primarily Kikuyu, seeking relief from population pressure in the reserves. The settlers had a cheap, reliable source of labor, and the Kikuyu earned use rights to the land by working for the European owner for about one-third of the year (Berman 1990:62).

The alienation of African land for European use was essentially complete by 1914, but enclosure continued up to the 1930s. Having acquired land, the settlers moved to secure it because they were concerned about restrictions regarding tenure and transfer of holdings. With regard to tenure, they were able to elicit a series of statements from several secretaries of state about the permanent and exclusive nature of white settlement in the Highlands. Eventually, the Highlands Order in Council of 1938 defined the Highlands as a European enclave (Dilley 1966:271–274).

The enclosure process had negative social, political, and environmental consequences. Some of this bubbled to the surface in the 1945–1952 period, as Africans were further excluded from land resources and livelihood opportunities. The European-controlled district councils imposed restrictions that placed squatters in a precarious position. They progressively limited the amount of land squatters were allowed to cultivate and forced them to dispose of most of their livestock. In addition, more Africans had to relocate as settlers shifted from squatter labor to contract wage labor. The reserves became more densely populated, and the number of landless Kikuyu increased as squatters were forced off European farms. Some of those who were not offered or would not accept wage contracts drifted back to the crowded Kikuyu reserves; others joined the ranks of the unemployed in the urban centers (Berman 1990:305–306).

No wonder then that clandestine militant organizations were easily able to find recruits from among the poor and landless peasants in the reserves, the displaced squatters of the Rift Valley, and the unskilled and unemployed in the urban areas (Berman 1990:334).

These dispossessed people formed the backbone of the Mau Mau nationalist movement (*The Ecologist* 1992:144). Land was certainly central to their concerns. Shortly before rejecting the "politics of petitions and resolutions," the Kikuyu submitted to the government a petition entitled "A Prayer for the Restoration of Our Land" (Berman 1990:336). Finding legal channels useless, the Kikuyu militants resorted to armed struggle. This led to a counterinsurgency campaign by the colonial state. The resolution of this conflict set the stage for Kenya's independence in 1963.

Postindependence land policy had only a modest impact on the landless and the land-poor. The colonial government set the tone for land reform in the period shortly before independence. Recompense for stolen land was not the goal of colonial policy; rather, the government wanted to ensure that the economic order and existing land titles would not be threatened by an abandonment of the concept of private property. As a result, a yeoman and peasant farmer scheme was initiated targeting the African petite bourgeoisie. Yeoman farmers were to be settled on 50-acre plots and peasant farmers on 15-acre plots. The capital requirements for participation in these programs were 10,000 shillings and 1,000 shillings, respectively. The implementation of this program was checked by the reaction from both the European and African communities. The European settlers were demanding inflated prices for their land, and a large landless and land-poor class was expressing discontent with the slow and inequitable process of land redistribution. A million-acre settlement scheme followed. It settled 29,000 families on small plots of land and 5,000 families on larger plots. A squatter settlement scheme was also designed to meet the needs of registered squatters. The Africans had to borrow from the state to purchase their plots, and Kenya borrowed extensively from Britain and international agencies to finance the resettlement (Berman 1990:410–412). African farmers had to pay a ransom for the property that had been taken from them decades earlier, and they were regaining private property, not the common property that they had lost.

By the early 1970s, 40 percent of the area of European mixed farms had been resettled. But the remaining 60 percent (about 2 million acres) was disposed of outside of this resettlement process. Some wealthy Africans, who disliked the paternalism of the settlement schemes, bought land on a straight commercial basis. To do this, they formed partnerships, limited liability companies, and farming cooperatives. As under the colonial system, a small elite benefited disproportionately, and the skewed land distribution patterns remained (Berman 1990:412).

Some of the environmental problems resulting from Kenya's enclosure were a consequence of agricultural systems that ignored the delicate balance between soil replenishment and plant growth. Crops like cotton and tobacco that required the clearing of vast amounts of land were particularly harmful. After harvest, the bare earth was left to bake in the sun. With root systems gone, soils were easily washed away, leaving behind degraded land (Lofchie 1989:6–7). Land scarcity and population pressure resulting from enclosure also brought their own environmental consequences, including soil degradation, deforestation, and desertification. With a large proportion of the population limited to a small segment of arable land, this area became environmentally stressed (Smith 1976:120; Kitching 1980:88, 103–105; Tignor 1976:305–306; Berman 1990:237, 302).

To date, Kenya has not recovered from the consequences of the century-old enclosure. Enclosure was the basis of the inequity between the European and African populations of Kenya. In addition, to support enclosure and related policies, the Europeans increased inequity within the African population. People and nature were given short shrift in the quest for profits.

Enclosing Local Knowledge of Neem

As capitalism deepens, the focus is shifting from the enclosure of material resources such as land to the enclosure of nonmaterial resources such as knowledge. Corporations are moving to enclose local knowledge, often benefiting from centuries of indigenous experimentation as well as local scientific research. For example, over the last several years patents have been sought or granted with regard to a variety of plants cultivated by third world communities for many generations. These include kava, linked to some Pacific island communities; barbasco, cultivated in the Amazon; turmeric, an Indian ayurvedic medicine; mamala, from the Pacific region; ayahuasca, cultivated in the Amazon basin since pre-Columbian times; j'oublie from Gabon; and endod, cultivated in a number of African countries, including Ethiopia (RAFI 1998; Shiva and Holla-Bhar 1996:155; Aoki 1998:52–53; Coombe 1998:88–89).

The controversy regarding the neem tree (*azadirachta indica*) in India illustrates this process of enclosure. For centuries, products made from the neem tree have been used locally for medicine, contraception, toiletries, timber, fuel, and insecticide. Its branches, leaves, and seeds are used to treat, among other things, leprosy, diabetes, ulcers, skin disorders, and constipation. The seeds' pesticidal powers, exploited by farmers for centuries, have been studied by scientists for at least fifty years. In the last fifteen years, corporations have been paying particular attention to this characteristic. The azadirachtin compound in neem has been recognized as an effective insecticide that is also biologically selective. Neem also contains salanin, another potent pest controller (*Hindustan Times* 1998; Shiva and Holla-Bhar 1996:148–149). Growing concern about dangerous pesticides has raised interest in the ecologically friendly neem products. Since 1985, U.S. and Japanese firms have taken out more than a dozen U.S. patents for a variety of neem compounds.

Patents allow the investor the right to exclude all others from making and using the invention for a limited time. This monopolistic right highlights the conflict between private gain and public interest. Countries have a variety of policies regarding patents, but the property rights regime of the World Trade Organization (WTO) seeks to harmonize intellectual property rights among all its member states. WTO's Trade-Related Aspects of Intellectual Property Rights (TRIPs) Agreement[9] is a comprehensive multilateral agreement addressing several areas of intellectual property, including patents. The new regime will require member countries to extend patent protection to products as well as processes.[10] Under the TRIPs Agreement, patent protection will expire twenty years from the filing date. The agreement is already in effect in the industrialized countries, but third world states have been granted a ten-year transition period in which to extend intellectual property rights to sectors not previously subject to intellectual property protection.[11]

Because this property rights regime allows the patenting of final products, anyone using new processes to develop those products would still be required to pay fees to the patents' holders (Prashad 1994). U.S.-based firms have favored product-based over process-based patenting laws because the former tends to give monopoly rights to the most technologically costly production process. Consequently, the high-technology product owner still benefits from fees even if there is a breakthrough involving a less costly process.

Essentially, a product patent discourages the kind of innovation suited to the resources of many third world countries—the development of low-cost, labor-intensive alternatives.

The patenting of neem tree products raises several concerns. The most important are the following: multinational corporations are usurping traditional knowledge; patents lead to erosion of diversity for the neem tree; neem seeds will become too expensive for poor farmers; and developing countries will be robbed of their rights to use natural products like the neem tree as they see fit.

Much of the controversy regarding neem has centered on W.R. Grace & Company. Beginning in the late 1980s, the company acquired at least four neem patents. While the first patent was originally assigned to Vikwood Limited, Grace is the original assignee for the remaining three. The company's patents claimed an innovative process based on its modernized extraction method. In addition, Grace has claimed that its more storage-stable pesticide product is not the same as the formulations traditionally used. The patents have drawn the ire of critics who confront the company with questions regarding intellectual ownership and failure to respect religious beliefs and cultural mores. Neem's insecticidal uses and properties are a part of India's common lore, and this is one reason why the Indian Central Insecticide Board did not register neem products under the 1968 Insecticides Act (Shiva and Holla-Bhar 1996:152). The tree also has religious significance. Small and medium-sized Indian businesses marketed neem-based commercial products such as pesticides and medicines, but they did not acquire proprietary ownership of formulae because, until it was changed in 1999,[12] Indian law did not allow the patenting of agricultural and medical products. Critics question Grace's claims of innovation, pointing out that, over the centuries, complex processes have been used to make neem available for specific uses. In addition, over the last three decades, Indian scientists have made advances in the area of storage stability (Lok Swaasthya Parampara Samvardhan Samithi n.d.).

The neem-related patents have caused considerable concern among farmers and scientists in India in light of the drive to standardize intellectual property rights. Corporate interest is already having adverse economic consequences for some local farmers who have to compete with transnational firms for access to neem seeds (Miller 1995:111). One result of the increased interest in neem has been an increase in the price of neem seeds from 300 to 8,000 rupees per ton (Shiva n.d.). Some marketing analysts predicted that by the year 2000 the price would rise to about 10,000 rupees per ton (*Hindustan Times* 1998). Such an increase might put neem out of the reach of farmers who do not have their own neem trees.

Because the patents are seen as enclosing local knowledge, corporations have been accused of biocolonialism. Individuals, NGOs, and some governments are challenging the granting of patents for products and technologies that make use of the genetic materials, plants, and other biological resources that have long been identified, developed, and used by farmers and indigenous peoples, mainly in countries of the third world. While corporations stand to reap huge revenues from this process, the local communities are unrewarded and in fact face the threat of having to buy the products of these companies at high prices. Corporations rush to patent in order to secure their place in what is being referred to as the biotechnology century, when products derived from biological materials are expected to replace many now made from metals and chemicals. When the intellectual property rights system grants patents on genetic and biological materials and on living organisms to corporations, the knowledge, innovation, efforts, and ownership of these communities are not acknowledged (Khor 1998; Coombe 1998:305–309).

Another concern is that enclosing neem through the use of intellectual property rights could not only enclose knowledge but also reduce genetic diversity. This loss of biodiversity results both from monoculture and from the alienation of the local community. For cash crops, the tendency is to focus on a few strains, while other strains are neglected and may be lost. Enclosure also undermines the traditional rights of local communities and thereby reduces their capacity to conserve biodiversity. This loss of genetic diversity leads to decreased resilience to pests, disease, and environmental stress (Shiva 1997:88). In addition, if this environmentally benign pesticide is priced out of their reach, farmers could be forced to employ cheaper and more hazardous substitutes.

An alternative perspective suggests that India has much to gain and little to lose from this heightened interest in neem. Corporate activity may mean increased employment and taxes. In addition, even if W.R. Grace's patent rights are recognized in India, a patent cannot remove the tree or the old formulations from the public domain. A farmer can still choose to use the old formulations or pay a premium for the new formulations. In addition, some farmers may have a new cash crop (Terry and Woessner n.d.).

But many remain unimpressed by this perspective. An assortment of NGOs have mobilized to protect third world indigenous knowledge systems and biological resources from piracy by the West (Khor 1998). These groups include the Third World Network, Rural Advancement Foundation International (RAFI). and Cultural Survival Canada. A series of legal challenges have been filed against patents granted on biological products, some targeting W.R. Grace and its neem products. In September 1995, more than 200 organizations from thirty-five countries filed a petition at the U.S. Patent and Trademark Office calling for the revocation of a patent given to W.R. Grace for a pesticide extract from the neem tree. They argue that the company has wrongfully usurped an age-old biological process used by millions of farmers in India and other countries for generations (Khor 1998). In Brussels, another legal petition was filed in June 1995 at the European Patent Office (EPO) against a patent (Patent No. 436,257 B1) granted to W.R. Grace for a method that extracts neem oil for use as a fungicide. The petition argues that the extraction method is decades old; in addition, the antifungal effects of neem oil have been known in India for centuries, so it cannot be a "discovery" as the company claims (Khor 1998). The petition to the EPO met with some success. In its September 1997 preliminary assessment, the EPO indicated that the neem fungicide was not sufficiently novel. An oral hearing on the case is expected to follow (IFOAM 1997).

Campaigners against the enclosure of knowledge have also been encouraged by the repeal of a turmeric patent (No. 5 401 504) on 23 August 1997, after the U.S. Patent Office found the claim to novelty to be false. Mississippi Medical obtained a patent for turmeric, claiming that it had discovered its healing properties. After a challenge by India's Council of Scientific and Industrial Research (CSIR), the patent was revoked. The CSIR used ancient texts to help prove that the claim of discovery was a false one (Raj 1998).

In the past several years, India's official government position has changed considerably as it has tried unsuccessfully to balance the interests of farmers and environmentalists on the one hand, and those of corporations and the global trade and property regimes on the other. India's Patents Act of 1970 did not permit the granting of patents for substances in the fields of agriculture and horticulture, or for curing or enhancing human, animal, or plant life. As a result, patents on pesticides and fungicides were disallowed (Terry and Woessner n.d.; Patel 1996:314), and India has been slow to harmonize its patent regime with WTO requirements. In March 1995, India's upper house of parliament forced the government to defer a Patent Amendment Bill. But 1998 saw a radical change in policy. India acceded to the Paris Convention and Patent Cooperation Treaty and, effective 7 December 1998, it became a member of the International Patent Cooperation Union (Remfry and Sagar 1998). In addition, a bill to amend the Patents Act of 1970 and bring India's patent regime in line with the demands of the WTO was passed by both houses of parliament in March 1999 (Remfry and Sagar 1999). It is retroactive and effective as of 1 January 1995.

India will now comply with and abide by the rulings of the Disputes Settlement Body of the WTO. The TRIPs Agreement requires India to offer patent protection to products related to agricultural, pharmaceutical, and chemical fields. This is an issue on which there is substantial disagreement in India. Some argue that India should accept only process patents and not product patents. But the WTO terms require the government to enact a Product Protection Act. The acceptance of product patents will further enclose local knowledge. Corporations are likely to claim that the items produced with appropriated knowledge are sufficiently novel to merit patenting. This would significantly limit the options of the local community, which would then run the risk of violating those patents.

The Indian government is trying to balance this change with proposed legislation to provide for the protection of indigenous communities' traditional systems of medicine and the plants used in such systems.[13] There were also plans to introduce a bill for the protection of plant variety and farmers' rights in April 1999 (Remfry and Sagar 1998), but the government did not meet this deadline. With its plans for the plant variety protection and farmers' rights bill, the government is signaling that it is sensitive to the sentiments of those represented by the thousands of farmers who protested against India's accession to the property rights regime. The farmers were concerned that the regime would destroy India's agricultural infrastructure and the Indian farmer. In addition, they felt that the country's biodiversity would be threatened (Rediff 1998). As part of the effort to fight the enclosure of community resources, an alliance of farmers and scientists has proposed an alternative form of intellectual property—collective intellectual property rights, or the collective patent. This would recognize knowledge as a community product subject to local common rights rather than as a commodity available for expropriation by corporate biopirates (Shiva and Holla-Bhar 1996:157–158).

The enclosure of neem is incomplete, but the process already reflects some of the features of the Kenyan land enclosure. Once again, the enclosure process is putting control of local resources in the hands of outsiders. As corporations and their allies make regulatory and policy changes to enclose knowledge, some local people experience decreased options, and some find their means of production threatened. Enclosure is likely to increase the inequity between corporate actors and their allies who have technological and political advantages, and local people without such advantages. Enclosure also threatens biodiversity, giving people and nature short shrift in the quest for profits.

Enclosure and the Consequences for the Commons

The enclosure of land in Kenya and the enclosure of neem in India share some common features. Both cases address the issues of property, access, and equity. They involve the enclosure of common property resulting in reduced or lost access as well as increased inequity. In each case, the enclosure of property is consistent with the libertarian doctrine of John Locke, who sought to justify the private ownership of property as a natural right obtained from combining man's labor with the natural commons. Locke holds that others do not suffer loss or injury as a result of this taking of property from the commons "where there is enough, and as good left in common for others" (Locke 1988:288). This view still influences political and economic decisions, even though its cornucopian assumptions have proven faulty. Indeed, an alternative perspective argues that Locke was articulating "capitalism's freedom to build as the freedom to steal" (Shiva 1997:3). With regard to natural resources, the rights of those who own capital supersede the common right of others even if the latter have prior claims (Shiva 1997:3).

In each of the cases examined, enclosure means dispossession. For both, dispossession has more than material consequences. It also affects social and cultural life.[14] Both knowledge and land, which are seen by members of the respective communities as having a measure of the sacred, are commodified and secularized. In addition, both enclosures have had negative consequences for the environment. In Kenya, enclosure resulted in deforestation and degradation of soils. In the case of neem, there are concerns regarding loss of biodiversity. In addition, as enclosure makes neem less affordable and accessible, farmers may turn to cheaper pesticides that are not environmentally benign.

Both cases are reflective of colonialism, signifying actions to possess and control the particular territories. Kenya's land policy was a part of Britain's colonial strategy. With regard to neem, corporate strategy and the supportive neoliberal policy of the WTO have been described as biocolonialism. In each case, resources are being used primarily to benefit the metropole and its representatives.[15] Both cases also involve resistance to enclosure by people reluctant to give up material and cultural values. In the Kenyan case, military means were used to deal with resistance.[16] And in the neem case, economic sanctions are available if India does not comply with WTO provisions.

The Kenyan enclosure took place during the second wave of colonialism. In the late nineteenth and early twentieth centuries, the major industrial countries competed for raw materials, cheap labor, and markets for surplus goods. As a result, colonial incorporation involved the enclosure of land and the transformation of production processes so that the territory would become integrated into the commodity chains of the world economy through the production of cash crops. This process was assisted by the transfer of material resources from the colonial power to the colony to build the requisite infrastructure for exploitation. In addition, existing political structures were reconstructed to ensure the territory's operation within the interstate system of the capitalist world economy.

The neem enclosure is occurring in the late twentieth century, a neocolonial period characterized by the continued dependence of periphery states and the persistent, albeit reorganized, influence of core states. Control of the core has become less overt and more indirect,[17] and economic relationships bear a greater share of the responsibility for overall system integration than they did earlier in the century. The structural advantage of the core states is reinforced by transnational corporations (TNCs) and intergovernmental organizations (IGOs) such as the WTO and the International Monetary Fund

(IMF). These institutions exercise authority that reduces the autonomy of peripheral states. At this point in the capitalist era, all territory has already been enclosed, and India is already significantly integrated into the world economy. There is no room for further spatial expansion so the emphasis has shifted to the deepening of capitalism. Actions such as the enclosure of the knowledge of biological products and processes serve that end.

Knowledge as an integral part of the capitalist project is not a new feature. In the early days of the Industrial Revolution, it was a component of the value of any product or service that was not strictly materially based. What is different in this phase of capitalism is the level and type of knowledge being utilized. Because of its need to expand opportunities for accumulation, capitalism is penetrating into previously noncommodified sectors. The enclosure of a resource such as knowledge within a regime of property rights may appear to change the form of capitalism because of the new commodities created, but the logic of capitalism as a system remains unchanged (May 1998). Because of this, the Kenyan experience may foreshadow the likely consequences of the enclosure of knowledge.

Enclosure transforms knowledge of nature into a resource for national and global production. With enclosure of these commons, the balance shifts from a community economy where innovations are the product and property of the group to a market economy based on competition and focused on the accumulation of capital (Gudeman 1996:103). Control of these resources is held by actors outside the community. As a result, enclosure redefines community and devalues local expertise and knowledge. Where common property regimes recognize the intrinsic worth of biodiversity, intellectual property rights systems see value as a product of commercial exploitation (Shiva 1997:67). The new property rights regime privileges the rights of corporations that function as plant breeders over the rights of farmers who have had a long-term nonproprietary relationship with the genetic material of the fields and forests. As a result, farmers cannot benefit from their comparative advantage in the context of the new agricultural technology.

Local knowledge is bound by contextual and moral factors and cannot be separated from larger moral or normative ends. Enclosure opens the way for bureaucratization and accords power to those who master the language of the new professionals. As local ways of knowing and doing are devalued or appropriated and local forms of governance are eroded, state, professional, and corporate bodies are able to insert themselves into the commons, taking over areas of life that were previously under the control of individuals, households, and communities. These changes favor or create local actors who are attuned to the interests of the core. Enclosure, therefore, provides another tool for control.

Those trying to slow the process of enclosure are active at a variety of levels. They have been mobilizing support at the local level, working primarily through NGOs. At national and regional levels, they have targeted political leaders as well as institutions such as the U.S. Patent and Trademark Office and the European Patent Office. At the international level, the WTO and the Biodiversity Convention are two critical forums for establishing the principles and legal framework for patenting biological materials and life forms. The WTO's TRIPs Agreement will have a decisive influence over national laws.

The TRIPs clause addressing living organisms is ambiguous: Article 27(3b) states that parties may exclude from patentability

> plants and animals other than micro-organisms, and essentially biological processes for the production of plants or animals other than non-biological and microbiological processes. However, Members shall provide for the protection of plant varieties either by patents or by an effective sui generis system or by any combination thereof.[18]

This clause is up for review after four years.

The Biodiversity Convention's language recognizes farmers' rights to their knowledge of biodiversity, but its language regarding intellectual property rights is an effort to balance the need to implement intellectual property rights and the need to ensure that those rights do not threaten the sustainable use of biodiversity. Despite the ambiguous language, intellectual property rights have the advantage. Article 16 of the convention addresses what constitutes access to and transfer of technology. It says that technologies should be transferred under fair and favorable terms, including concessional and preferential terms, when mutually agreed. However, other provisions present barriers to the transfer of biotechnology. According to the convention, if patents and intellectual property rights are involved, access and transfer should be provided on terms consistent with the protection of those rights.[19]

Those campaigning against life patents seek to affect the evolution of the patent regime and the Biodiversity Convention. They want to ensure that the WTO does not make it compulsory for member countries to patent living organisms, and they want the Biodiversity Convention to address the issue of biopiracy (Khor 1998).

Conclusion

The enclosure imposed by imperialism and colonialism has been complemented by the enclosure imposed by TNCs supported by modern-day neocolonial rulers and institutions. Then, land was targeted; now, life forms, species, and local knowledge are the focus of enclosure movements. As was the case 500 years ago, private property is being created through the appropriation of other people's common wealth. The freedom that corporations are claiming through intellectual property rights is the same freedom that colonizers claimed centuries ago to acquire control over the lands and livelihoods of indigenous peoples.

The British enclosure of land in Kenya had devastating social and environmental consequences, and the repercussions are still being experienced. In the case of the neem tree, the enclosure process is incomplete, but the negative consequences for the affected communities are already evident. These two cases appear to have significant differences: one addresses the enclosure of land, and the other examines the enclosure of knowledge. But both enclosures had similar functions in the separate stages of capitalist expansion. Contextual similarities suggest that information from the first case can be important in predicting the consequences of the increasing enclosure of knowledge. Both are stories of dispossession that include the coercion or cooptation of a local elite. As a result, elite policy and actions support enclosure. In the Kenyan case, the British colonial system coopted and coerced the local Kenyan elite; in the Indian case, transnational capital and its allies coopt and coerce the Indian political elite. With the enclosure of land, peasants in Kenya lost control of the means of production, and many became wage laborers; the enclosure of local knowledge is likely to have similar consequences for Indian farmers. Essentially, both cases reflect the remorseless logic of the capitalist marketplace.

Capitalism depends on continuing enclosures to weather periodic crises. But enclosure has tragic consequences for both nature and society. The enclosure of land has fundamentally restructured society and people's relationship to nature. Similarly, the enclosure of knowledge about nature will exacerbate social and economic inequities and further alienate people from nature. The inherent logic of enclosure inevitably leaves tragedy in its wake.

Notes

1. For example, see Berkes et al. (1989), Ostrom (1990) and Stevenson (1991).

2. As explained in Heilbroner (1985:24–27), in this context, logic is used in a causal sense. A system's logic "expresses the potential energy created by its nature." The logic of capitalism is shaped by the imperatives of accumulation, with its relentless search for profits.

3. Marx (1906:106–185) describes this continuous process involving the transformation of capital-as-money into capital-as-commodity, followed by another transformation of capital-as-commodity back into capital-as-money.

4. The Statute of Merton in 1236 is regarded as the first enclosure act.

5. The rent was an equivalent for labor services that had been obligatory, rather than a payment for the land the tenant occupied.

6. The Kikuyu did have family-owned tracts of land, but individuals had no right to sell without consulting family members. See Tignor (1976:27,307).

7. Rinderpest was introduced into the continent for the first time in 1889. Since the cattle had developed no resistance to the disease, it caused tremendous loss of life and famine, particularly among the Maasai and Kamba. See Tignor (1976:15–16).

8. See Marx (1906:41–96) for a discussion of labor as a commodity.

9. Agreement on Trade-Related Aspects of Intellectual Property Rights (1994).

10. Agreement on Trade-Related Aspects of Intellectual Property Rights, Article 27(2).

11. Agreement on Trade-Related Aspects of Intellectual Property Rights, Article 66(1).

12. This was one of the changes made after India became party to the Paris Convention and the Patent Cooperation Treaty, effective 7 December 1998.

13. Other third world states have been exploring this option. *The Ecologist* (1997:C3) gives the example of Thailand, which drafted a bill aimed at recognizing and protecting traditional healers and medicinal genetic resources. The United States reacted by warning Thailand that it could be in violation of the TRIPs Agreement.

14. In the Kenyan case, the alienation of land destroyed social cohesion and modified their culture. For example, the Maasai were moved to land that was inadequate for pastoral people, and they had to change their land use practices. See Tignor (1976:30–39). In the case of neem, the increases in price have had social consequences because of the resulting reduction of access.

15. With regard to the Kenyan enclosure, the economic benefits flowed to Britain. With neem, the enclosure of neem has neither the intent nor the effect of benefiting the Indian population. Indeed, the Indian population already has access to a wide variety of products made from neem.

16. See Tignor (1976:16–21). In the process of establishing control over Kenyan land, the British launched a series of attacks against the Kikuyu and Kamba.

17. The role of IGOs as well as "private" forms of authority may be considered quite overt and direct but does not involve the formality of colonialism and empires. See Chapters 3, 4, 5, 7, and 8 for additional treatment of the roles of IGOs and ENGOs.

18. Agreement on Trade-Related Aspects of Intellectual Property Rights, Article 27(3b).

19. United Nations Environment Programme (UNEP), Convention on Biological Diversity, Article 16 (UNEP 1992). See Chapter 3 for further discussion of multilateral environmental agreements and the WTO.

Valérie de Campos Mello

7

Global Change and the Political Economy of Sustainable Development in Brazil

Deforestation in the Brazilian Amazon is without a doubt among the world's greatest environmental problems and has attracted a great deal of attention from governments, international institutions, nongovernmental organizations (NGOs), and the media. It is also a topic that has received extensive treatment in the international relations (IR) literature on global environmental politics, with a special emphasis on the role played by the international community in helping to solve the problems of Amazonia. Many studies point to the internationalized or even globalized character of Amazonia and Amazonian policies. Yet, while a lot of attention is drawn to the role of international regimes, transnational social movements, and foreign pressure in explaining policies and politics in Amazonia, little attention is given to another major international link between Amazonia and the world, namely, the impact of liberal globalization on environmental standards and policies.

The mainstream literature on international environmental politics, a literature dominated by neoliberal institutionalism, tends to emphasize cooperation and interstate bargaining. It thus neglects international systemic factors, such as the redefinition of Brazil's insertion into liberal globalization, and domestic factors, such as state reform, conflicts, and resistance by actors excluded from global or domestic governmental processes. By focusing on global environmental management, mainstream approaches tend to overlook the effects of global economic processes on domestic environmental standards and policies.

135

The institutionalist literature also tends to emphasize the *positive* and potentially *integrative* effects of globalization, highlighting the benefits of the widespread acceptance of the concept of sustainable development as the foundation for a model of global environmental management (see Chapters 2 and 3). Yet, there are also negative relationships between the globalization process and the environment. The link is both direct—global economic processes such as production, trade, and investment put pressure on the world's natural resource base—and indirect—economic globalization is accompanied by a liberal consensus that promotes economic policies with environmental implications. Both materially and ideationally, the globalization process is redefining the historical context within which environmental standards and policies are made and transformed. By neglecting this major link between Amazonia and the world, mainstream IR approaches fail to account for some of the very sources of environmental problems, resulting in what Robert Cox calls a problem-solving perspective (Cox 1986:208).

This chapter examines the changes in domestic environmental standards and policies that have been taking place in Amazonia. It argues that the most appropriate approach to understanding this policy shift is one that bridges the domestic-international divide, linking global change and local actors in the making of environmental politics in Brazil. While recognizing the importance of international factors stressed by both neoliberal institutionalists and realists, such an approach intends to critically assess the new environmental policy that is emerging in the context of global change.

After a brief theoretical summary of the debate, the second section of this chapter explores links between social structure and economic globalization. It first locates Brazilian environmental policy change in the domestic context of the return to democracy. It then links it to the liberalization process, to the shift to market-oriented reforms, and to global change, showing the different channels that have enabled transnational actors and alliances to have an impact on Brazil's environmental policy reform. The chapter concludes by emphasizing the limits of policy change in the context of globalization and the consolidation of a free market model of development. It shows who is controlling and managing the reform process and highlights the persistence of structural obstacles to long-term sustainable development in Amazonia.

Critical Versus Mainstream Approaches
to Environmental Policy Change in Amazonia

During most of this century, deforestation in the Brazilian Amazon was a nationally led process resulting directly from patterns of state intervention in the region manifested in large-scale colonization and integration projects. In a few decades, the region was transformed from a completely forested and sparsely populated region into a region with a high urbanization rate and an important role in national production and income. This modernization was achieved at high social and environmental costs. At that time, the Brazilian government placed particular emphasis on asserting its sovereignty over Amazonia and protecting itself against external interference. In the early 1980s, the first environmentalists concerned about the preservation of the Amazonian rainforest met with strong resistance from the Brazilian government.

Yet today, on the eve of the third millennium, Amazonia is deeply internationalized. Recent years have seen the development of a variety of institutional and economic instruments, often resulting from international cooperation or pressure, aimed at strengthening environmental protection in the region. This could be interpreted as evidence of positive international influence (de Campos Mello 1996). There has also been an undeniable shift in the Brazilian government's policies regarding Amazonia that has affected the dynamic of deforestation in the region. This shift seems to indicate a change in the determinants of Brazil's environmental policy, demonstrating the growing role of international factors in decisions affecting the political economy of environment and development in Amazonia.

Considering the nationalistic character of Brazil's reactions to international interference in the past, it is interesting to investigate the reasons for this policy shift and ask how it became politically possible. What interplay between national and international factors accounts for the transformations in Brazil's policy regarding Amazonia? How do major IR approaches explain and interpret such a change? And what role do they give to the global historical context of economic liberalization within which these transformations take place?

Realist Interpretations: Power, Hegemony, and Security

As shown in Table 7.1, realists would interpret policy change in Brazil as resulting primarily from factors linked to hegemony and

Table 7.1   Competing Approaches to Amazonian Policies

	Realism	Neoliberal Institutionalism	Critical IPE
Causes of forest destruction	1. Imbalance between population and resources; settlement plans and frontier expansion	1. Market failures; externalities, inadequate pricing of forest products 2. Bad management, subsidies	1. Model of accumulation: developmentalism in the past, globalism today 2. System of political and social relations
Causes for policy reform in Brazil	1. U.S. and G7 hegemony: role of forests as carbon sinks and in biodiversity 2. Strategic opportunities for Brazil; Amazonia as a bargaining tool, providing comparative advantages	1. Shift in Brazil's interests; influence on economic relations 2. Role of public opinion and NGOs; epistemic communities 3. Role of the international forest regime	1. Evolution in the Brazilian social structure; redemocratization, social movements in Amazonia 2. Reform of the state 3. Redefinition of accumulation model; liberalization, market reforms
Major solutions considered for Amazonia	1. Reconversion of military 2. Decrease in population growth rates	1. International regimes, ITTO guidelines, international cooperation projects; PPG7, PANAFLORO, carbon sequestration projects 2. Correction of market failures 3. Removal of inefficient regulation and subsidies	1. Change in the model of accumulation: redistribution at global and national levels 2. Change in land tenure system, local solutions 3. Democratization, participation of local actors 4. Regulation at the global level; control of activities of TNCs, of IOs (WTO, WB, IMF, and UN agencies)

security.[1] If Brazil has changed its stance on environmental policy and policies affecting Amazonia, it is first because hegemonic powers have pressured it to do so and, second, because Brazil itself perceived the issue as an opportunity to make claims within the international power system.

In the realist perspective, the changing agenda of the United

States in relation to Latin America could be seen as influencing the Brazilian government's decision to carry out environmental policy reform. The trade-dominated orientation of U.S. foreign policy in the post–Cold War years contributed to the establishment of linkages between trade and nontrade issues such as environmental protection, social rights, and human rights. Trade negotiations became the forums where all issues would be addressed, providing the United States with sustained leverage over the bargaining process and allowing it to include the issue of environmental protection in many international discussions (MacDonald and Stern 1997:5).

The focus on tropical deforestation also served U.S. strategic goals, because emphasizing deforestation as a major factor contributing to global warming diverted attention away from the role of emissions caused by industrial activities. Another reason for the special attention given by the United States and other developed countries to Amazonia was its importance as a reservoir of biodiversity. Deforestation in Amazonia could mean the reduction of biological diversity and of the genetic materials that are the basic sources of medicinal and chemical products, representing a potential loss for pharmaceutical remedies and other chemical processes as well as for agriculture. The pharmaceutical lobby actively supported measures to preserve rainforests in general and in Amazonia in particular. From a realist perspective, this configuration of interests at the international level would explain the high degree of pressure exerted on the Brazilian government to fight deforestation and redirect its policy toward Amazonia.

A second factor put forward by realists would be the perception by developing countries, such as Brazil, that international environmental negotiations could provide a unique forum for discussing development and the international economic order. The perception was that many of the factors that had fed interdependence were losing their force since the end of the Cold War; the emergence of global environmental interdependence was seen as an important exception to this trend (Hurrell 1992:418). In addition, the South has the largest share of natural and biogenetic resources in the world, and Amazonia is the richest ecosystem on earth in terms of biological diversity. Its national biodiversity reserves, and Amazonia in particular, can be seen as one of Brazil's few strong cards in its efforts to reposition itself in the global geopolitical scenario. Strategic considerations stressed by realist analysis could thus have played a role in determining the recent focus of the Brazilian government on environmental protection and forest preservation in Amazonia.

Neoliberal Institutionalism:
Interests, Public Opinion, and International Institutions

According to the neoliberal institutionalist viewpoint, one of the major reasons for the environmental policy shift in Brazil is the perception that it was in the country's national interest to improve environmental protection at the domestic level. The very nature of environmental issues has contributed to the Brazilian government's abandonment of its view of forests as purely national resources and its recognition of their role as global resources. It was not just the direct political and economic costs of external pressure, but rather their impact on Brazil's broader foreign policy objectives that was decisive in helping to shift Brazilian policy. At the end of the 1980s, Brazil was beginning a liberalization process aimed at better integrating the country into the world economy, a project that could succeed only if cooperative relations were established with developed countries. Thus, Brazil's change of stance on the environment reflected the will to preserve its main political interests in trade, debt, and development (Hurrell 1992:417).

The neoliberal institutionalist approach also views international public opinion as affecting the shift in environmental policy in Brazil. At the beginning of the 1990s, public opinion in developed countries grew increasingly aware of the extent of environmental destruction, especially with respect to tropical forests. Media campaigns were launched to support the ongoing debate over environmental protection. Another important factor was the development of an alliance between Brazilian and international NGOs allowing grassroot movements and national NGOs to bypass the national government. This formed a transnational social movement network with broad international support.

Finally, the role of the nascent international forest regime is stressed by neoliberal institutionalists as a main reason for Brazil's change of stance on environmental policy. Though there is no international regime *strictu sensu* because no legally binding convention or treaty regulates the problem of deforestation, several instruments exist that together constitute a sort of informal regime (de Campos

Mello 1997). This regime encompasses a wide variety of instruments, including the application of conditionality in the concession of new loans and credits that limits Brazil's access to multilateral finance; the use of unilateral trade measures; the move toward including environmental clauses in the World Trade Organization (WTO); and the development of an international certification scheme for tropical timber to discriminate against timber extracted in an unsustainable manner. All these factors contributed to the awareness that preserving Amazonia was in the country's national interest and that failing to reverse deforestation would negatively affect its international image.

Critical International Political Economy (IPE): Linking Social Structure and Globalization

Both neoliberal institutionalism and realism shed light on important aspects of the internationalization of Brazil's environmental policy and contribute to an accurate picture of the international setting within which the policy shift took place. Yet, they provide an incomplete account of the changes taking place in Brazil today with respect to its Amazonian policies. Both approaches are notable for their uncritical appraisal of global environmental politics. Thus, globalization is often assumed to be a process that includes a globalization of values.[2]

Globalization is considered by neoliberal institutionalism as a progressive process that will ultimately bring higher environmental standards to the third world (see Chapter 2). Realists perceive that structural constraints arising from economic interdependence can be used to institutionalize environmental protection and promote sustainable development. To be fair to both approaches, it seems plausible to assert that globalization has in a sense helped to create conditions for the development of policy mechanisms and institutions to universalize and promote the concept of sustainable development. But the way the environmental debate has been framed by the international development establishment to legitimize market reforms is not questioned by mainstream IR authors, and existing alternatives to the liberal sustainable development approach are seldom addressed.

As a consequence, there seems to be limited concern in the mainstream literature about the impact of globalization on the political economy of environmental reform in developing countries. Although problem-solving discourses emphasize the benefits arising from the globalization of the environment—that is, the inclusion of environmental concerns on the international political agenda—these approaches fail to establish a concrete link between global change, restructuring, and state reforms on the one hand, and the type of sustainable development in the third world on the other. The nature of this link and, even more, its empirical measure are difficult to establish. There are, however, some signs that global change is exerting a structuring influence on the redefinition of environmental politics in the South. The kind of sustainable development being promoted seems to represent more the consolidation of a liberal project of environmental management than a real shift away from destructive practices. Globalization tends to consolidate a market-friendly view of sustainable development, one that gives priority to growth and to the amelioration, rather than prevention, of environmental damage. This is carried out at the expense of ecological sustainability and a view of sustainable development that stresses not only development but also social equity and participation.

In order to understand the transformations in Amazonian policies in the 1990s, it is useful to consider the dynamic interaction between local, national, and global factors. Deforestation and the socioecological crisis in the Amazon are first of all linked to the broader issues of economic development and patterns of state intervention in Brazil. While the influence of global factors—such as the pressure of international NGOs, IGOs, and foreign governments—on environmental concerns in Brazil appears quite clear, the role of endogenous factors should not be neglected. The aim of a critical IPE perspective is not solely to show the influence of international actors and liberal economic globalization on state policies in the Amazon region, but also to investigate how global change interferes with the political trajectory of environment and development in the Amazon region and to make explicit the responses of those domestic actors affected by global change. This aim is what distinguishes an approach interested in theorizing social change from problem-solving approaches, such as neoliberal institutionalism, and also from a great deal of the literature on third world politics.

The academic literature on third world politics has been dominated by the belief in the primacy of exogenous factors in explaining political changes. As stressed by Jean-François Bayart (1989), this type of analysis is limited to the short duration of events. Instead, a critical analysis starts with Fernand Braudel's (1969) concept of *longue durée*: contemporary politics should be viewed in the light of layers of slow history. In order to restore historicity to the analysis of politics, it is useful to situate politics at the crossing of inside and outside dynamics as in Georges Balandier's approach (1971:39). By investigating the continuity of civilizations and the underlying *longue durée* structures of present forms of civilization, it becomes possible to overcome erroneously universalist interpretations.

In today's Amazonia, the clash of different temporalities is the key to understanding the social and political conflicts deriving from unequal access to natural resources (for use of temporalities, see also Chapter 8). One major conflict is caused by the coexistence of primitive forms of accumulation (extractive activities) and modern capitalist types of social relations. The process of globalization interferes with every level of temporality because pressures for the universalization of liberal capitalism produce social conflicts and violence between actors operating according to different temporalities. By reshaping the insertion of various social forces in the international political economy, globalization affects the domestic political economy and in this sense helps to shape the political trajectory of environment and development in countries such as Brazil.

The critical approach I adopt is centered on three basic assumptions. First, it accepts plurality in understandings of nature and rejects the prescription of universal solutions to ecological problems. Second, it notes the inadequacy of concentrating exclusively on interstate relations. And third, it identifies economic development and globalization as the underlying causes of the ecological crisis and thus as major factors to be taken into account in the analysis of responses to that crisis. It is also an IPE approach in that it looks at the interaction between states and markets from a perspective that tries to overcome the classic domestic-international distinction (Gilpin 1987:11–14).

Although the ecological dimensions of global structural transformation have not penetrated the core concerns of IPE, there have been attempts to develop an IPE approach to ecological change (Bernard 1997; Paterson 1996). In particular, the work of Karl Polanyi (1957) has been used as a basis for understanding the contradictions of capitalist development and its impact on ecology in the context of global change. The greatest contribution of Karl Polanyi is his insight that markets are not mechanisms arising naturally but, rather, are products of the exercise of state power. As far as global political ecology is concerned, a starting point for a critical approach is Polanyi's argument that the "Great Transformation" process associated with the emergence of capitalism provoked a disembedding of economy from society that took the form of the commodification of labor and nature. While realism and neoliberal institutionalism view ecology as an exogenous and passive sphere to be controlled and managed, isolating ecological problems from the sphere of power and ideology, the critical IPE approach borrows from Polanyi's conceptualization of the interrelationship between social organization and the natural world, in which nature becomes commodified with the advent of market society.

Such an approach focuses on the globalization process as the key to understanding the transformations in state-society relations taking place in the 1990s and shows that the globalization of Amazonia is not simply limited to international negotiations or the diplomatic pressure of epistemic communities. A critical IPE approach thus provides a more comprehensive analysis of environmental politics as related to international restructuring and to the transformations in the political economy of environment and development in Brazil. In this sense, it is able not only to account for the *causes* of social change, but also to explain the nature of the reactions to that change.

The Interplay of Domestic and Global Factors

Today, Brazil is experiencing a period of transition at different levels: transition from economic populism to economic pragmatism; transition from developmentalism toward a more sustainable kind of growth; transition from an interventionist to a coordinating type of state; and transition from nationally led Amazonian policies to more internationalized ones. These processes are still incomplete. However, a historical analysis of the political economy of Amazonian development and of its determinants allows one to detect some general trends in this transition as far as Amazonia is concerned.

Political Change in Democratic Brazil

Environmental policy reform must first be situated within the context of a change in the structure of social and political relations in Brazil. At the end of the 1980s, political support for a policy shift at the internal level was beginning to emerge. With the return of the country to democracy, the ecological movement established itself as a permanent political actor, and the environmental issue became a locus for the exercise of citizen rights (Pádua 1991). Today, the movement is fully institutionalized, with a well-established network of activists and organizations, and public opinion is increasingly receptive to environmental protection. In a 1993 survey, 71 percent of the population declared an interest in environmental issues, and deforestation was singled out as the major environmental concern. In addition, 47 percent agreed that what occurred in the Amazon had an impact on the whole world and could not be decided by Brazilians alone (Crespo and Leitão 1993). A more recent survey reveals that only 27 percent of Brazilians believe that economic development should have priority over the environment.[3] Finally, the role of the media in building public awareness should also be noted. During the UN Conference on Environment and Development (UNCED), the Brazilian media played a crucial role in increasing public awareness.

This growing environmental awareness, rendered possible by democratization and international pressures, thus contributed to the trend toward environmental policy reform in Brazil. Yet, to fully understand the new directions of Amazonian policies in the 1990s, it is necessary, in Cox's terminology, to situate them in their historical structure. Global change constitutes a key factor in explaining the shift in Amazonian policy, contributing to the modification of the political economy of development in 1990s Brazil and leading to a redefinition of patterns of state intervention, of state-society relations, and of the country's insertion in the international economy. In Amazonia, this process has led to a shift away from the traditional "state-led development-sovereignty" approach and toward a managerial approach to environmental protection. This market-friendly approach has been translated into a policy that, while still poorly implemented, recognizes environmental protection as a central issue.

Beyond the acknowledgment of a policy change and the recognition of the role of international determinants in the phenomenon, three issues seem particularly interesting here with regard to the interplay between domestic and global processes. The first issue is the impact that economic liberalization will have in Amazonia as Brazil becomes increasingly globalized. Will environmental policy reform affecting Amazonia, considered as a step forward (albeit modest), be fostered in a context of growing economic globalization? How will the liberalization of the 1990s affect Amazonian political economy?

The second issue is a corollary of the acceptance of liberal, market-oriented policies—that is, the reform of the state and its institutions and the redefinition of their role. Will the state's capacity to provide a sustainable model for Amazonia be enhanced and will it improve policymaking and implementation?

The third issue concerns the structural factor lying at the root of Amazonian social and environmental conflicts, namely, the lack of democracy in access to and control of natural resources. Is policy reform altering this situation and promoting democratization in Amazonia? And, as the international insertion of Brazil is redefined, will new connections be made between international factors, actors, and forest depletion, with what effects and for whom? To sum up, will current Amazonian policy be able to promote long-term sustainable development in the region, understood as a development that is both socially and ecologically conscious?

Globalizing Amazonia: The Obstacles to Sustainability

Global change was a major determinant of both the adoption of economic policy reforms in the 1990s and the nature and orientation of these policies. It combined with the generalized crisis of the state that had marked Brazil in the 1980s, a crisis affecting the state's structure, functions, and pattern of intervention. With the exhaustion of import substitution industrialization as the motor of development and the failure of various policies to stabilize the economy and restore growth, liberalizing policies were adopted in the 1990s. This new policy framework, put into action with the 1993 Real Plan, included stabilization, trade liberalization, privatization, and state reform and is currently being implemented in a rather aggressive manner by the Brazilian state. The state is seeking to redefine Brazil's insertion in the international political economy in a favorable way and to master a transition from a developmentalist to a coordinating type of state (Bresser Pereira 1996). Despite a slowdown after the Asian financial crisis of August 1998, the present international conjuncture has ensured an abundant flow of foreign direct investment to the country. Combined with the normalization of domestic economic life after the end of inflation and initial gains in the population's purchasing power, it contributed to the relative success of President Cardoso's enterprise, guaranteeing his October 1998 reelection. However, the persistence of structural problems, such as the reproduction of patterns of exclusion and the uneven character of Brazil's globalization, poses serious threats to the chances of a development model that would be socially just and ecologically sustainable.

The impact of trade liberalization. While it is still too soon to fully evaluate the real impacts of the Cardoso administration's National Integrated Policy for Amazonia and the economic liberalization process, it seems clear that the optimism generated by the policy shift must be tempered. First of all, a look at the figures indicates that the shift itself was limited. The fires in the Amazon have not stopped; on the contrary, after a substantial decline over the period 1989–1991, the deforestation rate is speeding up again, showing that the decline in the early 1990s was more the result of a slowdown of economic activity than of coherent government policy. Deforestation data actually show a "spike" in 1995, a direct consequence of the 1994 Real Plan for economic stabilization.[4] Indeed, with the stabilization of the economy since the plan, the demand for timber, meat, and cereals has increased, placing new pressure on land. Present policies focus on economic growth and integration of the region as ways to improve environmental and social conditions. In this sense, the "new" policy for Amazonia does not represent a real departure from previous policies, as it stresses sustainable growth rather than sustainable development (GTA 1996).

In addition to concentrating on economic growth, the liberalizing reforms introduced by Cardoso correspond to a shift to predominantly market-oriented approaches to environmental problems. The view is that export markets will demand better environmental performances from exporters and thus contribute to higher environmental standards in the exporting country. There is a risk, however, that easy access to world markets will increase pressure on the natural resource base and accelerate the pace of deforestation in Amazonia. Finally, export markets tend to marginalize small-scale traditional production. Competition could lead small producers to abandon sustainable production and turn to less sustainable activities (GTA 1996:84).

The expansion of timber exploitation.   Another serious obstacle on the road to long-term environmental sustainability in Amazonia is the recent boom in timber exploitation and the arrival of Asian logging companies. Although the direct contribution of logging to deforestation is not as important as that of agriculture and cattle raising, its indirect contribution through the opening of roads and its multiplying effect on the economy is very significant. Historically, forest products have not played an important role in Brazil's economy. However, exports of these products have been growing steadily, mainly due to the increase in tropical timber trade facilitated by trade liberalization and the opening of the economy to foreign investment. Thus, the role of timber in the Brazilian economy is expanding and experiencing a real boom, encouraged by strong international demand for tropical hardwoods. A recent World Bank analysis indicates that Brazil is poised to increase its supply of wood products on the global market.[5]

Federal authorities now have to deal with Asian logging companies. They are moving into the Amazon in search of new timber sources because of the exhaustion of raw material in countries such as Malaysia, another clear example of the effect of economic globalization and trade liberalization on the environment. According to the Instituto Brasileiro do Meio Amblente e Recursos Renovaveis (IBAMA), 1.9 million hectares of Amazon land are now owned by foreign firms (*O Estado de São Paulo* 1997). These firms bought bankrupt local companies and are using advanced technology to transform the Amazon into a major timber extraction center. A hot debate has been going on in Brazil about Asian logging firms, as they have been accused of smuggling, illegal extraction, falsification of import guides, and irregularities in the purchasing of land.[6] However, illegal logging is by no means the monopoly of foreign companies. Attempts to regulate the timber market have long been rendered difficult by illegal logging by Brazilians.

The Impact of State Reform

Economic liberalization and state reform undertaken by the Cardoso administration are redefining the state's ability to pursue environmental policy. The reform of the state, considered to be a necessary condition for economic liberalization, has led to an effort to limit its competence in several areas in order to accomplish a transition from an interventionist to a coordinating type of state. Environmental policy was redefined, revising and eliminating state regulations and replacing them with economic instruments. Changes in land policy and the introduction of instruments such as the Green Protocol, which subjects bank lending to environmental impact assessments, are examples of this tendency. The environmental policy of the Cardoso administration seems to be market friendly, stressing the benefits of liberalization, privatization, and market mechanisms. This orientation could pose new challenges and constraints on the state's ability to promote sustainability in Amazonia.

At the institutional level, the resources available for environmental protection during a period of fiscal crisis in the state are very limited. Cardosos's policy shift was not effectively translated into a budget reallocation in favor of the environment, and the fiscal crisis is reducing the resources available for environmental protection. In October 1998, in the context of the adjustment plan negotiated with the IMF to protect Brazil from speculative attacks after Russia's collapse, the government announced cuts in all public spending, including a 20 percent reduction in the environmental budget.[7] This leaves Brazil in the situation of relying almost exclusively on external sources for funding its environmental projects. Under these conditions, funding agencies and, in particular, international organizations are actually in a position to determine the shape of projects and to define priorities.[8]

A second set of concerns has to do with monitoring and enforcement deficiencies of government agencies, which are often understaffed and badly equipped to control such a large territory. IBAMA's former president himself, Eduardo Martins, recently admitted that Brazil does not really have a forest policy. For Martins, the country could, with some effort, succeed in controlling timber production using economic instruments that focus on pricing and conservation measures. Eventually, Brazil could even become a forest power. Yet, the lack of resources and poor implementation and monitoring do not allow for a real improvement in forest management.[9] Another institutional weakness is the lack of an effective body to coordinate environmental policy. In general, there has not been a real incorporation of sustainability goals in public policies or in public administration practices.

The trend toward deregulation and privatization is another worrisome aspect of the Cardoso administration's policy, one that could undermine the control of pollution and environmental degradation. While privatization favors a short-term focus and immediate gains over long-term environmental concerns, it is considered an important instrument in the new Amazonian policy, confirming the market-oriented strategy. To date, however, the private sector has not demonstrated enough interest in moving toward more sustainable forest practices, because they incur high investment costs. Privatization seems premature because the administrative reforms necessary for the consolidation of the regulatory capacity of the state are still lacking. In Amazonia, some sectors of public administration need to be expanded and strengthened to ensure effective implementation (GTA 1996:35). In the context of reform of the state, there seems to be little room to undertake the policies necessary to ensure long-term sustainability in Amazonia.

Global Versus Local: The Limits of the Managerial Approach

Finally, the third aspect to be considered within a critical IPE framework is how policy reform is affecting democracy and access to common resources in Amazonia. I have argued above that one of the primary obstacles to sustainable development is the lack of democracy in access, use, and control of natural resources in Amazonia. As observed by Roberto Guimarães (1991b:90), a main characteristic of ecopolitics in Brazil has been the exploitation of Brazilian common property resources according to a developmentalist ideology that is guided by private criteria for the allocation of resources. In the mid-1990s, the advent of the Cardoso government meant the arrival of a modernizing discourse stressing the need to promote democratization and decentralization on the one hand, and social justice on the other. Yet, in Amazonia, far from the more fully globalized parts of the Brazilian economy and society, democratization and redistribution are difficult to find. Thus, environmental policy reform under Cardoso seems to be privileging international solutions and programs that do not fully address the basic needs of local populations, while allowing for the perpetuation of the role of the military and traditional elites in the definition of priorities and strategies for the region.

Limited democratization through international influence. While the influence of international factors in explaining policy change in the

Brazilian Amazon has been accounted for and analyzed, the magnitude of international influence should not be associated automatically with progress in fighting the ecological crisis. First, the impact of the action of international NGOs is sometimes problematic. In Brazil, NGOs are to a large extent financially dependent on international funds (Cordani et al. 1997:294). As a result, the agenda that prevails reflects the concerns of environmentalists in developed countries and not necessarily the priorities of local and national populations.

The market orientation adopted by the Cardoso administration also makes governmental environmental policy dependent on foreign resources. In this context, the World Bank is assuming a growing role in Amazonian policies. In response to heavy criticism by environmentalists worldwide, the World Bank has undergone some environmental reform. Yet, the poor results of programs such as *Plano Agropecuário e Florestal da Amazônia* (PANAFLORO) show the limits of environmental reform at the World Bank and other international organizations and highlights the risks involved in relying excessively on international actors to ensure sustainability in Amazonia. While small farmers, rubber tappers, and indigenous communities were supposed to be the main beneficiaries of PANAFLORO, the project actually resulted in a deterioration of their living conditions, an intensification of environmental degradation, and damage to extremely fragile ecosystems. The project has excluded the very groups that it was intended to benefit, depriving them of access to their sources of subsistence and of control over their natural environment. It also threatens the very future of these natural resources. The World Bank itself has recognized that it has not been very efficient in the approaches it has pursued, recognizing that "even the Bank's high-quality economic and sector work and the evaluation of its own projects have had negligible impact on Brazilian Policies" (Lele et al. 2000:84). In addition, the Bank acknowledges that it often appears to be an advocate for global objectives, such as the protection of biodiversity and the defense of indigenous people, even if they are at the cost of national and local interests, such as the direct survival of poor, nonindigenous populations" (Lele et al. 2000:83–84).

The globalization of Amazonia encompasses another worrisome aspect. Brazil's patent law, a result of intense pressure from the U.S. government and lobbying from pharmaceutical companies, authorizes the patenting of genes from plants, animals, and even indigenous peoples for commercial use.[10] The transformation of tropical flora into a market product under the control of large international pharmaceutical companies illustrates once again the ongoing commodification of nature that ultimately penalizes populations that depend on nature for subsistence and have developed the knowledge now being patented by others. In this case, international pressure, which took the form of the United States lobbying for the approval of the patent law by the Brazilian congress, has meant the victory of corporations and powerful economic interests over local populations, depriving them of control over their lives.

Limited democratization: The state, local elites, and the military in environmental management. While some international actions and channels certainly represent impediments to the prospects of sustainability in Amazonia, major responsibility must be assigned to the continuation of old practices and discriminatory state policies. First of all, the political practices in the region are still undemocratic. A traditional oligarchy maintains control over the political apparatus. There is also a tendency toward a militarization of environmental protection that is justified by a realist definition of environmental security.

While ensuring the survival of the oligarchy and the military's interests, the Cardoso administration has not developed a strategy to strengthen disenfranchised local actors and allow them to fully participate in decisionmaking processes. During the 1994 electoral campaign, Cardoso promised to consolidate the decentralization process and to base his government on a state-society partnership.[11] However, participation has been restricted and NGOs seem disappointed with the environmental performance of the Cardoso administration. Finally, the initiative presented by the state as a real solution for the region, the Pilot Program for the Tropical Forests of Brazil (PPG7), does not constitute a real strategy to strengthen the role of small producers and extractors, the actors who are best prepared to fight deforestation since they depend on the forest for their living. The program has been criticized for lack of participation by both state agencies and NGOs and for failing to address major policy issues such as the long-term sustainability of these activities (GTA 1996).

Most state and IGO initiatives have failed to consider the real causes of deforestation and to take into consideration the needs of local people who depend on the forest. They are not reversing the structural conditions that have led to deforestation, promoted capital concentration, and aggravated social inequality. In Amazonia, more than elsewhere, the weight of tradition perpetuates elitism. The power structure remains concentrated and exclusionary, and decisionmaking processes respond to the particular interests of the best-organized groups of society who tend to privatize common resources for their exclusive benefit (Guimarães 1991b:75–78). To a large extent, actions undertaken by the government and by international organizations in Amazonia have tended to benefit the best-organized sectors of society or the ones with the easiest access to power in a manner that seems to be a continuation of the politics of the previous military regime.

Conclusion

This chapter has presented a critical perspective on environmental policy reform in Brazil. Reviewing both neoliberal institutionalist and realist approaches, it has shown that these approaches fail to link the adverse impact of global economic processes with the environmental situation of Amazonia; rather, they concentrate on the positive and integrative effects of globalization. The critical perspective adopted here concentrates on the role of globalization in influencing the political economy of policy reforms that occurred in Brazil during the 1990s and promoted a redefinition of Amazonian policies along the lines of the liberal consensus reflected in a managerial type of sustainable development.

This critical approach better accounts for the determinants of policy reform, stressing mutual interaction between national and international processes; this approach also explains the nature of the new policy and its implications in terms of ecological sustainability and social equity. By focusing on the contradictions of the sustainable development consensus, it is able to explain why managerial approaches to the environment will not succeed in bringing long-term sustainability to Amazonia. Understanding "global Amazonia," the changing dynamics of deforestation, its contradictions, and the resistance it is encountering requires an approach that restores historicity to the analysis and stresses the underlying structural factors responsible for social change. It is thus useful to consider not only the historical structure within which change takes place in

Amazonia—that is, the particular configuration between ideas, institutions, and material forces—but also the pressure and resistance this configuration is encountering (Cox 1986).

I have argued that globalization places serious limits on sustainable development in Amazonia for three reasons. First, globalization has significantly affected policy reform and transformed the Brazilian state. It favors market-oriented strategies that marginalize environmental concerns, fostering an economic restructuring that strengthens the same model of accumulation that causes environmental destruction and pollution in industrial countries. Second, the ongoing reform of the state, launched in the context of the transformative process of the 1990s, is not likely to improve environmental standards, because it reduces resources allocated to environmental programs and hampers the implementation of legislation. And third, present policy is not promoting democratization of access to natural resources and the control of resource management processes. On the contrary, it tends to reproduce exclusion and to deny entitlement to a large part of the population.

In Amazonia, globalization has contributed to the exacerbation of conflicts, raising them to a new scale that goes beyond the mere fight for land. The conflicts that feed deforestation in the Amazon are, above all, conflicts about justice and distribution. Deforestation corresponds to processes with a logic and trajectory rooted in Amazonia's social and economic history. Since privileged groups maintain preferential access to natural resources owned by the state, the Amazonian development strategy of the present government seems to be a continuation of, rather than a break with, the strategy designed during the authoritarian years.

In this setting, Brazil's policy toward the Amazon appears to be increasingly affected by liberal globalization. It addresses the needs of an international audience rather than those of 20 million Amazonians. It is not based on a political analysis of how to make Brazilian society more sustainable and equitable, and it does not institute progressive environmental standards. In Brazil, environmental considerations have become part of a conservative modernization strategy benefiting the globalized sector of the Brazilian society and perpetuating social conflicts in the Amazon region. In arbitrating the conflicts between alternative uses of the natural resources in Amazonia, the Brazilian state in the 1990s has tended to reproduce the exclusionary logic that denies the existence of a diversity of views on how to relate to the forest. Doing that, it strengthens a "globalized Amazonia" that, because it depends on the extraction of resources and commodities, is perfectly inserted in centuries of dependency and globalized economic history.

Notes

1. Neoliberal institutionalist analyses have tended to dominate. This section reconstructs the realist and neoliberal institutionalist interpretations of the situation in Amazonia rather than summarizing these literatures.

2. I am referring here to the dominant mainstream approach to international environmental politics represented by Haas, Keohane, and Levy (1993), among others. For critical IPE approaches to global environmental politics, see, for example, Bernard (1997), Doran (1995), Lipschutz and Conca (1993a), and Paterson (1996).

3. Survey by IISER/IBOPE/Ministry of the Environment, quoted in *Gazeta Mercantil* (1997a).

4. Instituto Nacional de Pesquisas Espaciais, quoted in Lele et al. (2000).

5. Since 1980, the relative importance of the forest sector to Brazil's international trade has increased from 5.42 percent of total exports and 1.2 percent of total imports to 7.14 percent and 1.98 percent, respectively. Forest-related exports in Brazil have grown from $100 million in 1985 to about $500 million in 1997 (Lele at al. 2000:11).

6. According to a report by an external commission created by Congress to investigate the activities of the Asian companies and other irregularities, the companies are processing 30 million square meters a year, five times more than they have declared, indicating that the companies might be lying in their reports to IBAMA. In *O Estado de São Paulo,* 22 June 1997.

7. Rede Verde de Informações Ambientais, 1998.

8. Nogueira-Neto, quoted in *Gazeta Mercantil* (1997b).

9. Interview of IBAMA's president, Eduardo Martins, with *Veja,* no. 1052, July 2, 1997. Available online at http://www2.uol.com.br/veja/020792/sumario.html.

10. See Chapter 6.

11. See Cardoso (1995).

Barbara Lynch 8

Development and Risk: Environmental Discourse and Danger in Dominican and Cuban Urban Watersheds

New juxtapositions of human settlement and industrial activity in third world cities have important implications for urban environmental risk and its distribution. To understand this international political economy of risk, we need to know how material conditions, discursive formations, economic projects, and political actors interact at and across four levels of analysis: the world system, the nation-state, the municipality, and the neighborhood. In this chapter, I discuss the risk transition models that inform international development debates and suggest an alternative analytical framework that relates risk to participation in the global economy and exclusion from political decisionmaking. I then use this framework to analyze risk in two urban watersheds: the middle basin of the Río Yaque del Norte, encompassing the city of Santiago de los Caballeros in the Dominican Republic, and the smaller Río Almendares basin, which contains Havana's largely undeveloped Metropolitan Park.

The Dominican Republic and Cuba occupy similar positions in the global economy, although their development trajectories and dependencies have diverged as have the political ideologies that inform their urban environmental management practices. The comparison allows us to ask (1) how the timing and nature of insertion into the global economy affect the nature of risk; (2) how national urban and economic policies mediate the neoliberal prescriptions of international development agencies to alter the nature of risk and its distribution; (3) how discourses about risk employed by international, national, and municipal policymakers shape decisions about what kind of environmental science gets done and whose risks get addressed; and (4) how environmental management practices include or exclude majority interests and influence efforts to reduce risk or change its distribution.

Urban Environmental Risk in International Development Discourse

Environmental crises in third world cities have drawn increasing attention in international development circles since Jorge Hardoy and David Satterthwaite (1991) reviewed the field. The Urban Management Programme, created by the World Bank, the UN Development Programme (UNDP), and the UN Centre for Human Settlements (UNCHS), designed a strategic framework for urban environmental programs; the World Resources Institute dedicated its 1996 report to the urban environment; and the Inter-American Development Bank (IDB) sponsored a seminar entitled "Urban Greening in Latin America and the Caribbean" (World Resources Institute 1996). Unfortunately, these policy documents, mired in developmentalist rhetoric, rely on risk transition models that render new urban risks invisible.

Risk Transition Models

These models are based explicitly or implicitly on Walt Whitman Rostow's (1960) notion that all countries pass through similar stages of development on the road to modernity.[1] They treat urban environmental risk as a temporary effect of the early stages of development and view urban environmental concern as a luxury reserved for societies that have experienced "takeoff."[2]

Ulrich Beck (1992:ch. 1, 1996:29), for example, argues that transition to a risk society occurs when conflicts over the distribution of wealth are managed successfully through technological innovations. As a result of these innovations, risks tend toward globalization, and scientific knowledge about risk is contested and politicized. However, Beck cannot explain the seemingly contradictory processes occurring in third world cities that are riven by conflicts over the distribution of wealth yet are highly permeable to external economic influences and the unpredictable risks of late modernity.

The risk transition models that underlie international urban environmental policy documents (especially Smith and Lee 1993; McGranahan et al. 1995) are even more problematic. These models distinguish between traditional risks—associated with disease attributed to poverty and lack of basic infrastructure in poor neighborhoods—and modern risks—associated with pollution and attributed to traffic, energy consumption, and smokestack industries. They assume that with development overall levels of risk will decline. Because they view "traditional risks" as obstacles to, rather than products of, development, these models (1) do not ask how global economic projects set the parameters within which risks are created or how these projects interact with national economic strategies and social policies; (2) fail to consider ways in which global economic integration affects municipal governments' ability to reduce urban environmental risks; and (3) neglect the role of discourse in problem identification, prescription, and delimiting the sphere for public participation in the search for solutions (Blowers 1997:849).[3]

However, despite their limitations, risk transition theories dominate international urban environmental discourse. As a consequence, they shape urban environment programs funded by international development agencies and policies formulated by international agencies and third world states (Harvey 1996:373–376). The result has been an almost exclusive emphasis on bacterial contamination and solid waste, and neglect of issues like industrial siting, land markets, and sociospatial segregation.[4]

Toward an Alternative Understanding of Risk

Several social scientists have sought alternative explanations for urban environmental degradation and risk. Some attribute environmental degradation to state failure (Stillwaggon 1998; Guimarães 1991a). Indeed, state resources, cultures of governance, and state interests may have a significant impact on urban environmental risk, but state influence is constrained by powerful subnational and international actors. Others blame international capitalism while slighting political and social factors (Olpadwala and Goldsmith 1992). Weaving elements of both into his analytical framework for urban sustainability, David Drakakis-Smith (1995, 1996, 1997) acknowledges the roles of government, industry, foreign investment, and land markets in shaping urban environments. However, he overlooks

problems arising from differential rates of transfer of polluting technologies and knowledge about their control as well as from ways in
which environmental discourse and funding have defined arenas for
environmental action.[5]

These alternative explanations improve upon risk transition
models but share with them an evolutionary bias that "naturalizes"
risk in third world cities by associating it with the traditional or less
evolved. Thus, the most frequently cited sources of risk—even in the
progressive literature—are wood, dung kitchen fuel, diseases transmitted in untreated water, raw sewage, and insects. These risks are
visible precisely because they seem more "natural" and therefore
more typical of "backward" societies. The transfer of used equipment and obsolete plants from core to periphery may lend additional
credibility to evolutionary understandings of risk. However, the rapidly changing global division of labor makes it dangerous to assume
that today's risks in the urban periphery will look like yesterday's
risks in the core.

Risk and Hybridity

To avoid the developmentalist trap, I start from the assumption that
environmental risks are the products of specific urban and economic
policies. The contemporaneous and social nature of seemingly natural risks becomes evident when we associate them with their source
rather than view them as a stage of development. Risks associated
with human settlements may seem traditional, but they are not ves-
tigial. They are functions of location, density, and inadequacy of
urban services and are associated with informal or illegal settlement
and neglect of housing stock and infrastructure in the central city.

Risks associated with economic activity—industry, hazardous
materials storage, and consumption of industrial products—coincide
roughly with those that risk transition theorists call modern. These
vary depending upon the industrial technologies introduced, the timing of technology transfers and, equally important, the transfer of relevant information about how to monitor and control their related
risks.

Risks associated with industry are experienced in the workplace
and in the neighborhood. In the United States, polluting industries
and toxic facilities are concentrated in poor, minority neighborhoods
(Bullard 1990; United Church of Christ 1987). Evidence for this

phenomenon in third world cities is mounting (Reich 1994; Walker 1994; Lupton and Wolfson 1994). Economic liberalization measures since the 1980s have also ensured that the risks of industrialization will be disproportionately borne by poor nations and regions and that states and municipal governments will find it increasingly difficult to pay for environmental regulation or for infrastructure in working-class neighborhoods (Mitchell 1997).

These dense interactions between local and global, old and new, and residence and workplace are captured by Néstor García Canclini's (1995) concept of hybridity—the simultaneous existence of the premodern, modern, and postmodern in which each is reshaped by the presence of the other.[6] Hybridity suggests that we ask how political and economic *integration,* rather than marginalization, generates new risks, creates new routes of exposure, and affects the distribution of protection from risk. It also implies a historical specificity that requires that we ask questions germane to particular times and places.

Using hybridity as a starting point, we can ask how economic and political projects at global, national, and municipal levels, initiated at different historical moments, have shaped Dominican and Cuban urban landscapes. These projects have entailed successive transfers of industrial plants, processes, and technologies, each associated with specific forms of pollution. They have also entailed new patterns of urban land use. Because risk is a function of the interactions between production of toxic emissions and residential patterns, policies and programs that have determined the location of industry and urban settlements in relation to one another are key factors in determining the distribution of risk.

Equally important in the nature and distribution of risk are programs intended to improve urban environmental quality. Their efficacy depends on three interrelated factors: the conduct of international urban environmental programs at the municipal level; the state of environmental science in the nation; and the degree to which urban governance is inclusive rather than exclusive. To the extent that international agencies subscribe to a developmentalist discourse on risk, they are more likely to fund projects that address "natural" or "traditional" risks—notably water- and insect-borne diseases. Because they are the major funders of urban environmental programs, we can expect that they will influence national and subnational discourses and, as a consequence, the choice and transfer of risk abatement technologies. Where the latter are imported, we can also expect that environmental science, data collection, monitoring, and abatement will be shaped by international actors and their funding priorities and will be mediated by national states. This in turn raises questions about the utility of imported science for municipal decisionmakers. Finally, where government policies and programs are exclusionary, risks are likely to fall most heavily on the excluded. Where they are based on an inclusionary notion of citizenship, we can expect more equal sharing of knowledge about risks and, therefore, greater attention to risk mitigation.

The Dominican Republic:
Integration, Exclusion, and Risk

Economic Development and Urban Policy

Since 1929, the Dominican economy has moved from relative autonomy to full integration into the global economy. Meanwhile, urban policies have isolated the urban poor, limited their access to urban services, and excluded them from political decisionmaking (Derby 1998; Mitchell 1997).

Development has been governed by three successive economic models, each with different implications for urban environmental risk (Ceara Hatton 1996; Chantada 1996; Espinal 1998). Import substitution industrialization (ISI), promoted by President Rafael Leonidas Trujillo (1929–1961), meant factory construction beyond the city's edge. Thus, despite the absence of pollution controls, plant location kept cities from the brunt of ISI's urban environmental impacts (Chantada 1996). Trujillo's assassination and the Cuban Revolution spurred North American investment in Dominican mining and agribusiness. Mine tailings and pesticides fouled water supplies in Santiago and smaller cities. The Dominican state began to promote export-platform industrialization in the 1970s; the sector expanded in the 1980s with structural adjustment and the U.S. Caribbean Basin Initiative (Reyes Castro and Dominguez 1993; Santana 1994), and migration for work in the *maquilas* drove rapid growth of secondary and tertiary cities (Itzigsohn 1997).

Urban policies since 1929 have emphasized large-scale public works, urban land speculation, class separation, and token efforts to demobilize opposition. Trujillo favored the development of a socially segregated, monumental Ciudad Trujillo (Santo Domingo) but permitted the simultaneous, if slower, growth of Santiago. President Joaquín Balaguer (1966–1978, 1986–1996) encouraged the growth of unregulated urban land markets and urban sprawl. He also promoted large public works projects as concrete symbols of his regime's journey toward progress and modernization, sources of employment and benefits for political supporters, and instruments for demobilizing potential opposition (Pérez 1996; Ceara Hatton 1996). Balaguer continued to privilege investment in the capital and to initiate showy construction projects until his final days in office. At the same time, he promoted privatization of basic urban services (Mitchell 1997).

Santiago: Risk in the Hybrid City

Industrial development and the production of risk. Santiago grew up as a commercial center for the tobacco sector of Cibao, the rich agricultural region surrounding Santiago (San Miguel 1997). A modest industrial sector grew on the city's edge after World War II. Factories for cement and building materials, food processing plants, distilleries, and tanneries dating from this period are still in production and account for some of the city's most visible environmental problems. The 1960s and 1970s saw the concentration of tobacco, food, and agricultural input industries in the Cibao. In 1973, the first industrial park or *zona franca* was established, and by 1979 Santiago housed 16.8 percent of Dominican manufacturing plants (Santana 1994; Chantada 1991:19).

By 1998, nine zonas francas with 323 industrial plants were located in the Santiago metropolitan area (Consejo Nacional de Zonas Francas de Exportación 1998). More than 70 percent of firms manufacture textiles and apparel; the rest produce leather goods, electronics, packaging, and cigarettes. These are not typical smokestack industries, but they do produce wastes that require special handling. Industrial parks are owned by the Dominican state or by private landowners; the firms are tenants. The former are responsible for basic infrastructure and service provision; the latter handle removal of solid wastes generated in the plants. In principle, park owners are responsible for wastewater treatment but, in 1999, Santiago's largest zona franca still had no wastewater treatment plant and discharged industrial waste directly into the river (Castillo 1996). The zona franca also produces about 30 metric tons of untreated solid waste daily, which are deposited indiscriminately in the city's open dump (Garrido et al. 1997). Yet, the privileges accorded to export-platform industries in the 1970s and 1980s by the Dominican government have precluded effective regulation of industrial waste. The government may be even less inclined to regulate as these industries face heavier competition from Mexican firms.

Speculation, settlement, and the distribution of risk.   Urban sprawl, the juxtaposition of incompatible land uses, and residential polarization have produced an inequitable distribution of risk in Santiago. Major forces producing this reconfiguration of urban space have been export-platform industrialization and real estate speculation.

Santiago's real estate boom began in the 1960s, with appropriation of public lands by speculators allied with construction and financial interests. Construction companies built housing for the middle and upper classes, particularly for returning migrants from the United States (Hernández 1997:8). Builders used their substantial political clout to secure for their subdivisions preferential access to garbage collection and drinking water but took little interest in what happened downstream. As a result, urban sprawl consumed scarce municipal government resources.

Real estate speculation also reduced the amount of land available for low-cost housing just as the demand for labor was expanding. By the early 1990s, 30 percent of the urban population occupied 75 percent of the residential area of the city, leaving to the rest undesirable remnants of the public domain (Rodríguez et al. 1993). Some poor settlements were constructed on river banks subject to flooding. Others were built in *cañadas*—gullies that collect industrial discharges and solid wastes from their own microwatersheds. Poor settlements suffer from both inadequate sanitation and close proximity to polluting facilities: industrial plants, garbage dumps, and sewer outlets.

Many settlements lack streets, garbage collection, and legal access to potable water or electricity due to municipal neglect. At the same time, land tenure insecurity discourages individuals and communities from investing in infrastructure. Residents of the poorest neighborhoods are vulnerable to two kinds of takings. First, as land prices rise and building technologies advance, land once considered unusable may gain value and pass into the hands of developers. Second, as municipal authorities seek to make the city more attractive to investors, they raze informal settlements considered unsightly, environmentally degrading, or havens for "undesirable" elements.

In sum, we find no evidence of a risk transition in Santiago, despite economic modernization. The urban poor are vulnerable to eviction, natural hazards, and environmental risks resulting from inadequate infrastructure *and* uncontrolled industrial emissions— problems that can be traced to Dominican urban and industrial policies.

Environmental Science and Monitoring

Dominican environmental science reflects the discourse and funding priorities of international donors. As a result, transfer of new technologies is occurring much faster than the transfer of knowledge about how to monitor, regulate, and dispose of the wastes produced by these technologies. In our effort to map potential sources of pollution in Santiago and chart monitoring efforts, we found no air pollution data, despite ample evidence of factory and automobile emissions. The Secretariat for Social Security and Public Health gathered data on diarrhea and infectious disease but none on diseases related to toxic exposure. Water quality data emphasized coliform content but neglected heavy metals or organic compounds. International aid programs did little to enhance Dominican capacity to monitor industrial pollution. Rather than addressing the hybrid nature of risk, monitoring efforts focused primarily on natural or traditional risks.

A major barrier to the transfer of accurate information about industrial risk and the development of local environmental science capacity has been the persistence of developmentalist explanations of urban environmental risks that emphasize traditional risks and self-help projects and blame the poor for environmental degradation.

Urban Environmental Discourse and the Politics of Exclusion

Despite official indifference, industrial pollution is a concern for Santiago residents. Barrio organizations have filed petitions to protest chemical effluents from fabric-washing plants. The president of a local environmental NGO calls his organization "the department of environmental complaints for the city of Santiago." "Ecos de la

Comunidad," a neighborhood news column in *La Información,* Santiago's daily newspaper, documents complaints about pollution from neighborhoods in the city's industrial belt. Women's groups and neighborhood associations have raised concerns about water contamination, air quality, noise, and garbage. Residents and workers in riverine barrios have implicated tanneries and distilleries as major polluters, citing fish kills as evidence. But interviews with community leaders revealed that most complaints go unanswered or are addressed through small, isolated public works projects.

If poor neighborhoods are concerned about domestic waste *and* industrial pollution, the dominant environmental discourse emphasizes the former and discounts the latter. It attributes urban environmental degradation to bacterial contamination of the water supply, open sewers, and informal solid waste dumps and assigns blame for these failures to informal settlements. This discourse is largely the product of an alliance involving institutional members of the municipality's elite Asociación para el Desarrollo, Inc. (APEDI), bilateral assistance agencies, and international foundations (Paniagua 1998).

Its exclusionary bias is evident in a campaign to clean up the Río Yaque del Norte. The campaign began with a nostalgic and passionate call for cleanup.[7] The German Gesellschaft für Technische Zusammenarbeit (GTZ) financed a one-shot effort to monitor river contamination in 1992 (INDRHI 1993), and the U.S. Agency for International Development (USAID) launched a poorly funded environmental program centered on water quality issues in 1993. A 1992 presidential decree named the Instituto Superior de Agricultura (ISA) as the river's steward and made it head of a national commission for safeguarding its watershed. In that capacity, ISA issued a report attributing water pollution to settlements on the river's edge and in the cañadas and pressed for eviction (Carrasco et al. 1993). CONORDEN, an organization created by APEDI in 1994 and charged with developing a strategy for cleaning up Yaque del Norte tributaries, drafted a plan to control effluents flowing into Santiago's cañadas and sought support from USAID and the World Bank (Peralta and Fulcar 1994). Like the ISA report, CONORDEN documents attribute pollution mainly to new, informal settlements. The one agency concerned with industrial water pollution on a continuing basis is CORAASAN, the parastatal water and sewer corporation for the municipality of Santiago, but it lacks sophisticated instruments needed to identify a broad range of pollutants.[8]

Private sector initiatives show similar limits. The ethics committee of the Asociación Impresarial Region Norte (AIREN), a regional business association, asked its members to report on chemicals used, discharges, and treatment plants. Months after circulating its questionnaire, AIREN received no responses. Some enterprise managers in the zonas francas have asked park managers to install wastewater treatment facilities. Those most concerned with the environmental performance of zona francas are branch plants of large transnational corporations (TNCs)—potential targets of corporate responsibility campaigns.[9] But to date, pressure from these highly exposed firms has produced no significant changes in waste management.[10]

The Dominican state has had limited success in controlling industrial pollution. The Comisión Nacional para el Saneamiento Ecológico (CNSE), created by presidential Decree Law No. 226 to control industrial discharges into the nation's rivers, established emissions standards. The CNSE briefly and zealously enforced these standards in 1992, closing polluting plants and dispatching advisers to recommend treatment options. In some well-publicized cases, its recommendations were technologically unsound. More important, the CNSE targeted ISI factories but not the zonas francas, despite ample signs of problems in this sector (Cobb et al. 1991). Since then, government interest in industrial pollution has ebbed.

In 1997, national media and government attention turned to the highly visible problems of domestic solid waste. In Santiago, informal dumps are a persistent problem. Only 60 percent of solid wastes are collected, and 40 percent of the urban population has no access to garbage collection (Ponton 1995). Pilot projects undertaken with Kellogg Foundation and U.S. Peace Corps support mobilized community labor for local trash collection and recycling efforts but did not address its ultimate treatment and disposal. Industrial solid waste and municipal waste treatment practices have received almost no attention from nongovernmental organizations (NGOs), government agencies, or international development agencies.

In sum, industrial pollution was a major concern for poor Santiago residents. However, the narrow framing of urban environmental discourse, coupled with the exclusion of the urban poor from municipal policy discussions, kept their concerns from influencing municipal or international programs. Exclusion took several forms. Because industrial pollution was excluded from regional and international urban environmental agendas, local groups did not view the risks that they faced as environmental issues. Second, their economic marginality made neighborhood residents worry about the implications of environmental actions for jobs. Finally, by confining urban environmental activity to education and small-scale, self-help public works projects, donors, NGOs, and politicians were able to isolate local activists and impede environmental action at the municipal level. In this context, the multiplying risks associated with industrial pollution and the hybrid nature of risk constituted significant, but largely concealed, problems.

Cuba: Isolation, Inclusion, and Risk

Economic Development Models and Decentralization

Like the Dominican Republic, Cuba is a small, import-dependent nation with a relatively weak manufacturing sector, but the timing and nature of its insertion into the global economy differs from that of its neighbor, as do the values that undergird state economic and urban policies. Before the revolution, direct U.S. investment in Cuba exceeded $1 billion. About a third was concentrated in public utilities, followed by agriculture and mining (Pérez 1997:219–231). At first, the revolutionary government favored ISI investment in the polluting metallurgical, chemical, machine, and automobile assembly industries (Barraclough forthcoming), but with the U.S. blockade and military threat, Cuba entered the Council of Mutual Economic Assistance (CMEA) in 1961. Economic relations with the Soviet Union and its Eastern European allies meant access to cheap oil and also dependence on Eastern Europe for technical assistance and imports of machinery, heavy equipment, trucks, and automobiles (Zimbalist and Brundenius 1989). Technology transfers included plans for a Chernobyl-type reactor, plans that came to symbolize the negative environmental implications of CMEA membership.

With the 1989 demise of the Soviet Union, the Cuban economy collapsed, and housing, food, and consumer goods production slumped. The crisis impelled a shift to an economic strategy that encouraged foreign investment in tourism, mining, and, increasingly, real estate, while fostering self-sufficiency in agriculture and production for domestic consumption (Carranza Valdés et al. 1996; CEPAL 1997).

If Batista's urban policies favored Havana's hyperdevelopment, the revolution represented a triumph of the country over the city. Revolutionary urban policy has consistently favored investment in provincial cities. Incentives to locate outside of Havana and low birth rates on the island helped Havana to avoid the growing pains suffered by Dominican cities. At the same time, the antiurban bias of the revolution resulted in a neglect of central city housing that ultimately exacerbated urban sprawl (Nuñez 1997), and the economic policies of the 1990's unwittingly fostered migration to the capital.

Risk and Depression: Havana and the Río Almendares

Part of Havana's greenbelt, the Río Almendares basin is a large wedge of land, narrow at its outlet and broadening toward the south. In the southern part of the city, the river flows through the Metropolitan Park, a once largely undeveloped area that now houses recreational facilities, farms, informal settlements, and industrial plants.[11] As it nears the sea, the Almendares borders Havana's Vedado and Miramar neighborhoods.

Industrial development and the production of risk.   The Almendares basin housed U.S.-owned distilleries during Prohibition and became a site for ISI industrialization in the early 1960s. Local factories produce construction and building materials, paper, beer, and bottled gas. Other industries in the zone include food processing, an industrial laundry, and auto repair shops. Since 1989, agriculture has become an increasingly important economic activity in the watershed, which now contains several state agricultural production units and numerous market gardens. Pollution in the Almendares basin is much like that encountered in the urban reaches of the Río Yaque del Norte. Both areas receive agricultural wastes and similar industrial effluents. Both abut open municipal dumps that release toxic gases through uncontrolled burning and cement plants that emit large quantities of particulates.

Housing shortage, settlement, and the distribution of risk.   By the early 1980s, it became apparent that government emphasis on decentralization contributed to urban sprawl in Havana by allowing the deterioration of central city housing stock and encouraging construction of new housing on the urban fringe. The general plan for Havana, approved in 1984, sought to control sprawl by recommending development in areas where adequate services existed. The plan also called for new public parks, recreational areas, environmental zones, and protection of the city's environmental patrimony (Nuñez 1997:17). It did succeed in reserving for public use large tracts of parkland, but it was not implemented in a way that adequately protected urban watersheds.

With the economic crisis, deterioration outpaced construction in Havana despite efforts to spur reinvestment in central city housing.[12] As in Santiago, municipal poverty limits the ability of public agencies to serve new settlements. The Havana water supply deteriorated, and by the mid-1990s many residents relied on truck deliveries for drinking water.[13] At the same time, growing opportunities for earning hard currency income in Havana spurred in-migration from Cuba's poor eastern provinces. By the mid-1990s, new housing production met only about a third of the annual demand.

One response to the housing shortage was informal settlement in undeveloped portions of the Almendares basin (Cruz et al. 1997). The Cuban government hoped to slow the proliferation of informal settlements by encouraging migrants without employment or housing in the capital to leave the city, but not at the expense of maintaining civic peace. So, rather than emphasize eviction and resettlement, the government launched programs to formalize land tenure and improve sanitation and basic services in spontaneous settlements.[14] Still, the new urban settlements in the Almendares basin suffer from deficient infrastructure and service provision.

As in Santiago, risks in the Almendares basin are hybrid products of Cuban integration into the global economy and national economic and urban policies. They are exacerbated by the close juxtaposition of settlements and polluting industries. River basin studies, more comprehensive than their Santiago counterparts, identify the following sources of contamination: the municipal dump, leaky sewers, informal settlements without infrastructure, informal solid waste dumps, masonry waste, high lead concentrations, and air pollution (Cruz et al. 1997). However, management approaches differ radically, partly because Cuban science has a strong social orientation, partly because state legitimacy depends on broad citizen participation in urban management, and partly because neighborhoods are not highly segregated along class lines.

Environmental Science and Monitoring

The Cuban government has consistently prioritized science and medicine; as late as 1997, Cuba spent 1.2 percent of GDP on research and development, placing it ahead of Brazil, Venezuela, and Mexico (Schulz 1999). Until the 1990s, environmental science was largely limited to disease control and forestry, but the field gained ground in the 1990s for three reasons. First, the Chernobyl accident offered Cuba a chance to reject the Soviet development model (one it never wholeheartedly embraced). It also offered an opportunity to advance the state of nuclear epidemiology and a reason to integrate environmental analysis into urban planning at a time when the country could have been expected to choose nuclear energy as the path of least resistance toward energy self-sufficiency.[15] Second, the economic crisis of the early 1990s afforded opportunities to develop and test low-input technologies. The scientific community responded with innovations in low-input agriculture, alternative energy, and low-energy forms of transportation and construction. Finally, the 1992 UN Conference on Environment and Development (UNCED) provided President Fidel Castro with the platform from which to initiate a process of environmental planning and stimulate the growth of an indigenous environmental movement. Cuba's Agenda 21 report helped to legitimate the urban environment as an arena for scientific inquiry by outlining goals for the greening of industry, toxic waste control, solid waste management, and safe handling of radioactive waste. It identifies women, youth, workers, peasants, and NGOs as key environmental change agents (CITMA 1995).[16]

Risk in the Almendares Basin: The Politics of Inclusion

Unlike Santiago, where local concerns about industrial pollution were systematically excluded from municipal environmental agendas, in Havana, local involvement in environmental management was encouraged. This was facilitated by a tradition of neighborhood mobilization and the absence of severe sociospatial segregation, which in turn permitted the diffusion of organizational talent and political resources across all urban neighborhoods. The result is relatively strong local organizational capacity that has been effectively utilized to initiate self-help housing, infrastructure, and environmental programs in poor outlying neighborhoods (Coyula 1996).[17]

The Almendares cleanup illustrates Cuba's inclusionary approach to urban environmental management. In the early 1990s, a working group was formed to improve the environment in the Metropolitan Park, and a citizens' group, SOS Almendares, was formed to clean up the river. In June 1995, the Cuban government signed an international agreement with Canada's Urban Institute to assist with park planning. The working group, together with the new Foundation for Nature and Man, initiated a planning process that included park residents in diagnostic analysis, planning, and, ultimately, implementation and evaluation of the plan. With some support from international NGOs and bilateral assistance agencies,[18] the municipality of Havana prepared a development strategy that would establish a joint program to monitor and control industrial pollution involving local communities, polluting industries, and government regulatory agencies.[19] The cleanup program had technical, educational, and expressive components. It called for communities to reduce the volume of untreated domestic wastes entering the river, but recognizing that the most damaging contaminants come from industrial sources, it gave priority to seven plants for pollution reduction (Cruz et al. 1997).

The inclusionary emphasis of the program was strengthened by a 1996 directive requiring all government-funded projects to address environmental issues and include plans for popular participation. Monitoring was not sophisticated and did not include testing for heavy metals or organic compounds. It did, however, entail substantial institutional collaboration among agencies and enterprises. Some of these agencies lacked a tradition of environmental engagement, but their involvement in the cleanup project was an indicator of a micropolitics of environmental management in Cuba that allowed scientific institutes to protect their funding by demonstrating social utility.

Participation in environmental planning took two forms. Planners invited four popular councils in neighborhoods surrounding the park to list and prioritize problems. Council members complained of river contamination, informal dumps, deterioration of local roads, deforestation, insufficient water supply, distance from services, and lack of recreational facilities (Cruz et al. 1997). The park planners also asked groups composed of doctors, union officials, managers, economic functionaries, workers interested in the environment, and workers in key environmental roles from five local industries—two breweries, a paper mill, and two gas bottling works—to make parallel diagnostic analyses of park problems and to identify clean technologies. The industrial groups helped to formulate and implement projects to reuse waste materials, eliminate sources of contamination, and carry out environmental education programs.

To conclude, urban environmental risk in Cuba is a function of both its isolation from and integration into the global economy. The combination has resulted in the proliferation of underserved urban neighborhoods and dependence on polluting plants close to residential areas. However, urban policies that favored nonmarket mechanisms for the allocation of housing have also prevented extreme sociospatial segregation. As a result, risks are broadly shared. By emphasizing the social role of science and self-sufficiency and rejecting the Soviet emphasis on massive, polluting technologies, Cuban development discourse has legitimated efforts to control industrial as well as residential pollution. Finally, revolutionary experience with building local institutions and the relative absence of sociospatial segregation have enabled greater local participation in problem identification and environmental planning.

Comparison and Lessons

Urban environmental risk is conditioned by the nature of a city's insertion into the global economy over time and by national urban policies that can either cushion or exacerbate problems experienced by the urban majority as a result of that insertion. In Havana and Santiago, the nature of insertion into the global economy is shaped by the interests of international investors, the development community, and national and municipal policymakers.

Both Cuba and the Dominican Republic experienced technology transfers from the core that increased environmental danger without affording resources for remediation. These transfers include export of extractive and polluting industries, obsolete technologies, and inefficient or half-spent equipment in the absence of information about their consequences or control (Platner 1997). For this reason, despite differences in the timing and nature of their integration into the global economy, both societies face similar hybrid risks. However, Cuban and Dominican urban and economic policies reflect divergent development strategies and responses to their similarly dependent positions in the global political economy.

One major difference between the two countries lies in the way in which environmental discourse is embedded in a larger political discourse. If Dominican urban environmental policies are informed by a modernization-driven rhetoric of order, progress, and *exclusion*, Cuban policies seem driven more by a rhetoric of order, progress, and *inclusion*. In the Dominican Republic, progress is defined solely in terms of economic growth; poor urban dwellers are stigmatized as polluters and their participation in environmental management is limited to labor contributions.[20] In Cuba, progress implies high performance on quality of life indicators like education and infant mortality (Guevara 1968; Feinsilver 1993), and contamination is viewed as a broader societal problem to be solved collectively by polluters, scientists, government agencies, and urban dwellers.

Cuban and Dominican approaches to informal settlements also differ sharply. Unlike the Dominican emphasis on removal, Cuban policies reflect a tacit understanding that government authorities will not try to remove existing informal settlements even as they seek to discourage new ones. In return, community residents are asked to work with the state to identify and rectify environmental hazards. In both countries, informal settlements remain at the pleasure of the state, but the Cuban state sees itself not as the patron of public works, but as the mobilizer of citizens to protect the environment.

This comparison has two implications for development planning. First, urban environmental problems seldom respond to quick technological fixes. They require the generation of knowledge about risks associated with technologies and how to monitor and control them in cost-effective ways. Cuban science emphasizes this kind of knowledge, but international development assistance programs based on risk transition models rarely if ever recognize the need for or support collection of these kinds of data. However, technology transfer implies an obligation on the part of exporting nations and the international development community to ensure that technology is used safely. This means that technology transfers that strengthen science in the public interest are a sine qua non if urban environmental risks are to be controlled.

Second, a politics of inclusion bodes better for risk reduction than a politics of exclusion. Risk reduction cannot be accomplished through eviction or scapegoating. As long as employment opportunities are better in the city than in rural areas while access to affordable urban housing is limited, people will settle in risky locations (Hardoy and Satterthwaite 1991). Risk reduction requires regulation of land and housing markets in ways that ensure that services, infrastructure, and environmental risks are equitably distributed among neighborhoods.

A three-part urban environmental strategy is needed, one with implications for the international development community, state and local governments, and neighborhood organizations. This strategy must address discourse, practice, and material conditions by (1) disseminating accurate information about hazards associated with different economic activities and challenging the authors of developmentalist discourse to address risks as they are and not as they imagine them to be; (2) improving state and municipal capacity to identify, monitor and regulate, and restrict movement of risky industries and products; and (3) encouraging local groups to see neighborhood environmental issues within a broader sphere of environmental action and to join national and transnational alliances in support of their agendas.

Notes

I am grateful to María Paniagua, Pedro Juan del Rosario, José Miguel Fernández, Marcia Hawa, María Caridad Cruz, and James Platner for their intelligent collaboration in data collection and analysis and to the Ford Foundation for its generous support. The conclusions drawn in this chapter, however, do not necessarily reflect the views of my collaborators or the foundation.

1. These models do not fall within the ecological modernization perspective described in Hajer (1995), Harvey (1996), and Blowers (1997), which calls for a general greening or ecological enlightenment to enhance the efficiency of capitalist production. In contrast, the risk-transition model described here suggests that the nature and locus of environmental problems will change with development.

2. A memo, written by Lawrence Summers when the secretary of the Treasury was chief economist for the World Bank, presents the extreme case of this approach (*The Economist* 1992a, 1992b). It suggests that poor countries should be pollution havens because environment is an aesthetic concern only for the well-off, most third world residents do not live long enough to experience the ill effects of pollution, and, even if they did, their lives are worth less than those of their counterparts in developed nations.

3. Dryzek (1997:8) uses the word "discourse" to connote "a shared

way of apprehending the world" that allows its adherents to interpret information and create coherent stories about the world. I do not use discourse to refer to this common worldview, but rather to the narratives of environmental change consistent with this view, the code words that refer to actors and events in the narrative, and the causal explanations derived from these narratives. I view discourse as a shaper of practice and material conditions, but as distinct from them. For example, the word "traditional" invokes a story about the world that places the nations of the South at a lower point on an imagined evolutionary ladder that they will ascend as they emulate the more progressive nations of the North. Like Harvey (1996:78), I consider discourses to be manifestations of power.

4. See, for example, Easterbrook (1994) in the *New York Times Magazine*. He mentions industrial emissions and ambient lead levels in third world cities but identifies population growth as the "core environmental problem for most of the world" (1994:63) and dirty cooking fuels and bacteria-laden water as the most immediate problems. His cures are large hydro and coal-fired power plants, oil field development, and large-scale water and sewer infrastructure.

5. Drakakis-Smith (1995) argues that the environment in a given city will reflect (1) population growth and demand for services; (2) the nature of economic growth and environmental regulation; (3) the ability, capacity, and willingness of local and national governments to control industrial growth; and (4) the physical landscape (see also Drakakis-Smith 1996, 1997).

6. "How do we study the cleverness with which the city attempts to reconcile everything that arrives and proliferates, and tries to contain all the disorder—the peasant's exchange with the transnational corporation, the traffic jams in front of protest demonstrations, the expansion of consumption together with the demands of the unemployed, the duels between commodities and behaviors from all sides?" (García Canclini 1995:3–4).

7. A seminar entitled "Past, Present and Future of the Río Yaque del Norte," sponsored by the Ecological Society of the Cibao (SOECI). See also Veras (1991).

8. Information on pollution control efforts in Santiago comes from interviews with key agency officials and community leaders undertaken in 1996–1997, unpublished project documents, and local newspaper accounts. Interviewers included myself, María Paniagua, and James Platner.

9. In Chapter 5, Newell attributes this lack of effective regulation of TNC pollution to complicity on the part of third world states and to limits to the role that transnational NGOs can play in shaming companies into cleaning up. His conclusions are supported by this study.

10. Information on private sector initiatives comes from interviews with *zona franca* plant managers, AIREN members, and CORAASAN technical staff conducted in 1996 and 1997. Interviewers included myself, Marcia Hawa, and Pedro Juan del Rosario.

11. Information on the Metropolitan Park comes primarily from a comparative study by project collaborators, María Caridad Cruz Hernández, of the Foundation for Man and Nature, Havana, and María Paniagua.

12. In principle, urban residential property is allocated on social rather than market principles to discourage sociospatial segregation, although no attempt was made to do away with private property (Hamberg 1998; Núñez 1997).

13. This situation is exacerbated by the blockade that has made it impossible for Cubans to obtain spare parts for water and sewer systems built by U.S. firms to U.S. specifications before the revolution (Schulz 1999).

14. Some planners fear that the recent liberalization of land markets may displace Havana residents to informal settlements on the periphery. However, it is not clear to what extent land market liberalization has played a role in the expansion of informal settlements within the Río Almendares basin.

15. Benjamin-Alvarado (2000) asks why Cuba has continued to pursue nuclear power as a development strategy. He argues that recent government efforts to develop conventional alternatives to nuclear power do not signal an abandonment of the latter and that the nuclear option may be the only rational energy choice for Cuba. From an environmental standpoint, it makes sense to turn his argument on its head: why, given the compelling logic of nuclear power in a small, oil-poor island nation, has there been so much opposition to plant development and so much emphasis on oil exploration and conservation?

16. One response to UNCED was the formation of ProNaturaleza, an NGO founded in 1993, which had about 8,000 dues-paying members in 1995. Its leadership drew heavily from the Cuban research establishment, and its agenda included control of local industrial pollution (Collis 1995). For recent Cuban reporting on achievement of Agenda 21 goals, see www.un.org/esa/agenda21/natlinfo/countr/cuba.

17. Like NGO projects in Santiago, these programs address very local problems and transfer infrastructure environmental management costs to local volunteers, but integration of local activists into government and party structures permits information trickle-up and the aggregation of local environmental interests.

18. Including the Canadian International Development Agency (CIDA), UNDP, the World Wide Fund for Nature (WWF), the Spanish Junta de Andalucía, the Canadian Urban Institute, Oxfam-Belgium, Oxfam-Canada, and Bread for the World, a German NGO (Cruz et al. 1997; Montané 1995).

19. The Water Resources Institute, Ministry of Agriculture Institutes for Forest Research and Soils, the Institute of Nuclear Science and Technology, the Institute of Hygiene and Epidemiology, and the Water and Sewer Authority for the province of Havana.

20. An exception is a Kellogg Foundation–supported public health program that provides water-testing equipment to health promoters in poor neighborhoods and trains them to test tap water for chlorine.

Part 3

Theoretical Challenges

Gabriela Kütting

9

A Critical Approach to Institutional and Environmental Effectiveness: Lessons from the Convention on Long-Range Transboundary Air Pollution

The effectiveness of international environmental institutions is an issue of growing political significance. Regime analysis has dominated environmental research in recent years, and a major focus has been the effectiveness of international environmental agreements (Young 1997; Victor et al. 1998). The two goals of this chapter are to assess the regime approach to effectiveness and to propose alternative paths for assessing an agreement's environmental effectiveness. The Convention on Long-Range Transboundary Air Pollution (LRTAP) is considered to be one of the best examples of an effective international environmental institution. For this reason it provides a fitting case study for the examination of environmental and institutional effectiveness.

The analysis of the effectiveness of international environmental agreements is important to international political economy (IPE), although this may not seem immediately obvious. The connection, however, is apparent since environmental degradation is a by-product of the IPE. As Robert Cox argues:

> The global economy, activated by profit maximization, has not been constrained to moderate its destructive ecological effects. There is no authoritative regulator, so far only several interventions through the inter-state system to achieve agreements on avoidance of specific noxious practices. (Cox 1996c:516)

Here, Cox makes the link between unconstrained productive forces and the limited power of regulatory intervention through state actors, highlighting the incompatibility between what he calls the production structure and ecological requirements. However, he continues to see the impacts on the state system and sovereignty as the primary issue (Cox 1999) rather than the effect on the environment or the effect of environmental degradation on global society. This means that Cox's critical approach still operates within the traditional concerns of the international relations (IR) discipline—that is, it is mostly concerned with actors and their ability to change outcomes or structures in the international or global arena. This chapter takes an alternative critical approach, focusing not only on the actors in the international system but also on environmental degradation itself. It thus broadens the IPE discourse on the environment by linking effectiveness to ecological rather than political concerns. This is clearly a difficult task, because it goes against prevailing concepts and prevailing preoccupations with political and institutional factors rather than environmental necessities. However, a social and critical approach to environmental effectiveness allows us to "restate" the nature of environmental problems, ensuring that relevant social factors and forces are not marginalized and externalized. In addition to its important theoretical and ideological implications, then, such an approach also allows us to identify important methodological and practical shortcomings of conventional problem solving.

Because it is a well-established and well-researched institution that is open to external analysis as a result of its policy of readily giving researchers observer status at negotiating sessions, the LRTAP Convention is a good case study for evaluating an agreement's effectiveness. Acid rain became a prominent issue in Scandinavia from the late 1960s onward. The convention itself is a brainchild of the 1972 UN Conference on the Human Environment (UNCHE) in Stockholm. An Organization for Economic Cooperation and Development (OECD) study commissioned in the early 1970s in response to the Stockholm Conference showed that industrial air pollution from Western and Central Europe traveled in the atmosphere and was deposited in Scandinavia as well as other places.[1] Scandinavian appeals for international regulation in the early 1970s were resisted as Western states asked for more evidence. An unrelated initiative by Leonid Brezhnev, during the 1976 round of the

Conference on Security and Cooperation in Europe (CSCE) requesting more East-West cooperation in a low politics area, led to the choice of transboundary air pollution as an issue for this occasion. Since the CSCE has no organizational infrastructure, the United Nations Economic Commission for Europe (UNECE) was chosen to host the agreement.

The convention was signed on 13 November 1979 in Geneva by thirty-four UNECE member states. It was the first multilateral agreement on air pollution and the first international environmental agreement involving nations of both Eastern and Western Europe as well as North America. There are seven protocols to the convention, with the signing of another protocol imminent.[2]

While the LRTAP Convention is generally considered institutionally effective (Gehring 1994; Sprinz and Vaahtoranta 1994), this chapter shows that, because the agreement concerns itself more with institutional feasibility than environmental necessity, its environmental effectiveness is questionable. Although recent protocols take a more environmental focus, environmental aims have always been subordinated to political and economic necessities.

To demonstrate this claim, I briefly outline the most prominent regime approaches to effectiveness and put forward a new approach. There are two strands of regime effectiveness studies to which I refer: institutional effectiveness and modified institutional effectiveness. These two approaches are broadly similar but differ in their focus on environmental improvement. According to what I call the institutional effectiveness approach, effectiveness is viewed in terms of creating and maintaining cooperative rules and behavior (Young 1992, 1997; Jakobeit 1998). According to what I term the modified institutional effectiveness approach, effectiveness is also measured on the basis of environmental impact (Wettestad and Andresen 1991). However, this study of environmental impact remains embedded in institutional concerns. The discussion that follows seeks to illustrate two important weaknesses of both approaches that are not rectified by their incorporation of environmental concerns: first, it is argued here that their concern remains predominantly with the change that an institution can bring about rather than environmental quality per se; second, the object of analysis, namely the regime/agreement, is not embedded in the social, political, economic, and environmental context in which it operates, which means that related structural and exogenous factors and contexts do not form part of the analytical framework in which the regime/agreement is placed.

The Institutional Effectiveness Approach

As the name implies, this approach is characterized by a focus on institutions. Oran Young, as the major representative, asks the following question:

> How can we assess the significance of institutions as independent or intervening variables with regard to individual and collective behavior at the international level and, in so doing, resolve the conflict between these divergent points of view? (Young 1992:161)

He answers that an institution "is effective to the extent that its operation impels actors to behave differently than they would if the institution did not exist or if some other institutional arrangement were put in its place" (Young 1992:161).

Thus, Young defines effectiveness as solely located in the performance of the institution. Other determinants, such as environmental amelioration criteria, are reflected in institutional performance and therefore influence effectiveness indirectly. Young (1992:176–194) has established a list of factors that influence the impact of regimes. These are divided into exogenous factors relating to the social context in which the regime operates and endogenous factors relating to the character of the regime. An effective regime would need high transparency, high robustness, good transformation rules, high capacity of governments to implement provisions, equal distribution of power, high interdependence, and a constant intellectual order (Young 1992:176–194). All these factors can enhance the effectiveness of a regime, while their absence impedes it.

Along similar lines, Levy, Young, and Zürn (1994:21) name three dimensions of regime consequences: direct versus indirect effects; internal versus external effects; and positive versus negative effects. The separation of factors into endogenous and exogenous categories and into internal and external effects poses a severe problem. Since, for regime theorists, order is a function of agency—that is, it is dependent on a willingness to achieve order—the achievement of effective order should be a function of agency as well. However, if effectiveness is largely dependent on exogenous factors as Young (and also Levy below) argue, then it is not a function of will but rather is dependent on the nature of the problem, the particular membership of the regime, and other circumstantial factors and thereby is historically dependent and fortuitous. From this it follows that it may not be possible to have an effective (in whatever way) regime even if all the members are inclined to form one. Therefore, effectiveness is not a function of will alone. Exogenous factors include processes, structures, and systems that are not directly related to actor behavior. This clearly means that actor-level analysis, as assumed by the atomistic institutional framework used in regime theory, is insufficient for an understanding of effectiveness. Moreover, regime theory cannot account for this weakness within the parameters of its internal logic.

This poses two problems: first, a change in actor behavior may result in action but no actual improvement of the environment (e.g., the 1985 LRTAP Convention Sulphur Protocol led to a 30 percent reduction in national sulphur dioxide emissions by 1993, but that did not stop the forests from dying or lower the rate of respiratory diseases). Alternatively, the change may result in an improvement in the environment as compared to the preagreement stage, but one insufficient to solve the environmental problem.

Second, it is impossible to isolate the processes that led to the conclusion of an agreement from larger social and environmental processes; therefore, the impact of an institution/agreement cannot be measured. After all, the larger social processes that led to the creation of the agreement quite possibly also led to changes on other levels, and therefore change cannot be attributed to the institution/agreement alone. Analytically, it is impossible to isolate the effects of the agreement from the broader consciousness of a particular kind of environmental degradation. For example, it is not possible to trace technological changes in car engines or exhausts to the LRTAP Convention, because concern with acid rain led not only to the creation of this regime but also to domestic policies, industry awareness, media campaigns, and changes in public opinion, among others. Therefore, an analysis based on institutional effectiveness alone is lacking in many respects.

The Modified Institutional Effectiveness Approach

There are several regime analysts who are conscious of the need to link effectiveness analysis to environmental concerns, although they still operate within the parameters of the institutional effectiveness approach. I refer to their writings as the modified institutional effectiveness approach. Marc Levy, for example, also follows the tradition of defining effectiveness in institutional-behavioral terms. However, he expands: "Effective international institutions, in the comprehensive sense, not only redirect behavior; they also solve environmental problems; and they do so in a more efficient and equitable manner than available alternatives" (Levy 1993:17).

This approach is similar to that of Peter Haas et al. (1993:7) when they ask: "Is the quality of the environment better because of the institution?" This implies that an effective institution should initiate change that would not occur otherwise. However, this point relates only indirectly to the environmental problem and its amelioration. The focus is limited to any type of change without indicating how it can be measured or how change can be causally attributed to the institution in question rather than some regime-external developments. Joergen Wettestad and Steinar Andresen (1991) have developed a series of indicators that make it clear that their main research question is whether the institution in question is actually dealing with the environmental problem it is supposed to solve or ameliorate. To date, their definition is the most detailed, and it includes institutional and environmental criteria by which effectiveness can be measured. These indicators are the achievement of the institutional goals set by its member states; the degree of correspondence between expert advice and actual decision taken; and the degree of improvement compared to the preinstitutional state of the environment (i.e., what the state of the environment would be without the institution) (Wettestad and Andresen 1991:2).

Wettestad and Andresen also differentiate between the effectiveness of a problem-solving effort and that of a solution—that is, between what the agreement sets out to do and what it actually does—and they focus on solution effectiveness. However, such an approach neglects the broader problem-solving goals of an agreement. This means that if the targets of the agreement are achieved, the agreement can be termed effective even if it may not actually aim at environmental improvement but is merely the result of diplomatic compromises.

The same authors (1991:2) mention two environmental indicators: goal achievement of the agreement (which doubles as a criterion for institutional effectiveness and becomes an environmental indicator only in an appropriate framework); and the degree to which the content of the agreement is consistent with expert advice on what measures should be taken. The first indicator faces the criticism of vagueness, because goal achievement can be measured over time and at different institutional or environmental stages. It is debatable whether it is the signing of an agreement, its ratification, or its implementation at the national or local level that constitutes goal achievement. The second indicator supplies a standard against which the contents of an agreement can be measured, but independent expert advice is only of limited use as a standard because of the controversial status of scientific advice.

Although Wettestad (1995), in a working paper, argues that the primary aim of an effective analysis of environmental regimes has to be their capacity to solve the environmental problems giving rise to the agreement, he realizes that environmental problems have "objective and subjective dimensions." These dimensions are not static—they change over time. Therefore, Wettestad (1995:16) argues that "this comprehensiveness strengthens the case for focusing most attention on the outcome/behavioral change part of the concept [of effectiveness]." However, this analytical solution puts emphasis on easy measurement rather than the importance of the issue, as it shies away from dealing with what Wettestad terms subjective dimensions and focuses on the relatively uncontroversial implementation of regimes. The case Wettestad makes for this focus is based on analytical comfort/feasibility rather than the improvement of the concept of effectiveness.

Likewise, the indicators used by Wettestad and Andresen, although introducing a strong environmental component on the implementation side, still place this environmental component within a framework that takes institutional performance as the main focus of analysis. In Cox's terms, they take for granted the boundaries of institutional performance and try to fit environmental criteria into it rather than developing a framework that is equally comfortable with environmental and institutional criteria.

A Critical Approach to Environmental Effectiveness

One insight that has emerged from a review of the various definitions of effectiveness is that there is no clear understanding of the concept and how it can be measured. As Paterson argues:

> Conventional approaches to regimes "depoliticize" international environmental problems by providing criteria by which responses can be judged in a supposedly neutral manner. . . . Yet these cannot be isolated from other criteria. Environmental questions cannot be neatly boxed off from other political questions. The regimes established to resolve transnational environmental problems always benefit some social groups more than others, whether or not they are successful from a purely environmental point of view and they also preclude the broader questions of whether the existing political, social and economic orders may themselves generate environmental crises. (Paterson 1995:214)

The alternative approach outlined below forces us to address the questions that Paterson identifies and can help improve our understanding and operationalization of environmental effectiveness itself. This is not to deny the importance of institutions but, rather, to highlight the absence of environmental criteria and the "social disembedding" of the problems and processes that bring forth institutions and environmental standards.

In simple terms, the environmental effectiveness of an international environmental agreement refers to the degree to which the degrading or polluting processes and consequences are arrested or reversed as a result of international action. Initially this definition does not seem any different from that offered by a number of regime theorists (Haas et al. 1993; Wettestad and Andresen 1991; Levy 1993). However, vital differences emerge once we take a critical look at the social contexts that inform environmental standards.

A focus on the social context of an environmental problem, what Young calls the exogenous factors, is important if regime theorists are to improve their problem-solving capacity. Most crucially, however, it is important because it allows us to focus on the problem-posing processes that have both practical and ideological implications. In fact, identification of an environmental problem leads to many responses, and the conclusion of an agreement to deal with this problem is just one social process among many.

As noted earlier, the reversal of environmental degradation is not necessarily directly attributable to the agreement in question. If the agreement set in motion other social processes that led to an arrest or reversal of degradation, then the agreement has been indirectly effective. The attribution of the solution of a problem to a specific policy, particularly one that does not address exogenous yet related factors, may be impossible to prove. For example, the turnaround of the British government in relation to the phasing out of chlorofluorocarbons (CFCs) stipulated by the 1987 Montreal Protocol, is generally attributed to the Imperical Chemical Industries (ICI) identification of CFC substitutes rather than to the protocol itself.

A social and critical approach places the environmental effectiveness of an agreement in the wider historical contexts that produce the problem, its definitions, and various policy preferences. In other words, the provisions of international environmental agreements are not solely actor driven; rather, both actors and policies are rooted in particular social and structural origins.

The omission and externalization of such structural factors has important implications. Such externalizations allow policymakers to focus on political feasibilities within existing parameters instead of environmental necessities that may challenge these parameters. Problems are evaluated and tackled within the framework of the policymaker's political and institutional margins, which means that politically feasible solutions prevail over environmentally necessary ones.

Institutional arrangements reflect negotiated compromises at the policy level and represent institutional feasibilities. However, these compromises also tell a story about priorities in policymaking that reflect the interests of the most powerful actors in this or, indeed, other overlapping policy processes. These priorities can be manifested in economic terms, in social terms, in agenda setting in general, and in evaluations or definitions of the environmental problem in question. The definition of acid rain as a problem of emissions rather than of the use of fossil fuels is a case in point.

A social and critical concept of environmental effectiveness also leads us to ask questions about the relations between the state, the market, and civil society and how they interact to deal with issues such as equity and ecology in economic decisionmaking (Camilleri 1996:138; Wapner 1997a). Joseph Camilleri (1996:139) summarizes the main tenets of a more environment-focused paradigm as opposed to the hegemonic liberal-materialist paradigm: a new paradigm needs to ensure the compatibility of technological innovation and social goals; it needs to be based on an equitable distribution of cost and benefit of economic development and on a form of social organization that gives equal value to integrity, stability, diversity, and balance of nature. This approach is obviously not unproblematic, as both equity and environmental effectiveness are expressed through political concerns that reflect hegemonic power constellations. Equity in this sense does not mean a form of objective social justice but implies an approach that takes into account the values and needs of more than the predominant views. This might even lead to potential conflict between environmental and social concerns, because some actors' values may not necessarily be compatible with the aims of environmental effectiveness. Hence, it is necessary to link effectiveness not only to actor-driven concerns but also to ecological standards as well. However, the proposed remedies for environmental degradation arising out of a concern with environmental effectiveness must take into account social and intergenerational equity and not impose a burden on only some social groups. As Nicholas Low and Brendan Gleeson (1998:180) put it, the relationship between "instrumental effectiveness and the wider context of governance" needs to be considered. The next section examines how far these aims have been achieved within LRTAP.

Evaluating the Effectiveness of the LRTAP Convention

Acid rain is a highly complex phenomenon that arises when sulphur and nitrogen oxides are released during the burning of fossil fuel. These oxides react in the air and produce acidifying substances that are transported by wind and weather patterns. These wet and dry deposits are referred to as acid rain. In ecosystems with high sensitivity to acidification, they cause substantial damage by upsetting the normal acidity of the soil or water area. Particularly vulnerable areas are the Scandinavian lakes and Central European forests, where overacidification has led to the death of flora and fauna. Cultural monuments, such as the Dome Cathedral in Cologne, have also been affected, and air pollution is the cause of respiratory diseases in humans, especially children. Some acid rain is deposited locally or regionally, but large proportions are also transported over large distances. Therefore, acid rain is a transboundary problem whereby airborne pollutants are deposited over entire ecosystems and have a cumulative effect.

Although the LRTAP Convention started off as a rather low-priority agreement, it has developed into a very active forum with many innovative initiatives and attempts to keep the process in motion. Its institutional structures are very strong, continuous upgrading takes place, and progress is constant. However, this efficient institutionalization also has its drawbacks, because a veritable political economy of science and technology has transformed air pollution regulation into an economic activity. Environmental considerations are subject to economic and technological feasibilities and are mostly referred to in percentage terms—the 60 percent gap-closure scenario. In addition, environmental needs are classified in terms of resource and health management. This means that economic feasibility and not environmental benefit drives the agreement. The critical loads approach used by LRTAP amply illustrates this point (Kütting 1998).[3]

The LRTAP Convention is a well-functioning agreement in the institutional sense. From an economistic/technocratic point of view, the agreement can even be called environmentally effective as demonstrated by its progressive emission limits. Since the agreement is only partially directed at ameliorating environmental degradation, however, LRTAP is not effective in an ecological sense.

Institutional and Technocratic Analyses

The aim of this section is to briefly outline the limitations of institutional and technocratic solutions in evaluating the effectiveness of the LRTAP Convention. In a typical example of the institutional approach, Levy concentrates on the institutional details and history of negotiations. As he states,

> National policy responses tell only part of the effectiveness story. It is necessary to go one step further and ask what causal role did the institution play in bringing about the national responses we observe? In doing so it is useful to perform the heuristic exercise of imagining the counterfactual case of a similar situation lacking an institutional response. (Levy 1993:115)

This assertion reflects the institutional assumption that the effectiveness of the LRTAP Convention is due to its success in changing actor behavior. It is not feasible, however, to measure LRTAP's effectiveness through imagining policy responses to acid rain in the absence of LRTAP. This technique presupposes that this institution operates as a closed system that is not influenced by, and has not influenced other, social processes and assumes that no action would have been taken without LRTAP. As such, it is not possible to prove causation but only correlation. Levy (1993:116) further argues that LRTAP signatories reduced their sulfur dioxide (SO_2) and nitrogen oxide (NO_x) emissions more than nonsignatories and therefore attributes policy change to the LRTAP Convention, since "to measure effectiveness one must estimate the reductions that would have taken place in the absence of a protocol." This point also establishes correlation but not causation. Furthermore, the reduction of SO_2 and NO_x emissions does not constitute effectiveness, as they may not have been reduced to the extent necessary to achieve environmental improvement.

This brief illustration suggests that, methodologically, regime theoretical approaches to the effectiveness of the LRTAP Convention are limited by the externalization of factors that may, in fact, play a very important role. This is also a problem with those approaches that place their emphasis on technological solutions.

Human innovation has created technologies that can vastly reduce the release of acidifying by-products, thus aiming to eliminate the existence of acid rain in Europe by the year 2010/2020. This case is amenable to technological solutions because the impacts of acid rain are not totally irreversible. While there are several problems with the technological approach, if transboundary air pollution were eliminated through technological solutions by 2010/2020, then an argument in favor of considering broader social factors would be significantly weakened. A number of reasons, however, suggest that a successful technocratic approach would have to deal with the social dimensions of the problem, in particular:

• While acidifying substances will be filtered out to a large degree, they will still have to be deposited somewhere. Thus, the problem is displaced either geographically or through the creation of different environmental problems not related to acid rain (such as disposal of air filters and catalytic converters or nuclear power).

• The convention does not adopt a holistic approach to the degree that it does not address the fundamental causes of acid rain, such as the fossil fuel economy and the transport sector. As a result, the narrow posing of the problem will also produce narrow technologies. The use of energy-efficient technologies in later protocols is a step in the right direction, but it still operates in an environmental management rather than a holistic framework.

The Social and Political Contexts of the Convention

The LRTAP Convention is just one institution in a web of other relations. First, it is part of the whole European integration project. Second, it also owes its existence to the rapprochement that took place during the last stages of the Cold War. Finally, it has been influenced by the broader General Agreement on Tariffs and Trade/World Trade Organization (GATT/WTO) system. The first two relations explain the presence of states that are not really affected by or interested in transboundary air pollution. Because they have integrated in other spheres, such as defense or the economy, they cannot exclude themselves in the acid rain case without jeopardizing the overall integration process or other related international linkages. However, the importance these countries attach to this specific policy process depends on their environmental values and perceived priorities and may indeed be low, thus leading to sluggish policymaking. For example, Greece does not have a serious acid rain problem and did not perceive itself to be affected by acid rain at all during the early stages of the convention. It, and other southern European states, persistently put economic development before environmental protection, believing that environmental protection follows economic development rather than precedes it (personal communication). This attitude implies a focus on environmental repair rather than environmental protection in the first place.

Another case in point is the disagreement between the United Kingdom and the northwest European states during the mid-1980s. The United Kingdom suffers from acidification damage but has a tradition of inciting industry to take voluntary action rather than imposing regulatory measures. In addition, there is no tradition of the use of the precautionary principle but a tendency to wait until a definite cause-effect relationship has been established—that is, until the damage has been done. This incompatibility has resulted in a lot of debate and tension, not just in LRTAP but in other policymaking domains as well (Boehmer-Christiansen and Skea 1991). This tradition also affects corporate policymaking (Dosi et al. 1991; Fagerberg 1988). More broadly, the Anglo-Saxon tradition believes that regulation hinders innovation, while the Germanic-continental tradition assumes that regulation will lead to innovation. These differences are part of national and regional traditions and thus shape the ways in which societies operate and in which diplomacy takes place.

The LRTAP Convention must also be situated within the context of global neoliberal institutionalization reflected primarily by the GATT/WTO. The convention is subject to GATT rules and cannot override them. The conflicts between international environmental agreements and the global trade framework are important issues that are addressed by Marc Williams in Chapter 3. Although the LRTAP Convention is not directly affected by these issues since it is not directly concerned with the environmental effects of tradable products, the Spanish case that follows illustrates that it is not immune to these problems.

In the final stages of the 1994 negotiations for the new sulphur protocol, a potential conflict arose when Spain wanted to insert a clause that allowed it to continue to use indigenous coal and apply the negotiated provision relating to the use of best available technology to imported coal only. The Spanish government felt it was not able to afford the import of low-sulphur coal and close down its own coal industries. However, Canada and the United States objected to this special option for Spain because it contravened GATT rules stipulating that indigenous products are not permitted to receive preferential treatment over imported products. The problem was finally solved by a change in phrasing that was not entirely acceptable in GATT terms but was left to pass.[4]

The above example is a case of an overt clash between trade and environmental considerations. However, a much more important aspect of the predominance of economic/market structures is already incorporated in agenda setting, relating to Lukes's third (structural) dimension of power (Lukes 1974). The rules and structures of the liberal market system give some actors an intrinsic advantage over others, leading to particular types of problem posing as well as problem solving. In this case, for example, the nature of energy production and its detrimental effects in terms of acid rain are not questioned. The competitive nature of the economic system, based on growth and innovation, leads to preferences that favor technical solutions such as best available technology over energy efficiency, alternative energy forms, and nongrowth-based economic practices. This leads directly into a second set of factors that affect the effectiveness of the LRTAP Convention: its embeddedness within particular social and economic constraints.

The Limitations of the LRTAP Convention

The above section has located LRTAP in a social and political context that shows the constraints within which it operates. This section critically assesses the framework within which ideas of feasibility and necessity of policy solutions are anchored.

The political economy of energy (national and international) is structured heavily in favor of fossil fuels. Their predominance is not questioned despite constant warnings that fossil fuel supplies are finite and seriously tax the capacity of planetary sinks. Petrochemical companies are very large and diversified conglomerates that penetrate the majority of international and domestic market sectors. Alternative energy forms are not cost competitive at the moment, partly because they do not have a support network nor are they subsidized in the same way as petrochemical companies. This does not mean that petrochemical companies receive direct subsidies because many fossil fuel products such as petrol are quite heavily taxed (although road building and the construction of the energy grid could also be defined as subsidies). Rather, the size and diversification of multinational corporations (MNCs) make it easy to offset gains and losses from different products and sectors, and petrochemical companies also have easy access to public decisionmakers. In addition, fossil fuels externalize environmental and health costs. This means that their price does not reflect their full cost, which is borne by the state and/or society. Alternative renewable energy forms do not externalize costs and are thus realistically priced, limiting their economic attractiveness.

These structures obviously influence international environmental policymaking, but at no time was the predominance of fossil fuels questioned in LRTAP. The more recent LRTAP negotiations have moved away from controlling fossil fuel–based emissions by technological means to controlling rather insignificant sectors such as ammonia emissions from livestock farming, as the 1998 protocol on Persistent Organic Pollutants shows.

Likewise, the transport sector is neglected in LRTAP. Although road transport is responsible for the lion's share of NO_x and volatile organic compounds (VOC) emissions, there has been no direct attempt to target the transport sector. In addition, there is no account of the proportional increase of transport emissions in overall emissions as documentation of the negotiation process shows. Again, petrochemical firms (fuel) and car manufacturers are major European industries, and the link between road transport and transboundary air pollution is not made explicit in LRTAP. Fossil fuel–based transport and the use of individual transport are deeply embedded in Western societies and elsewhere. It is assumed that this privilege is a corollary to development and can be extended to an unlimited degree.

What are the implications of these priorities/assumptions immanent in the convention? First, existing industrial structures and thus traditional protection of certain industries means that the nature of energy production is not questioned. This becomes especially apparent vis-à-vis the transport sector.

Second, and as a result, the reliance of the European economic system on fossil fuels means that the emphasis in LRTAP is on technology-based solutions to the problem of acid rain, leaving the fundamental structures in place. Thus, catalytic converters or other end-of-pipe solutions are preferred policy options, while precautionary solutions, such as changes in the production system or the subsidy of alternative fuels, are marginalized. In short, more radical policy options are rendered unfeasible and utopian.

Third, the nature of the economic system dictates which policy options are desirable and which are not. Therefore, a change in the mode of production cannot even enter the agenda as a policy option because it is outside the ruling economic paradigm. This explains why the dependence on fossil fuels is not questioned.

Conclusion

This chapter has reviewed the shortcomings of conventional regime-centric approaches to the effectiveness of international environmental agreements, with particular reference to the LRTAP Convention. It has demonstrated that approaches that focus only on the endogenous characteristics of an institution and treat it as a closed system can at most give a partial account of institutional and environmental effectiveness. An alternative approach that considers exogenous contexts and constraints has been put forward here and applied to the LRTAP Convention. This social and critical approach considers the origins both of the environmental problem and the agreement. It suggests that when policymaking procedures subordinate environmental concerns to bureaucratic and institutional feasibilities, the formation of environmentally effective agreements is doubtful and their success temporary and fortuitous, because these feasibilities embody specific types of bias. Environmental institutions, like all social institutions, must be examined in terms of the social relations that have significant and determinant effects on their substance and operation. While this focus on social relations does not negate the need for abstracting and theorizing, it requires that theory does not externalize precisely those factors that ultimately determine the institution's performance and social purpose.

Therefore, the approach put forward here adds to both a critical perspective of IPE and of the environment by embedding social relations in an environmental context. This widening of the research focus moves away from actor-driven analysis and raises opportunities for introducing alternative policy frameworks. At the same time, it raises equally important questions about the relationship between equity and environmental effectiveness.

Notes

1. The OECD Cooperative Technical Programme on Long-Range Transport of Air Pollutants ran from 1972 to 1977 and had eighty observer and measuring points in Western Europe (Mayer-Tasch 1986).

2. The seven protocols to the convention are (1) On Long-Term Financing of Cooperative Programme for Monitoring and Evaluation of the Long-Range Transmission of Air Pollution in Europe (EMEP Protocol 1984); (2) On the Reduction of Sulphur Emissions or Their Transboundary Fluxes by At Least Thirty Percent (Sulphur Protocol 1985); (3) Concerning the Control of Emissions of Nitrogen Oxides or Their Transboundary Fluxes (NO$_x$ Protocol 1988); (4) Concerning the Control of Emissions of Volatile Organic Compounds or Their Transboundary Fluxes (VOC Protocol 1991);

(5) On Further Reduction of Sulphur Emissions (New Sulphur Protocol 1994); (6) On Heavy Metals (1998); (7) On Persistent Organic Pollutants (1998).

3. Because the targets put forward by the RAINS model used for the critical loads approach were not deemed achievable in practical terms, a compromise solution was negotiated that foresaw that the discrepancy between the five percentile critical loads model and actual sulphur depositions in 1990 had to be reduced by 60 percent, hence the "60 percent gap closure scenario." Only in the grids where the model's aim had already been achieved (parts of Portugal, Spain, and Russia) were its figures used for the protocol. In practice, this process can be described as the economic and political integration of the model.

4. The final version reads: "In a case where a Party, due to the high sulphur content of indigenous solid or liquid fuels cannot meet the emission limit values set forth in column (ii), it may apply the desulphurisation rates set forth in column (iii)." This phrase does not explicitly state that there is preferential treatment for indigenous fuels, but it is implied. This can pass the GATT rules, although strictly speaking it is not permissible.

Eric Laferrière # 10

International Political Economy and the Environment: A Radical Ecological Perspective

For about two decades now, various thinkers in the fields of international relations (IR) and ecology have sought to establish the grounds for an interdisciplinary rapprochement. Few would disagree today with the argument that environmental issues form legitimate case studies for theories of IR. Furthermore, as attested by the flurry of environmental diplomacy, no one would dispute that environmental repair now requires international political solutions. In other words, there is little controversy in suggesting that theories pertaining to IR and to ecology should look for common ground. Political ecologists and environmental scientists and engineers have long recognized that "improving nature" requires political pressure, appropriate legislation, and often the allocation of public funds; to extend the argument to the international or global arenas is mere common sense.

Still, while university departments, state bureaucracies, and academic publishers now routinely sanction work on international environmental affairs or global environmental politics, one could argue that the theoretical links between IR and ecology remain relatively unexplored. I make two related claims: (1) that theorists of IR have been inspired only from the mainstream or conservative ecological literature; and (2) (consequently) that theorists of IR, and particularly those specializing in international political economy (IPE), have yet to acknowledge the existence of a radical ecological literature (which they might well reject, but which remains very pertinent to an understanding of global political and economic order). The purpose of this chapter, then, is to clarify the theoretical links between IR and ecology (with specific references to the subfield of IPE) and to demonstrate the descriptive power and prescriptive potential of radical ecology—a broad school of thought grounded in various forms of critical social theory.

In a nutshell, the argument is as follows: (1) IR theorists of all kinds aim at an understanding of political (dis)order on a large scale; (2) ecological order is a fundamental dimension of political order (no political order can survive and prosper in a collapsing habitat); (3) perspectives on ecological order emanate directly from long-standing views on the essence and purpose of nature—views both antecedent and current to modern science; and (4) radical ecological perspectives, specifically, are cobbled from an array of alternative world-views challenging the alleged culprits behind global disorder—especially capital accumulation and instrumental rationality (but also state power and various hierarchies). In sum, linking IR and ecology (as an exercise in theoretical foundation) entails nothing less than an unpacking of philosophical material that is often assumed (but rarely fleshed out) by IR theorists and policy analysts.

Developing an ecoradical approach to global order requires several steps: (1) indicating how mainstream IR and IPE studies have conceived of global order and how they insert the ecological problematique within that conception; (2) demonstrating a necessary caveat, namely that radical ecology is not a homogeneous literature; (3) arguing nonetheless for some common thread within that literature that can speak to IR/IPE, and thus stating some general ecoradical principles serving as a rebuttal to the mainstream.

IR, IPE, and Ecology: Mainstream Views

By definition, a mainstream view offers explanations of order according to assumptions and methods defended by a majority within a community—in this case, an academic community. What are those dominant assumptions and methods in the three fields of IR, IPE, and ecology? These largely pertain to a modern view of nature as categorizable, manipulable, and serving no ultimate purpose—a mechanist, materialist view. This is an ontology that indeed connects the apparently disparate fields of IR (including IPE) and ecology. It finds its origins in the rejection of Aristotelian teleology in the seventeenth century by such luminaries as Galileo, Newton, and Hobbes.[1] Newton's key contribution in defining the mainstream consisted in consecrating nature as a clockwork mechanism—set by God yet functioning on its own through the force of gravity.[2]

By mechanizing nature and thereby separating it from its human observers, the scientific mainstream eventually gave life to ecology as a scientific discipline. While many radical ecologists would invoke this science to support their claims, ecology did become a fundamental tool for the mainstream, manifested as conservationism: nature is above all a pool of resources to be properly managed by existing forces of production so as to prolong their usefulness to humankind.[3] Conservationist ecologists may well recognize the many interconnections binding nature, yet they show confidence in human ability to manipulate them. Such mainstream ecologists are not necessarily corporate apologists, but they will hardly be swayed by either elusive appeals to the intrinsic value of nature or pseudoromantic calls for the rollback of industrialism.

The celebrated concept of sustainable development emerges here as the flashpoint of a thoroughly utilitarian approach to nature. That concept is surely controversial when used (as is done commonly) as a synonym for sustainable growth,[4] and so it offers a good insight into the magnetism of mainstream ontologies and epistemologies. Just as the idea of sustainability was absorbed by the political mainstream, so has the general theme of ecology (as environment) attracted attention among IR and IPE scholars precisely because it is well suited for absorption. Widely read books and articles on international environmental politics tend to vindicate (with slightly different twists) established arguments about regime maintenance, collective action failure, or global authority.[5] As long as environment can stand for some quantifiable resource, classical political and economic problems pertaining to scarcity may be restated wearing different garb. While mainstream social theorists may well appreciate that the attack on nature can pose fundamental reconsiderations of the very fabric of social-scientific studies, they are more likely to invoke disciplinary boundaries and hence refer such ruminations to philosophers.

Presumably, then, mainstream approaches are likely to provide only partial explanations and solutions to the problems posed by ecological degradation. Why is that the case? How can we argue, in other words, that mainstream IR and IPE are missing part of the ecological picture and are likely to ignore the radical challenges that ecological crises pose to their discipline—and the world?

Consider the importance of Thomas Hobbes's writings for the field of IR and their link to the mechanical worldview, which Hobbes borrows from Galileo, Newton's immediate predecessor. Hobbes is often seen as the father of realist thought in IR; but he is arguably more than that, because liberal theory is also indebted to him. Beyond specific recommendations for a centralized, highly powerful authority that would regulate the aggressive tendencies of humankind, Hobbes must be remembered for the science of politics that he tried to present in the opening pages of *Leviathan*. If nature can be understood deductively, so can the social world be subjected to axiomatic logic—the conflictual state of nature acting as premise. If the world may be construed as a giant mechanism set in motion by God, to be analyzed part by part and prodded for its hidden laws dictating its eternal operations, then so can human beings—and Hobbes (1985:81) tellingly discusses the human being as an arrangement of wheels, joints, and strings. Furthermore, while *Leviathan* conjures up powers associated with medieval authorities, its form is eminently modern—produced by a social contract. Contract theory is liberal theory. Contract theory is problem-solving theory: the state is a problem-solving mechanism (an artificial body), designed not only to protect citizens, but also to make them prosperous—and Hobbes was no less committed to market expansion (aided by science and technology) than full-fledged liberals such as Locke or Smith.[6]

There is, then, a common thread in the IR mainstream that transcends the usual divisions stated in the literature.[7] It is indeed a foundation built on Newtonian science, contract, and capital accumulation that is very congenial to the mainstream ecological view of nature as use-value ("natural capital"). As modern political thought, its key assumptions include the egoistic (or self-interested) character of human beings; the view of natural determinism (change is explained as a function of matter responding to matter); and the view of nature as harnessable through the application of reason (technologies and political institutions thus are comparable forms of engineering). Beyond their many important debates, proponents of the mainstream agree that politics is defined by scarcity, not by the pursuit of virtue; that scarcity problems are solved rationally; that reason is manifested through the application of technical expertise; and that reason is by no means inimical to the use of force. All in all, there is a decided, common belief in the management of scarcity through scientific and technocratic means, which hinges on a literally despirited view of the world: a human being alone in a world of predictable matter, looking for the expert as a means to security, thus bound by endless contracts governing his or her life. This is a world surely amenable to a scientific theory of international relations—the goal that perhaps best defines the mainstream and its link to twentieth-century positivism.

Mainstream studies of IPE have clearly evolved from this science of IR, offering some important descriptions of the relationships between markets and governments as they unfold on a large scale. In so doing, they defend a Western worldview embracing realist and liberal poles.[8] In such an enlightened modernism, there is agreement as to the general soundness of the societal values and objectives upon which the interstate system and the global economy have been constructed.[9] Beyond the fundamental commitment to science, a clear consensus on such ecologically significant concepts as order, security, peace, freedom, and prosperity may also be discerned:

- *Order* requires a political hierarchy in which governments have a definite place, even if their regulatory roles may vary.
- *Security* is a combined function of economic growth and military might.
- *Peace* is largely seen in the limited sense, as the absence of war; in both realist and liberal cases, a long-standing commitment to the just-war doctrine consecrates the value of a militarized peace.
- *Freedom* actually eludes discussion, largely because its normative connotations are too overwhelming for a scientific theory, and so the role of entrepreneurial freedom as a necessary means for political order and economic security is not called into question.
- *Prosperity* (or progress) likewise stands as a given, as a cornerstone of all the basic values defended by modern social theory, measured by aggregate growth figures and delivered by forces of science and technology channeled into corporations and governments.[10]

In sum, while mainstream approaches aim at descriptive analysis, their prescriptive base cannot be ignored or underestimated—especially when not articulated. Critical approaches (including ecology) speak to both dimensions of theorizing, seeking a more nuanced view of process (less mechanical, more holistic) and calling for the use of theory as an emancipatory tool.

To sum up, this section has argued that the fields of IR, IPE, and ecology share a theoretical mainstream largely derived from the scientific revolution of the seventeenth century and the concurrent turn toward liberal philosophy and ideology. It is highly dependent on a view of nature as dead matter, of human beings and political communities as self-interested actors (an individualist ontology) and, ultimately, of politics and economics as essentially intertwined.

"A" Radical Ecology?

The hallmark of a radical intellectual movement is its critique of social order—that is, its strong questioning of various institutions around which a society has established some sort of coherence. For several decades now, the radical critique of modernity has extended to ecology. Moved by the plight of nature, radical ecologists sense that ecocide is a manifestation of a larger social problem. This is why radical ecology must be construed as a bona fide social theory, with obvious roots in the great nineteenth- and twentieth-century radical movements.

Radical ecology is a diverse field where, in most cases, concern for nature is grafted onto a more established political perspective (such as socialism, anarchism, or feminism). The attack on nonhuman life is seen as part and parcel of the attack on people. Thus, the logic of biocontrol is convergent: its purpose is presumably to extract resources from life so as to sustain the economic and political privileges of an elite. The ecological crisis serves as a reminder that, as constructed, the modern project is unsustainable—and that true freedom for the common individual entails a serious critique of the key bastions of modernity. Obviously included are industrialism, capitalism, statism, and instrumental rationality, but they also extend to long-standing forms of hierarchical control such as sexism, racism, and "speciesism" (Singer 1990). In offering a critique of modernity, ecoradicals obviously hold an organic (or holistic) view of nature that Newtonian science and the concept of sustainable development as growth cannot grasp.

As suggested above, "radical ecology" is a loose expression encompassing various critical currents. What qualifies as a radical ecology, and can one legitimately defend a convergent ecoradical critique of IPE studies? If the term "radical" is meant to invoke a commitment to a rational reconstruction of individual freedom within an appropriate social context (and one could disagree with such a definition), then, as discussed below, the well-known schools of deep ecology, ecoanarchism, ecosocialism, and ecofeminism would arguably qualify as radical strands and share a necessary base.

Deep ecology is perhaps the most controversial candidate. It is a naturalist philosophy with clear romantic roots, formally established in the early 1970s as an alternative to the "shallow" ecology of green consumerism and government-led environmentalism (Naess 1972). It traces its source at least to the nineteenth-century American activist John Muir, who was instrumental in establishing a network of national parks in the United States. It is also inspired by the celebrated land ethic of Aldo Leopold (1966). For Leopold, morality is a function of ecosystem preservation; an ecosystem actually has its own ways of "thinking," and so humans must harmonize their acts and institutions with that natural logic. Muir, Leopold, and their followers show a clear commitment to a biocentric worldview: undoubtedly, there are some truths about healthy and purposeful living that can be read in nature, and attempts at showing our ontological superiority (through technological arrogance) are futile, if not dangerous.

The question is whether the biocentrism (or ecocentrism) of deep ecology really contributes to a radical critique of the mainstream—a question that derives from the sheer breadth of the movement. The central criticism (not necessarily warranted) is that deep ecology is a reactionary philosophy and can entail misanthropy and political naïveté. Deep ecologists are usually favorable to the Gaia hypothesis (Lovelock 1979), whose unitary view of the planet would seem tantamount to the ontological marginalization of humankind: the planet is basically a unicellular entity that can easily withstand the extinction of highly differentiated species; humans are not essential to its survival. Thus, Gaia seems both disconnected from the necessary political engineering for ecorenewal and insensitive to human beings. This may explain why some self-avowed deep ecologists are ready to use violence as a tactic of resistance (e.g., Watson 1993) and others show little compassion for famine or AIDS victims (see Dobson 1995:62). Furthermore, there is a mystical side to deep ecology that clearly sets it apart from Western social movements;[11] while mysticism may help the individual to achieve communion with nature, it may also detract from the political task at hand.

This said, one may still salvage deep ecology in formulating an integrated ecoradical approach. Arne Naess, perhaps the key figure in the movement, shows that an ecocentric philosophy may well remain humanistic if it is understood as a philosophy of nonviolence and technological simplicity (Naess 1989). If radical thought is to be understood as political thought, then deep ecologists are decidedly not all insensitive to it (see Devall and Sessions 1985; Eckersley 1992). It is interesting to note that Naess's main inspiration was an active political figure, namely Mahatma Gandhi, whose own teachings reflected his appreciation of Western radical thought, particularly the anarchist tradition.

In sum, while deep ecologists are admittedly not prone to using an Enlightenment discourse, it may well be a mistake to interpret their romanticism and naturalism as a longing for paganism or feudalism. Their apparent distance from many other radicals thus is breachable (see Zimmerman 1994:151–152).

Other ecoradical candidates analyze much more systematically the social bases of ecological destruction. Murray Bookchin's ecoanarchism (1991, 1991a) insists on tying the plight of nature to all forms of social hierarchy. Bookchin reads history as a long process of elite control, though such a reading is not limited to the issue of production. For Bookchin, an ecological society must be a free society, and individual freedom demands the rejection of all established forms of authority—from gerontocracies to the nation-state. Bookchin looks fondly at experiences with direct democracy in ancient Greece and, more appropriately, in early American history; such is the context where political order can be secured from below and where the essential source of ecological destruction—elite control—may be kept at bay.

Ecosocialism, on the other hand, restricts the argument to capitalism, necessarily tempering the classical Marxist endorsement of industrial production and cautioning against violent revolutions (Pepper 1993; Gorz 1980).[12] Ecosocialism is the most avowedly anthropocentrist school within radical ecology. Yet, if ecosocialists resist attributing any inherent value to nature, they do not treat it as a mere appendage to (an expanding set of) human needs; abolishing capitalist exploitation will actually reinstate a more modest—and thereby ecologically respectful—set of needs.

Ecofeminists emphasize patriarchy, invoking the long-standing image connecting women to nature—which they do not necessarily accept (Merchant 1980; Plumwood 1986, 1993; Biehl 1991). In ecofeminism, the path to an ecological society requires recognition of the long-standing effects of male domination that treats women and nature as so much passive matter to be conquered by male rationality.

Obviously, this is a diverse body of literature and one does not wish to trivialize the differences within and among those currents. However, there is arguably sufficient convergence in both the analytic and prescriptive dimensions of those schools to warrant a unified ecoradical position that will address the IR/IPE mainstream. With some notable exceptions within ecofeminism (see Biehl's discussion 1991), all three schools agree that a mystical or Gaian ecocentrism is just as inappropriate as a utilitarian anthropocentrism as a basis for an ecological ethic/society. All decry the instrumental rationality of the modern industrial project, but they are not prepared to denigrate the essence of the Enlightenment ideal—which has sought to rescue the dignity and freedom of the human being (see Hayward 1994). All accept the wisdom of political and economic decentralization to reestablish a grassroots democracy and foster values of tolerance and diversity.[13] All are prepared to resist authority, yet all are aware that violence is self-defeating—pacifism and environmentalism are indeed twin movements.

In sum, radical ecologists claim that people, and the biosphere as a whole, are being systematically overrun by forces whose purpose is to extract raw material from living being. Radical ecologists construct a diagnosis of modern society that emphasizes the various pathways by which knowledge, capital, and elite power converge to manipulate nature in the name of freedom.

This is not, admittedly, a completely new analysis of political order. Radical ecologists do rely on strong philosophical precedents, which should be noted. Political critiques based on the themes of freedom and ecological sustainability date back at least to Rousseau. His fondness for the small agricultural community, his attack on the elitism of his time, his denunciation of the cult of money, his defense of direct democracy are all well known and appealing from an ecoradical point of view.

Nineteenth-century critiques are similarly worth noting. John Stuart Mill cannot be classified as a radical, yet he very much embraced the important romantic currents of the time that had sought to rehabilitate nature in the wake of runaway industrialization. And so his attack on facile utilitarianism, his defense of the stationary economy, his commitment to women and Irish peasants are all part of his views on freedom aimed at balancing the individual and the community—a balance that may be secured if economic needs are restrained, if nature can serve as a source of contemplation and introspection, and if transparent discourse can replace propaganda and verbal assault in lawmaking. The Marxist critique may have welcomed the productive prowess of capitalism. Yet, the attack on the bourgeois division of labor and the concurrent insistence on maximizing the wholesome, balanced character of human beings demonstrated how Marx longed for a society living at a reduced pace.

The anarchist tradition, finally, is particularly important from an ecoradical perspective. Bookchin is especially fond of Kropotkin, who articulated theses about mutual aid (rather than competitive struggle) in nature and in traditional communities. While still imbued with nineteenth-century confidence in science and modernity, and although some strands of the movement were equivocal on the issue of war and violent struggle (which is anathema to radical ecology), there is no doubt that anarchism served to focus efforts at rejecting capitalism and securing grassroots democracy.

Radical ecology thus is adapting to the late modern period old voices of wisdom, old forms of dissent resisting the current to varying degrees. To say that radical ecology is not an intellectual blank slate is to give added credibility to its arguments, which sit on quite solid foundations. Yet, the new millennium has its own reality, dominated by neoliberal globalization—and this is where radical ecology can project a distinct voice, one that must have relevance beyond the community or the national unit.

Nature and Nations: Radical Conceptions

In the following pages, the aim is to specify how radical ecology interprets key trends in the global economy and how it may offer a critique of mainstream interpretations and prescriptions. As political theory, radical ecology inevitably speaks to the international or global system. As ecological theory, radical ecology just as necessarily addresses the economic foundations of our global system. As critical theory, radical ecology further seeks to identify some of the positions within mainstream social theory that legitimize the antiecological processes defining global order.

We may first use radical ecology as a means to appraise the current ways in which wealth is generated and power is distributed. As mentioned, radical ecology holds an organic view of nature that may be expressed according to principles of ecological finiteness, wholeness, diversity, and temporality (Laferrière 1996): growth is a transient (not a sustainable) phenomenon; nature has no externalities of production; life thrives on biotic complexity; innovation is an extremely long process. Accordingly, any economic and political system that treats life as a resource to be extracted and processed quickly and on large scales is bound to be both unecological and socially repressive. The global political economy precisely points in this direction in its defense of liberalization and globalization. This dual momentum has exploded over the past decade, yielding several bilateral and multilateral free trade agreements, creating an extremely powerful structure in the World Trade Organization (WTO), and still pushing for a Multilateral Agreement on Investment (MAI) that may well erase all pretense at nation building and environmental protection (Hoedeman et al. 1998).[14]

Governments and corporations defend this momentum in the name of productive efficiency and international cooperation.[15] Yet, the radical critique not only points out that such cooperation is a euphemism for corporate alliance (an established neo-Marxist argument), but also that corporate growth is thoroughly "antibiotic." By favoring corporate rule, globalization sanctions extractive processes that cannot possibly help the cause of nature (including human beings).[16] Footloose corporations locate and relocate in the most hospitable economic and political climates, leaving a predictable trail of waste and human suffering in their midst—as may be seen in the *maquiladora* phenomenon in Mexico or the recent boom-bust cycle in Southeast Asia, where high growth rates have literally fed on environmental destruction (Goldsmith 1997b).

Obviously, modern technologies are essential to the globalized logic of efficiency, yet they also play an integral role in the evolving ecological crisis by treating nature aggressively, creating unemployment, and fostering cultural and biological uniformity (Shiva 1993). As Schumacher (1973) argued so well, such technologies do not respect natural cycles and limits and, in spite of all their wondrous achievements, actually stunt the creativity of human beings and lead to the latter's redundancy. Examples abound, and those include military technologies—an annual, trillion-dollar contribution to the global economy, whose furthering of global "security" carries the largest externalities of production of any industry in the world (see Thomas 1995).

Ecoradical critiques of on-the-field developments are the very fabric of radical ecological thought, and there is little point here in elaborating on material that is extensively covered elsewhere.[17] In contrast, much less has been said, from a radical ecological perspective, on the status of IR theory and studies of IPE. I have discussed elsewhere (Laferrière 1996; Laferrière and Stoett 1999) some of the possible avenues that an ecoradical reappraisal of IR theory could follow. I have referred to that discussion earlier in this chapter and will only briefly return to it here.

If the mainstream of IR theory may be broadly divided into realist and liberal streams, one can indeed use radical ecology as a means to illuminate flaws in the mainstream's discussion of the key issues that define the discipline of IR. The purpose of IR theory is to describe processes of international disorder and, consequently, to prescribe solutions for achieving order; order is indeed arguably the master concept in the discipline, one that ties it to the larger field of political theory and leads into discussions of related concepts such as peace and stability, or freedom and sovereignty. For our purposes, the point is that the IR mainstream cannot provide a convincing theory of global order because it neglects its ecological dimension; similarly, arguments about peace or stability ring hollow in the absence of an ecological account.

Realists can be criticized for their Hobbesian worldview, one that defines peace in minimal terms, treats nature as a mere source of energy, and seeks stability through strong states (i.e., by enforcing rigid domestic hierarchies and discouraging dissent). Realism "works" only if one assumes that the world can survive in the long run the various requirements of *raison d'État*—particularly its massive military dimension.

Liberals are no less keen to maintain an extensive military structure. While their emancipatory discourse is appealing to the many ecoradicals who still value the foundations of the Enlightenment, it is so blatantly rooted in an antiecological conquest of nature that it loses much of its credibility. Liberal theory is also universalist and institutionalist theory, in both cases posing problems from an ecoradical perspective. Universalism may encapsulate values of cooperation and tolerance that are welcome to ecoradicals, yet it clearly threatens the principle of diversity that is so essential to global order. As for institutions, if they are understood as intergovernmental networks of technical experts mandated to solve social problems, then they can only conjure technocratic visions that are clearly incompatible with an ecoradical view of order—problem solving is no substitute for real reform and individual freedom.

Finally, the radical ecological critique also targets the epistemological underpinning of mainstream IR theory. Mark Neufeld (1995) has discussed extensively the problems with positivist social science and its commanding presence in IR, and his warnings are fully heeded by radical ecology. It is surprising and unfortunate that the critical wave in IR theory is still fundamentally ignorant of the ecological literature (hence some mixing must be encouraged here), but its emancipatory message, echoed by Neufeld, rings a familiar tone. A science of IR, hiding usually conservative norms behind cold descriptions of "social facts," is not only an elitist enterprise that inevitably perpetuates the current global order, but is also a conquering enterprise—one that celebrates the dualism between mind and matter, between passive nature and active observer. This is not to say that an ecological approach to global order should reject science altogether, especially if one considers the links between ecological holism and the worldview of the new physics (Capra 1991). Rather, the particular warning is against the facile application of Newtonian science, whose mechanical worldview is ill suited to the fluidity of human phenomena.

If radical ecology can be invoked as a challenge against established wisdom in IR theory, then the subfield of IPE should also take notice. Both realists and liberals have tackled the related problematiques of production and state power, yielding an impressive body of literature analyzing the dynamics of functional integration, complex interdependence, and international regime formation. Such literature seeks to remind readers that much international politics takes place around economic issues and beyond formal state channels, and that international institutions may or may not develop autonomously as a response to political problems. Beyond the various points mentioned earlier in the chapter, the radical ecologist would urge the student of IPE to account for a critical IPE literature that embraces dependency theory and more recent neo-Gramscian analyses of world order, yet with a sharper eye for the ecological problematique.

There is much to be said about the congenial relationship between critical IR theory and ecology. By formally bringing Marxism to IR, dependency theory challenged the scientism of the field of IR (see Amin 1977; Cardoso 1977) and has opened critical channels concerning global state power and class formation. From an ecoradical (and particularly ecosocialist) perspective, neo-Marxist analysis of global relations naturally contributes to legitimizing a holistic and historicist language that directly taps into the organic view of nature; such organicism is inseparable from the extensive "temporality" of nature and from what Fernand Braudel has famously referred to as the *longue durée* of history—a concept that includes the geographical constraints that have shaped social formations through time—(Braudel 1969:51).[18] Dependency theory thus avoids the ontological reductionism of the mainstream—a necessary step toward a theory of IR and a study of IPE that would show ecological sensitivity. Furthermore, dependency theory is (obviously) emancipatory theory seeking to flesh out the limits to freedom exercised on the masses by global capitalist alliances; to break the shackles of dependence on Western capital and the Western cultural model is inevitably part of an ecoradical message. However, in traditional Marxist fashion, and in line with the dominant Southern call for economic justice, dependency theory has never addressed ecology per se.[19] If anything, it would see ecological concerns as a bourgeois plot to deny industrial autonomy to the South. In sum, dependency theory sought a decentralization of global power that is, at first sight, compatible with a radical ecological approach to global relations but that inevitably falls short in light of its unqualified anthropocentrism.

Critical works in IPE often seem to come back to Marx, and that much is true (in this case, through Gramsci) of Robert Cox's analysis of the evolving global political economy. "Coxian historicism," to quote James Mittelman (1998a), is now a fixture of critical IPE work and has moved closer to the ecological problematique than dependency theorists ever did. Still, ecology arguably remains an appendage to Cox's critique.

Cox can be praised for embracing the historicist ontology that is central to the Marxist tradition, for suggesting that the whole is not a mere static combination of discrete parts. As Mittelman (1998a:76) mentions, the Braudelian argument about *longue durée* is fully incorporated into Cox's work. It has drawn specific attention from several scholars of IPE who, inspired by Cox, have contributed to theorizing on globalization; in the case of Eric Helleiner (1997:93), this concern is directly informed by the ecological dynamic. Yet, while Cox's work is in line with ecoradical thinking, the ecological significance of his historicism must still be drawn out. Ecology was literally an afterthought to Cox's path-breaking book (1987), and while Cox has dealt with the issue more directly since then (Cox 1996d:24),[20] it is far from central to his argument. For instance, in his report to the United Nations University, Cox did not include environmental issues among the key global political developments of the 1990s (Cox 1997:103–104), though he did suggest that they should receive more attention (Cox 1997:109–110, 114). In his review of Cox's scholarly contribution, Mittelman (1998a) literally ignores the issue. True, both Cox (1996d:24) and Mittelman (1996b:236) occasionally address ecology (or environmentalism) as an element of globalization or with respect to the power of new social movements as agents of resistance to globalization (Mittelman 1998b). In any case, however, the descriptive account of new social movement activity is not the most radical aspect of this new globalism in IPE.[21]

All this said, critical studies of IPE are obviously close to a formal inclusion of ecology within their problematique. From the typically Western IPE literature, an article by Helleiner (1996) cogently argued for a specific "Green" alternative to the established IPE perspectives on liberalism, Marxism, and economic nationalism. Helleiner wisely indicated that his Green perspective may well gloss over important differences within ecological thought, yet he certainly captured the spirit of radical ecological thought by identifying anti-industrialism and communitarianism as key green values; the greens' reading of global political order is one of "life out of balance," in contrast with the liberals' view of harmony and in contradistinction to the conflictual/anarchical and exploitative readings of economic nationalism and Marxism, respectively (Helleiner 1996:72). Helleiner uses the term "neo-medieval" to describe the green political project (Helleiner 1996:60). This may not appeal to some ecoradicals, yet it is essentially correct; radical greens are quite fond of the communal-confederal model of medieval Europe, though without its feudal dimension. Works by Bookchin (1992) and Biehl (1998) on confederal municipalism form the pillar of the otherwise limited IR theorizing found in the ecopolitical literature, and they relate quite clearly to Helleiner's discussion. The need to reconcile global consideration and local action requires "political bodies above the local level . . . not [to] be powerful independent state institutions" (Helleiner 1996:65).

Helleiner's article is particularly important because it stresses the normative dimension of IR theory alongside its descriptive component. Southern political writings, beginning with dependency theory, have long recognized this dual character of theory. From an ecological perspective, Vandana Shiva's work is the most likely candidate for establishing a bridge between Northern and Southern globalist traditions and hence for legitimizing an ecoradical approach to IPE studies.[22] Shiva's ecofeminism is grounded in a solid analysis of late twentieth-century neoimperialism, focusing on the tight links between Western capital, technology, and culture—in other words, on those globalizing dynamics jeopardizing the integrity and diversity of Planet Earth and its inhabitants. Shiva's particular interest is in agriculture and the related dangers of genetic engineering and monocultural plantation (see Shiva 1989, 1997). Throughout her work, she delivers a consistent message whereby the North is denying Southern community existence by imposing its own version of globality. While Shiva is not part of the typical "IPE crowd," there is no doubt that her ecoradical work is highly pertinent to the understanding of the global political economy.

Conclusion

The purpose of this chapter was to briefly explore (1) the ecological limitations of established theories of global order; and (2) the possibilities of a radical ecological response to those theories. I examined the connections between mainstream IR theory and mainstream views on ecology prominent since the rise of modern science and the Industrial Revolution. Basically, I have argued that a view of order that feeds on ecological degradation is unsustainable in the long run and that radical ecological perspectives are best suited to explain that inconsistency. Radical ecology is admittedly a varied field, the components of which are debatable. Yet, it seems possible to identify a radical ecological core that speaks against the commodification and instrumentality of the modern project and that recasts the debate on global order around principles that account for both the limitations and complexities of nature.

Just as ecology and economics share common etymological foundations, and the ecological society requires global political efforts, then radical ecology can speak directly to the academic field of IPE. Obviously, no one would deemphasize the obstacles jutting into the path to such dialogue—or dialectic, more properly, since this would not be some friendly chat. While ecology had emerged as a racy topic for sundry theorists in the late 1980s, it quickly outlived its exoticism in the deflation of post-Rio politics. And much as critical IR theory has sought to question the feeble social purpose of mainstream IR, there is this nagging feeling that the traditional canons will withstand yet another assault.

Is this undue pessimism? Perhaps more pessimistic is the thought that the rise of the new dialectic—and its outcome—will require further, more telling demonstrations of the "antibiotism" of modernity, as scientists and engineers now literally tinker with the structure of life and as governments facilitate the growth of powerful conglomerates. While social theories can claim some input in shaping the future, it seems safer to say that they have traditionally followed political events. On the other hand, never has the world confronted a global, anthropogenic ecological crisis; and while new generations often believe that they have arrived at some momentous step in the course of history, perhaps the coming of postmodern doctrines truly shows a historical impasse—or watershed. Perhaps, in this sense, the needed meeting between IPE and radical ecology will soon take place, and social theorists can finally speak to practitioners in a moment of anticipation.

Notes

1. On mechanism, see especially Merchant (1980); on teleology and ecology, see Goldsmith (1997a).

2. On the legacy of Newtonianism, see, for example, Dobbs and Jacob (1995).

3. For conservationist sources, see, among other, Meadows et al. (1972), ICIDI (1980), WCED (1987), and Brown et al. (1996).

4. On sustainable growth as an "impossibility theorem," see Daly (1998).

5. From a long list, see, for instance, Soroos (1986), Caldwell (1988), Young (1989), Haas (1990), and Homer-Dixon (1994).

6. See MacPherson's thesis in his introduction to *Leviathan* (Hobbes 1985:48–51).

7. These are many, though one could make a case for dividing the mainstream into realist and liberal components.

8. This may be found more or less explicitly in Keohane (1984, 1989), Krasner (1985) and, earlier, Herz (1951).

9. For further details on this assertion, see Laferrière (1995, 1996) and Laferrière and Stoett (1999).

10. Again, for more details on this conceptual analysis, see Laferrière and Stoett (1999).

11. Deep ecologists' strong affinity with traditional native cultures largely explains this mystical side.

12. The ecosocialist literature has attracted a rather wide range of adherents through the pages of *Capitalism, Nature, Socialism*, a radical academic journal taking a specific position against "bourgeois ecology"—which should not be construed as a defense of Soviet-style socialism (O'Connor 1988:5).

13. See Schumacher (1973) and Sale (1985), whose "bioregional" approach to sustainability bridges deep ecology and the "social ecology" of Bookchin.

14. See Chapters 3 and 4.

15. See Chapter 5.

16. See Chapter 6.

17. The radical ecological journal *The Ecologist* is particularly resourceful in presenting tightly documented empirical research on the global economy, technology, and ecology.

18. See the treatment of temporality in Chapters 7 and 8.

19. See Chapter 2.

20. I thank Rosalind Irwin for pointing this out to me.

21. Ecological and other social movements are obviously to be encouraged as perhaps the only voices of dissent having the ear of governments, but ecoradicals are quite aware of the boundless possibilities for cooptation and of these movements' predominant appeal to some sections of the middle class in the North—the ecosocialist David Pepper (1993:247) bluntly calls them "bourgeois."

22. See Chapter 6.

Commentary: Some Reflections on International Political Economy and the Environmental Question

The Advantages and Disadvantages of Environmental Social Scientific Specialization

I have long favored reorienting the social sciences in order to take environmental issues more systematically into account. There have been some considerable strides taken toward this goal over the past twenty-five or so years. Virtually every social science discipline has well-established and growing groups of specialists who identify with and work within "environmental" subdisciplines. Sociology is a particular success story. There are probably about 500 to 600 U.S. sociologists—and several times that number elsewhere—who would identify with the labels "environmental sociology" or "sociology of natural resources and environment." There are no fewer than three large overlapping professional organizations of environmental sociologists (the Section on Environment and Technology of the American Sociological Association, the Environment and Technology Division of the Society for the Study of Social Problems, and the Natural Resources Research Group of the Rural Sociological Society) in the United States. The Environment and Society Research Committee of the International Sociological Association is similarly vibrant.

As much as the growth of environmental subdisciplines within the social sciences has been a positive development, there are also some downsides to this type of specialization. For example, in the case of environmental sociology, there has been a tendency for most of its practitioners to take a highly objectivist posture toward the notions of global environmental change and global environmental problems.[1] This has been largely because of the strong environmental sympathies among environmental sociologists and the fact that environmental sociology has strived to legitimate its existence in the larger discipline by claiming the imprimatur of the natural sciences of the environment (particularly when ecological knowledges point toward major environmental crises or risks such as global warming or rainforest destruction). Nonetheless, the predominance of objectivist views toward global environment change inevitably led to constructionist-type critiques (see, for example, Yearley 1991; Taylor and Buttel 1992; and Macnaghten and Urry 1998, who breezily dismiss most environmental sociology for its uncritical objectivism). These constructionist critiques were in some sense necessary but have also led to an unproductive polarization of views along the objectivist-constructionist dimension.[2]

It is also the case that most environmental sociologists, even those who have worked on global environmental issues for a decade and a half, have yet to develop a very nuanced or historically informed view of global politics, the international state system, international regimes, and international organizations. There has been a very long tradition in sociology to take the "society" or "nation-state" to be the self-evident unit of analysis, even though for only a small sliver of human history has the nation-state been the predominant form of large-scale social organization. Environmental sociologists, similar to their more mainstream sociological counterparts, have been ill at ease dealing with the "globalization" phenomena of the late twentieth century. Similar to the tendency to conceptualize the global environment in ahistorical and essentialist ways, environmental as well as more mainstream sociologists have tended to see globalization as a novel—but essentially an immutable or irreversible—trend. The rooting of sociology, both environmental and mainstream, in the institutions of the nation-states of mid-century is not only problematic on its own terms, but this presumption is an obstacle to a more satisfactory understanding of environmental issues and changes.[3]

It is perhaps no accident, then, that while political science/ international relations (IR)/ international political economy (IPE) is the social science discipline with the least well institutionalized "environmental" subdiscipline,[4] the authors of the chapters in this book are generally quite agile in avoiding many of the dualisms and essentialisms present in other environmental social sciences. The tendency in these essays, for example, is not to uncritically adopt the received definitions ("social constructions") of sustainability or global environmental problems set forth by either the international environmental "epistemic community" (Haas 1992) or by prominent ecological activists or organization officials. As political scientists, the authors are, not surprisingly, quite comfortable with the notion that states play critical roles in causing—and ameliorating—environmental problems, but they do so in ways that avoid the excessive state-centrism that has tended to manifest itself in much IPE. And while the authors tend to have a shared conviction that international social structures and power relations are important in shaping how environmental resources are appropriated from the biosphere and how environmental struggles are constituted, they avoid making a priori assumptions about the normality of the nation-state or about its imminent demise.

The chapters are also refreshingly ecumenical on the matter of whether there needs to be a wholesale restructuring of analytical schemes and categories for IR/IPE to be able to address environmental issues. Environmental sociology, by contrast, has at times been overly preoccupied with the matters of whether the classical tradition is incompatible with a truly ecological sociology and of whether bona fide environmental sociology must "deprivilege" social variables and include biophysical variables in causal models (see, for example, Foster 1999).

Reflections on the Chapters

I would like to make a few observations on the chapters collectively and some additional observations on some of the specific chapters. These observations take several forms: praise, criticism, or exhortations to follow up on promising leads.

First, to a greater or lesser degree, each of us in the environmental social sciences tends to fall victim to the tendency to assume that ecology and environmental science are essentially coherent domains of science. The environmental social sciences have tended to have an affinity with the Eugene Odum–style holistic image of ecosystems with a successional logic and homeostatic tendencies, and have tended to assume that this holistic perspective is the underlying "paradigm" of the ecological sciences. In fact, ecosystem biology has been marginalized in ecology over the past three decades or so and has been progressively supplanted by the highly mathematical approach of population ecology (Fitzsimmons and Goodman 1998; Trepl 1994). While several of the essays in this collection refer to the ecological sciences, with the partial exceptions of Chapters 6 and 10, they tend not to recognize their diversity or else ascribe the diversity of environmental knowledges to sources outside environmental science.

Second, however, the papers are generally properly skeptical of the conventional wisdom that environmental issues—or at least the most important environmental problems—are intrinsically global in nature and that, by functionalist leap of logic, global governance is "required" to solve them.[5] A corollary of this conventional wisdom—that global governance mechanisms, if properly designed, are superior to national state governance because international organizations are more enlightened or less parochial than national states[6]—is also largely eschewed in these chapters. The authors of Chapters 3 and 4 do particularly nice jobs of demonstrating that international policy arenas prove efficacious as much or more for transnational corporations (TNCs) as for nongovernmental organizations (NGOs).

Third, while several of the chapters (particularly Chapters 6, 7, and 8) stress the role of the South in international environmental politics and do so creatively, there could have been more systematic discussion of the role that the states and groups in the South play in international environmental politics. It should be noted that IPE has generally exhibited the weakness that it generates far more detail on the national and geopolitical processes that shape the North's positions in international organizations and regimes than it does on those that shape the South's (see, for example, Crumpton's [2000] review of Vig and Axelrod [1999]). There are some remnants of this tendency in this book.

There are important historical and contemporary dimensions to the role of the South in environmental politics that are worth noting. For example, since the late 1960s, dominant environmental ideologies have tended to be anchored in a global conception of environmental problems (the population bomb, limits to growth, global environmental—especially climate—change; see Taylor and Buttel 1992 and Yearley 1991 for analyses of why this has been the case). Each of these dominant environmental ideologies, however, has tended to generate criticism from the South, from both developing country states and civil society groups (as well as from TNCs and a variety of other groups). The exasperation of groups in the South with the late 1960s and 1970s pronouncements from Northern environmental groups about global environmental issues was a significant obstacle to global coalition making as well as to international environmental negotiations. While the states of the South are obviously not powerful actors in international environmental discussions, due to the numerical predominance of developing countries and the fact that such large shares of the world's population and resources are within third world borders, it is imperative for operational and legitimacy purposes that international agreements have some signatories and consent from the South. In the early 1980s, it seemed very unlikely that countries of the South would ever be strong supporters of international environmental initiatives.

Persistent criticism by the states of the South of Northern environmental agendas was one of the factors that led to the UN Secretary-General's appointment of the World Commission on Environment and Development (WCED) and to the eventual publication of *Our Common Future* (WCED 1987). *Our Common Future*'s recognition of the relationship between poverty and environmental degradation and its advocacy of "sustainable development" can be seen as, in part, a political compromise among environmental groups, developing country states, development-oriented NGOs, and mainstream development assistance agencies—especially the World Bank and the International Finance Corporation (IFC).

During most of the interval between the publication of *Our Common Future* and the 1992 Rio de Janeiro United Nations Conference on Environment and Development (UNCED, or Earth Summit) meeting, most of the developing world was tentatively on board the international environmental bandwagon. Ultimately, however, the demise in the late 1980s and early 1990s of the European state-socialist regimes undercut the geopolitical rationale for foreign aid (including but not limited to environmental foreign aid). The result was an effective end to the Cold War and the decline of foreign aid worldwide (with a few exceptions, such as Japan). The decline of foreign aid and the bleak prospects of generating green or any other color of foreign aid undermined the incentive for national states of the South to accept restrictions on resource extraction and environmental destruction as a condition of agreeing to international environmental accords. The result is that since the Earth Summit, developing countries have generally become very critical of the North's positions on international environmental issues and thus reluctant to ratify international environmental agreements such as the 1997 Kyoto Protocol of the Framework Convention on Climate Change (FCCC). In addition, the only conditions under which most nation-states from the South have been willing to ratify agreements are those that largely exempt them from the major strictures called for under these agreements. Consequently, the fact that the 1997 Kyoto Protocol largely exempted nation-states of the South from having to make major sacrifices as a condition of ratification has galvanized U.S. congressional opposition to Kyoto.

There is also a need to look more systematically at the contradictory roles played by the world order's hegemonic power, the United States. On one hand, the United States is the home to roughly half of the world's major environmental nongovernmental organizations (ENGOs) and a lesser but still sizable share of its ecological scientists. Depending on how one views market mechanisms such as emissions trading, one could say that the United States is in some sense an innovator in environmental policy. Due to the sheer size of its economy, a major share of "industrial ecology" research and development occurs in the United States. Most environmental "epistemic communities" are based heavily on U.S. expertise and its scientific and policy institutions. The United States is typically (though not always) on the environmentally progressive side (though seldom at the fringes) of international negotiations (with some exceptions, such as the Biodiversity Convention).

On the other hand, the United States accounts for a disproportionate share of antienvironmental activity. The active resistance by particular segments of U.S. capital and its ideological allies has arguably been the single most significant force in effectively derailing agreements such as the Kyoto Protocol. Further, the conservatism of the U.S. Congress has made it unlikely that most bills ratifying U.S. participation in international environmental agreements will be brought to a vote, much less be passed. The antitaxation fervor in U.S. right-wing circles makes it virtually impossible that there will be consideration of energy, BTU, or general consumption taxes, which are arguably the environmental policy levers of choice if one wishes to make environmental progress within a neoliberal policy framework. Right-wing groups in U.S. civil society have played a disproportionate role globally in delegitimating states and governments and thus in undermining the social rights of citizenship worldwide. The United States (with, interestingly, strong support from many third world primary exporters) has been the world's foremost champion of trade and investment liberalization measures (e.g., World Trade Organization [WTO], Multilateral Agreement on Investment [MAI]), which are a response to, and will have the effect of further deepening, the neoliberal policy thrust. These contradictory roles (and many others that could be mentioned) of the world's hegemonic power in international environmental politics deserve comprehensive treatment from a world-historical framework.

Another area in which a critical IPE can and must make contributions concerns identifying the possibilities and limits of "capitalist environmentalism" or "green capitalism." In the United States, the position of capital on environmental regulation and control is predictably negative; it is interesting to note the far more progressive role that capital plays in environmental improvement in countries such as the Netherlands and Germany. Environmental progress (particularly in terms of "dematerialization" of production and reduction of pollution) in Northern Europe has led to a quite considerable restructuring of environmental social sciences there, toward adoption of a theoretical point of view known as "ecological modernization" (Mol 1995, 1997).

Brutally summarizing, the key points of ecological modernization are threefold. First, in principle, capitalism possesses the institutional capacity to reverse the environmental destruction that it has created historically.[7] Second, ecological modernization holds that solutions to environmental problems will necessarily be found in greater modernization (sometimes referred to as "super-industrialization") rather than less. Third, ecological modernization (much like classic modernization theory in development studies) rests on an imagery of global diffusion; it is argued that ecological modernizationist knowledge and practices (e.g., environmental science knowledge, industrial ecology technologies, decentralized market-based environmental regulatory practices) have a strong tendency to diffuse globally from ecological modernization leaders to the laggard nations and groups.

Ecological modernization raises very interesting issues about the nature and future of capitalism. Industrial ecology, strategic environmental management, and dematerialization tendencies within capitalism should not be ignored. However, there are some parallels between the current excitement about ecological modernization and the trap of technocratic international environmental regime booster-ism that is scrutinized so effectively in this book. From a critical IPE point of view, the major problems with ecological modernization center on (1) its Eurocentricity, in that the relatively progressive environmental policies of the Northern European countries and the industrial-ecological progress made by some segments of capital are due to these countries' institutional specificities and are not replica-ble elsewhere, and (2) the likelihood that the major institutions and practices of global society (e.g., WTO procedures, the increased intensity of international economic competition) will ultimately mili-tate against diffusion of ecological modernizationist policies and practices in other countries (see Mol and Spaargaren's [2000] sum-mary of most of these criticisms and their response). Ultimately, the most important issues in ecological modernization are comparative and international political-economic in nature, areas where a critical IPE can make major contributions.

Finally, a number of the authors in this book have addressed one of the most interesting issues in international environmental politics: the role that environmental NGOs (or global civil society) will be able to play with regard to environmental governance. I am skeptical about all the attention currently being lavished on the notions of "civil society" and "social capital" and believe that the notion that solutions to international environmental problems lie in global civil society is somewhat utopian. I cannot help but agree with Yearley (1996), who has suggested that in contrast to WCED's notion of "our common future," the factors that lead to environmental problems as well as the consequences of these problems tend to result in *differen-tial impacts* among nation-states—thus portending the fracturing rather than the unifying of the peoples of the world.

This is not to suggest that environmental movements will not be important actors in shaping international environmental conflicts as well as decisions on issues (e.g., trade regimes, genetically modified organisms) that have an environmental dimension. My hypothesis, however, is that environmental movements ultimately are predomi-nantly creatures of nations. This does not negate the importance of a critical IPE of environment. It merely requires that this IPE resist essentializing the notions of environment and environmental politics, that it resist state-centrism, and that it not lose sight of the fact that global orders, the international state system, and nation-states are mutually constitutive (McMichael 1990). These chapters suggest that critical IPE is well on its way to contributing to this agenda.

Notes

1. Objectivism is a doctrine that the natural world exists apart from humans and that this natural world can be understood only through correct reasoning (i.e., the scientific method). Objectivism is typically counterposed with social constructionism. The characteristic social constructionist view is that humans are part of the natural world, that the distinction between the observer of nature and nature itself is artificial, and that nature can be known to humans only through concepts and abstractions that reflect language, culture, and belief systems of observers.

2. See the very vigorous attacks on constructionism and defenses of objectivism by Dunlap and Catton (1994) and R. Murphy (1994, 1997). There is a certain interesting parallel between the largely unproductive objectivism-constructionism debate in environmental sociology and the equally uninteresting and unproductive rationalism-constructionism debate in mainstream IPE, which Katzenstein et al. (1998) now contend is the most significant debate in the field.

3. For example, contemporary financial and monetary systems are at least in some senses no more globally integrated than they were during the heyday of the British finance-capital empire in the late nineteenth century, and much the same can be said about trade at the same time (Katzenstein et al. 1998).

4. Within APSA, for example, environmental politics essentially plays second fiddle to science and technology politics with the Science, Technology and Environmental Politics Section (STEPS). [Editor's note: The Environmental Studies Section of the International Studies Association has contributed greatly to raising the profile of international environmental politics.]

5. Stevis and Assetto are also properly critical of the notion that cross-border solutions to environmental problems are necessarily a challenge to the state system.

6. See Frank et al. (2000) and my critique (Buttel 2000).

7. This is ecological modernization's major "reflexive modernization" premise, which is shared by Beck's (1992) theory of the "risk society."

12

Commentary:
The International Political
Economy of the Environment
and the Subpolitical Domain

This book's editors and contributors identify a very worthy goal for themselves, namely, to prevent the discussion of international political economy (IPE) and the environment from either closing down into very narrow understandings of what "the environment" is or accepting very thin interpretations of how "the economy" works. Environmental problems are real, and most of them cannot be adequately addressed, much less effectively solved, without coming to terms with the social purposes of those who misconstruct political economy and the environment around the terms that are most commonly used today. The editors also hope to broaden environmental discourse as widely as possible so that the built environment of society and its production processes can be seen as a pervasive factor that should not be separated from the unbuilt environments of nature and its reproduction processes (Worster 1979). What defines, directs, and develops that built environment and its products clearly must be a central concern of IPE, because states and societies both try to capture and contain these social forces. Their interventions, however, rarely are decisive enough to succeed, even though entire academic disciplines, like environmental studies, green management, and applied ecology, are dedicated to guiding their efforts (Buchholz 1993; National Academy of Engineering 1989; Smith 1995).

The contributions to this book all are devoted to advancing and elaborating the critical analysis of how IPE might improve the environment. To initiate the collection's analyses, Chapter 2 retraces the theoretical and practical development of today's sustainable development policies out of the more traditional conservationist approaches of the past. Chapter 3 addresses the controversies surrounding the creation of the World Trade Organization (WTO) to construct an interpretative frame around the assumptions and actions of managerial forms of environmentalism in the public and private sectors. Chapter 4 follows up on those studies by recounting how the international regulatory approach to climate change does, and does not, respond to the Multilateral Agreement on Investment (MAI). Chapter 5, in turn, looks at the viability of various green nongovernmental organizations' (NGOs') dealings with transnational business as an alternative mode of green governance. The authors' findings answer some existing questions, while raising new worries, about the prospects of such arrangements.

These general treatments of the environment and IPE are followed with more concrete investigations in the next four chapters. Chapter 6 retraces the logic of land enclosure in England as it reverberates in the corporate closure over intellectual property in India with respect to communal knowledge about the neem tree. Chapter 7 recounts how sustainable development practices in Brazil have not done much to enhance the prospects of many in the Amazon, even though these rhetorics have changed how the Brazilian nation-state operates in the world system. Chapter 8 reveals how water policy in Cuba and the Dominican Republic reflect the weaknesses of those states in responding to larger transnational environmental debates. The study in Chapter 9 of the Long-Range Transboundary Air Pollution (LRTAP) Convention suggests these transnational forces also must be leveraged effectively if any environmental advances are to flow from international regulatory accords. Finally, Chapter 10 reviews how intellectual assumptions and policy practices now constitute some of the biggest roadblocks in the path of meaningful environmental change by forcing the problematic of IPE and the environment into rigid resource managerialist and bureaucratic instrumentalist terms. To short-circuit these shortcomings, it pushes the conceptual utility of nonmainstream forms of historical, institutional, and political reasoning, like Marxist or dependencia theories, to break the chokehold of conventional managerialist reasoning over most environmental policy analysis. In contrast to those who would forsake these theories (Rubin 1994; Lewis 1992), Laferrière underscores in Chapter 10 the value of alternative contested viewpoints for those who are truly committed to developing a critical political economy of the world environment.

The fusion of conflict studies, environmental policy, global diplomacy, and cultural change addressed by the contributors to this book implicitly underscores the importance of Ulrich Beck's vision of "the risk society." That is, "the social production of *wealth* is systematically accompanied by the social production of *risks*," and, as a result, "the problems and conflicts relating to distribution in a society of scarcity overlap with the problems and conflicts that arise from the production, definition, and distribution of techno-scientifically produced risks" (Beck 1992:19, emphasis in original). The world's ongoing modernization is forcing most political officials and economic structures to become reflexive. Ironically, then, modernity is making, and it already has remade, elements of technology/democracy/capitalism into an environment (Luke 1997). While the classical narratives of rationalization underpinning the modernization project have presumed that greater command, control, communication, and intelligence will come from applying more rationality to life, our experiences of living amidst these past, ongoing, and planned exercises of rationalization in the world environment actually find us living with many consequences far beyond anyone's command, control, communication, or intelligence. In other words, the allegedly growing calculability of instrumental rationality actually brings along with it new measures of incalculability—unintended and unanticipated—rooted in instrumental irrationality.

To comment on these studies in IPE and the environment, I want to develop two major points. First, as several of the contributors advocate, I will think more broadly about what "the environment" is and then position this understanding in the twenty-first century—a time, for many, coming at "the end" of nature. Second, I hope to indicate how such thinking about IPE must reexamine how the uneven globalization of technoscience has created a now all-pervasive subpolitical domain, in which the rules of economic profit and technical rationality either paralyze or predetermine the political—beneath, beyond, and beside the sphere of politics. And the imperatives of subpolitics may give a better perspective on the environmental crisis than thinking about how the incomplete globalization of civic activism in the political sphere, as many others have claimed, limits ecological improvements. An IPE of the environment cannot come to complete closure until or unless its practitioners carefully reconsider how the subpolitical domain constrains and confounds many policy initiatives aimed at protecting the environment's survival. Several of the chapters in this book anticipate this concern, but my comments are meant to highlight this theme for others who seek to advance the IPE of the environment.

International Political Economy and the Environment

The ties between IPE and the environment assumed considerable importance in the 1990s, because so much of the world's ecology had deteriorated during the past ten, thirty, or fifty years. This deterioration, in fact, has spread so quickly that neither John Muir's preservationism nor Gifford Pinchot's conservationism can do much to solve the pressing ecological problems of the present, as Chapters 2 and 10 both assert. After the Industrial Revolution, nowhere in the world holds out against machines: technology is everywhere. After the two world wars, few places around the world hold on to traditional formulas of authority: democracy is spreading everywhere. After the Cold War, nowhere in the world seriously holds forth as a real alternative to the market: capitalism is everywhere. So only a truly critical approach to IPE and the environment, as the editors suggest (Chapters 1 and 13), can unravel why these forces interact and maybe correct how they create ecological destruction. Improving the understanding of IPE as a scholarly discipline is one response to this new context, because the dysfunction of markets and states is, strangely enough, a key constituent component of the contemporary world system's environmental crisis.

The "environment" as a basic concept rarely captures, as Chapters 2, 3, and 6 argue, the full range of all human beings' interrelations with the terrains, waters, climates, soils, architectures, technologies, societies, economies, cultures, or states surrounding them. In most of its uses, the environment simply names a strong but sloppy force: it can be almost anything "out there," "everything" around us, something "affecting" us, a few things "within" us, but also a thing "upon which" we act. How, then, might this understanding be improved? The historical emergence of "the environment" as concept/word/idea proves suggestive here. This archeological move does not uncover a stable nominal essence. It simply reilluminates semiotic qualities carried in the expression today that, first, accompany the term from its earliest origins and, second, throw light upon its current applications. In its original sense, which is brought into English from Old French, an environment is the result of an action from or the state of being produced by a verb, "to environ." In fact, environing as a verb is a type of military, police, or strategic action. To environ is to encircle, encompass, envelop, or enclose. It is the physical activity of surrounding, circumscribing, or ringing around something. It even suggests stationing guards around, thronging with hostile intent, or standing watch over some person or place. Therefore, to environ a site or a subject is to beset, beleaguer, or besiege that place or person.

As either the means of such activity or the product of these actions, an environment can be read in a much more suggestive manner, especially in light of how most environmental knowledge is produced and consumed today. As each of the contributors tries to indicate, it can be the encirclement, a circumscription, or the beleaguerment of nonhuman places and human persons in a strategic disciplinary policing of space. An environmental policy is already a disciplinary move, and it often (re)constructs some domain of space—a locale, a biome, a planet as biospheric space or some city, any region, the global economy as technospheric territory—within a discursive envelope of policing regulation. Once placed inside such enclosures, environmental expertise might arm environmental activists, policymakers, or regulators who stand watch over these surroundings, hoping to include or exclude forces, agents, and ideas from these zones of encircled space.

The eclipse of natural otherness by capitalism, democracy, and technology often is misread in triumphalist terms as the foundation of Francis Fukuyama's "coherent and directional Universal History of mankind" (1992:xxiii). On the other hand, it could simply mark how these social forces now surround all living and nonliving things on the planet as their "environment." Accordingly, Fukuyama's vision of "accumulation without end" (1992:89–97) now captures the "omnipolitanization" of the planet through global economic and social development. Omnipolitanization flows, as Paul Virilio asserts, from the concentration of urbanized values and technified practices in a *"world-city,* the city to end all cities," and "in these basically eccentric or, if you like, *omnipolitan* conditions, the various social and cultural realities that still constitute a nation's wealth will soon give way to a sort of 'political' *stereo-reality* in which the inter-action of exchanges will no longer look any different from the—automatic—interconnection of financial markets today" (Virilio 1997:75, emphasis in original). In keeping with Fredric Jameson's observations about postmodernity, this omnipolitanization "is what you have when the modernization process is complete and nature is gone for good" (1991:ix). As the environmental critics of contempo-rary IPE all suggest in their chapters here, economy and society, cul-ture and politics, science and technology have all acquired environ-mental qualities as society engulfs nature, economy channels ecology, and human organisms beleaguer all environments. Some today, like Nicholas Negroponte (1995), exalt this global condition as "being digital" and see the omnipolis as essentially a "city of bits." However, as Chapters 3, 4, and 5 maintain, omnipolitan times could be better understood as how human and nonhuman beings must now coevolve with global markets, climate change, world trade, or transnational governance.

Indeed, as Zachary Smith suggests, toxic wastes are "a by-product of energy development, agriculture, and most industrial activity," which now "are found throughout the environment, in our air, water, and soil" (1995:170). So, like weather, water, and wildlife, as Chapters 4, 6, and 8 argue, waste is to be found everywhere in the planetary environment, making this by-product a new omnipolitan characteristic of the earth's ecology as it is being transformed by modern agricultural, industrial, and technological development (National Academy of Engineering 1989). Many mechanisms in the world's political economy dump toxic wastes outside specific locales, boost their concentrations beyond permissible thresholds, raise exposures so intensively as to threaten health, and disperse effects indiscriminately across space and time. These irrationalities come from human artifice, and they now are negatively affecting fac-tors on a global scale. Some are intended, most are unintended, and many have not all been comprehended, but they all now surround human and nonhuman life as elemental qualities of their environment.

The Subpolitical Domain

Virilio's ideas on omnipolitanism are compelling, because they cap-ture the ever changing chaos of technoeconomic infrastructures running just beneath, behind, and beside the world's many great, but still quite different, urban places. These turbulent worldwide webs move matter, energy, and information from everywhere to anywhere, while at the same time piling up most of these goods and their services in a few places to the detriment of many other places that pile up even more bads. They work underneath, above, and apart from the polis, but they are also structures of power, systems of exchange, and signs of culture. These subpolitical realms, as Beck indicates, are often misrepresented as the black boxes of "science" and "technology," but their power effects, social values, and cultural practices can be quite enlightening.

IPE may not make much sense of the ecological crisis without acknowledging the subpolis, which is the collective assembly of rationalization practices in technoscience that "preprograms the permanent change of all realms of social life under the justifying cloak of technoeconomic progress, in contradistinction to the simplest rules of democracy—knowledge of the goals of social change, discussion, voting, and consent" (Beck 1992:184). It represents the continuous workings of operational powers layered under politics, occluded in technologies from ordinary political understandings, hidden from politicians by the mechanics of markets. Like the polis, the subpolis is a built environment, but its constructs, as Chapter 7 suggests, all too often are depoliticized in the professional-technical development rhetorics of civil engineering, public health, corporate management, scientific experiment, technical design, and property ownership. It discloses the quasi-objectivity of subjects as they engage practicably in technical activities, but it cannot be separated from the quasi-subjectivity of objects circulating en masse in globalized economies of scale. The workings of the subpolis constitute much of what is international political economy, but academic IPE rarely reads the risks attached to its social contracts of technological action.

The subpolis takes shape in the vast sprawl congealing in suburbia, the gridlock freezing flows of traffic, the maldevelopment rising out of rapid growth, and the toxic by-products coming from desired products. As the editors anticipate (Chapter 13), Beck worries about how "the possibilities for social change from the collaboration of research, technology, and science accumulate," when one finds that the locus of social order and disorder *migrates from the domain of politics to that of subpolitics*" (Beck 1992:223, emphasis in original). In the subpolis, what begins at an individual level as a rational plan combines at a collective level into the irrational, unintended, and unanticipated. Still, it is difficult to resist these outcomes inasmuch as the workings of modern technics and markets are "institutionalized as 'progress,' but remain subject to the dictates of business, science, and technology, for whom democratic procedures are invalid" (Beck 1992:14). Unlike the polis, which is a collective of people situated in a specific locality or particular nation-state, the subpolis is an ever shifting general assembly of people and machines interoperating with many other technical assemblies and people elsewhere along multi/trans/supernational lines as well as within inter/infra/intralocal spaces. While the authors of Chapters 3, 4, and 5 want to hope for global governance, believing it might address the irrationalities of the subpolis, most of its workings escape the frameworks of IPE, as the radical critiques of mainstream environmentalists discussed in Chapter 10 all suggest.

Within the world's continuously revolutionized built environments, industrial production and by-production contribute to the construction of a transnational subpolis of technoscience acts and artifacts—as the analysis of air pollution in Chapter 9 or the study of water use in Chapter 8 both document—set beneath, within, and above each territorial polis still being composed out of political acts (Luke 1999a). This technified mode of mounting revolutionary changes in everyday life is the work of the subpolis. More specifically, narratives of chemical, industrial, nuclear, and ecological revolution, like the comments from the editors indicate, simply underscore how thoroughly

> now the potential for structuring society migrates from the political system into the sub-political system of scientific, technological and economic modernization. A precarious reversal occurs. *The political becomes non-political and the non-political.* . . . The promotion and protection of "scientific progress" and of "the freedom of science" become the greasy pole on which the primary responsibility for political arrangements slips from the democratic system into the context of economic and techno-scientific non-politics, which is not democratically legitimated. A *revolution under the cloak of normality* occurs, which escapes from possibilities of intervention, but must all the same be justified and enforced against a public that is becoming critical. (Beck 1992:186, emphasis in original)

Democratic institutions in the territorial polis ordinarily accept these changes without much contestation, because such technoscientific revolutions are believed to bring the good life (albeit at times with a few risks) or those unwanted, but still allegedly quite controllable, noxious by-products of technological innovation. In fact, however, the subpolis of technoscientific artifacts undercuts the workings of conventional political life (Luke 1997).

Beck worries about the unintended effects in the radical subpolitics implied by continuous change in advanced industrial technics. That is, the political system, on the one hand,

> is being threatened with disempowerment while its democratic constitution remains alive. The political institutions become the administrators of a development they neither have planned for nor are able to structure, but must nonetheless justify. On the other hand, decisions in science and business are charged with an effectively political content for which the agents possess no legitimation. Lacking any place to appear, the decisions that change society become tongue-tied and anonymous. . . . What we *do not* see and *do not* want is changing the world more and more obviously and threateningly. (Beck 1992:187)

Chapters 2, 5, 8, and 9 make the same point about those technoscientific revolutions taking place under the cover of normality within industrial production: what we do not see and do not want from industrial by-production obviously is changing the world quite thoroughly. Nobody and everybody is, at the same time, deciding to make this happen as the market's democracy lets consumers "vote" with currency to circulate and accumulate more products, often without effectively containing or legitimating their by-production processes. Even though we do not immediately see and ultimately do not want the negative by-products, we will get them anyway.

In the subpolis, ordinary processes of democratic legitimation fail. Modern industrial revolutions with all of their toxic by-products are highly technified economic actions. Each always "remains shielded from the demands of democratic legitimation by its own character" inasmuch as "it is *neither politics nor non-politics,* but a third entity: economically guided action in pursuit of interests" (Beck 1992:222, emphasis in original). Still, as the authors of Chapters 2 and 5 assert, most inhabitants of this planetary subpolis have yet to realize fully how "the structuring of the future takes place indirectly and unrecognizably in research laboratories and executive suites, not in parliament or in political parties. Everyone else—even the most responsible and best informed people in politics and science—more or less lives off the crumbs of information that fall from the tables of technological sub-politics" (Beck 1992:223). The subpolis evolves in the machinations of many industrial ecologies, whose "machinic" metabolism, in turn, entails the planned and unintended destruction of many nonhuman and human lives.

Because the machinic metabolisms underpinning the world's economy create such by-products, and they do not change easily, everyone must, on the one hand, resign themselves, like Chapter 4 claims, to the fact that such dangerous by-products now are a fixed environmental feature in the mix of useful products delivered to them in the marketplace. On the other hand, when coping with harmful risks, as Chapter 8 indicates, recognizing that science can render fairly reliable probabilistic statements about the rates of their incidence or the levels of their relative severity provides a guide to individual and group behavior. Risk is simultaneously naturalized (turned into an ineluctable background condition), socialized (reduced to a collective cost born by all), and personalized (transformed into a multidimensional game of various lifestyle choices). To live is to play the odds in large numbers as the overall environment of technological artifacts, democratic agents, and capitalist acts now encircling us are approached through the *illusio* of data structures with their statistical statements about multiple arrays of risk. IPE, as the editors note (Chapters 1 and 13), increasingly adds its voice to these registers of reflexive risk management. Risk analysis creates the advisories, and citizens thereby become the advisoried masses, struggling to determine the path of maximum likely survival from a stream of health news, economic forecasts, food scares, trade agreements, and hazard warnings about the world's noxious encirclement by technology/democracy/capitalism.

As early as the sixteenth century in Europe, princes and their retainers introduced notions of economy into political affairs as an essential aspect of statesmanship with the practices of government. Government, as Foucault argues, became understood as "the right disposition of things, arranged so as to lead to a convenient end" (Foucault 1991:93). By the age of enlightened despotism, codes of governmentality effused collective life in "the proliferation of political technologies that ensued, investing the body, health, modes of subsistence and habitation, living conditions, the whole space of existence" (Foucault 1980:143–144). The rise of complex global markets and dynamic national economies in the twentieth century blurred the boundaries between political and economic, technological and social, public and private. Hence, the modern regime of biopower must assume that technology/democracy/capitalism will act as environmental forces. In turn, a clear understanding of IPE and the environment becomes a new means to organize "the conduct of conduct" for citizens and consumers.

The acts and artifacts produced by Fukuyama's "accumulation without end" in transnational modernization constitute the things that government must rightly dispose of and arrange so as to serve convenient ends in the globalized civil society of the global economy.

> What government has to do with is not territory but rather a sort of complex composed of men and things. The things with which in this sense government is to be concerned are in fact men, but men in their relations, their links, their imbrication with those other things which are wealth, resources, means of substance, the territory with its specific qualities, climate, irrigation, fertility, etc.; men in their relation to that other kind of things, customs, habits, ways of acting and thinking, etc.; lastly, men in their relation to that other kind of things, accidents and misfortunes such as famine, epidemics, death, etc. (Foucault 1991:93–94)

The subpolis shapes, and is itself shaped, in this imbrication of the polis for humans and the market for things. And, as "the possibilities for social change from the collaboration of research, technology, and science accumulate," the organizational mission centered in governmentality, once again, as Beck suggests, *"migrates from the domain of politics to that of subpolitics"* (Beck 1992:223). Consequently, as the editors claim (Chapter 13), IPE and the environment must be even more closely connected in policy theory and practice to correct these contradictions.

IPE must critically and comprehensively address as a discipline how all of the contradictions in the subpolis bring their disruptive influence into our public life. As all the contributors to this book imply, technology predetermines collective ends without much, if any, ethical discussion or political deliberation. This occurs because those who "know-how," as well as those who "own-how," in the subpolis are permitted to prejudge everyone's actions in the polis. Their expert knowledge and private ownership give them the capability to decide for all. Democracy, in turn, finds dictatorial administrative rationalities turned into collective ends in themselves without much, if any, ethical debate or political discussion. Environmentalism is one of the last remaining discourses available for us to provide some ethical consideration or political reflection about the effects of the subpolis on the overall civic life of the society. As we perhaps stand at the end of nature at the opening of the twenty-first century, I concur with the contributors to this book that we cannot continue on this track if the earth's ecologies are ever to be mended. Fortunately, the contributions here provide many insights into how the subpolitical domain can begin to be regulated and directed by a new critical political economy intent upon protecting the global environment and its inhabitants.

Dimitris Stevis
Valerie J. Assetto

13

Conclusion: History and Purpose in the International Political Economy of the Environment

A few years ago, there was a brief exchange between Robert Cox and Kenneth Waltz over the purpose of international relations (IR) theory. Cox divided international relations theories into "problem-solving theories" and "critical theories." Problem-solving theory "takes the world as it finds it, with the prevailing social and power relationships and the institutions into which they are organized, as the given framework for action" (Cox 1986:208). Critical theory, on the other hand, "is critical in the sense that it stands apart from the prevailing order of the world and asks how that order came about" (Cox 1986:208). In his response, Waltz (1986:338) states, "I have no quarrel with Cox's concern with counter and latent structures, with historical inquiry, and with speculation about possible futures. Ashley and Cox would transcend the world as it is; meanwhile we have to live in it."

To read Cox's statement as a call for utopias and Waltz's response as an affirmation of hard-nosed realism is equally misleading. Since the social construction of the world we live in remains a central question of social analysis, the issue is not merely adjudication among competing solutions to well-known problems. (See Elliott 1998:chapter 10.)

Motivated by the above assumptions, we have pursued two related goals in this book. Our first goal has been to contribute to the prevention of closure of the discourse over the international political economy (IPE) of the environment; our second goal has been to give social purpose the centrality that it deserves.

In this concluding chapter, we outline the parameters of an approach that is sensitive to both historical context and purpose, drawing upon the broader literature on environmental politics[1] and from the contributions of our collaborators. Our approach points to specific ways in which one can investigate environmental politics systematically. Equally important, it does not prohibit the adoption of a wealth of useful insights from a variety of productive research programs, such as regime analysis, with which one may disagree in a number of ways.

Bringing in History

In recent years there has been a proliferation of good work on the social and historical contexts of the environment from scholars committed to its cause (McCormick 1989; Grove 1995; Crumley 1994; Cronon 1996a; Miller and Rothman 1997; Goldfrank et al. 1999; Ross 1998; Biersack 1999). Insights from other disciplines are beneficial for the IPE of the environment for a variety of reasons. First, they allow us to reflect on our particular research agendas and enrich our substantive repertoire, thus enhancing the empirical foundations of our theorizing. Contrary to some assertions, for instance, modern environmental politics did not start in the 1960s. Even if we did accept this view by using some narrow definition of environmentalism, post-1960s environmental concerns have clear and practically relevant genealogies, depending on the issue area (for example, Boardman 1981; McCormick 1989; Gottlieb 1993; Sellers 1997; Ross 1998).

Second, evidence from disciplines with broader historical and cultural horizons compromises the facile excuse of ignorance and forces us to reflect on the politics that have brought us to the present. For example, the adverse impacts of tobacco were known to the British Crown as early as the beginning of the seventeenth century; the environmental and human impacts of deforestation and enclosure have long been the subject of debates (Grove 1995; Chapter 6); the health hazards of gasoline fumes were a major issue in the United States in the 1920s (Gottlieb 1993); post–World War II environmental politics were quite diverse (Chapter 2; McCormick 1989); the U.S. government is not impervious to the reasons for and environmental implications of the proliferation of utility vehicles and the increasing size of houses. These examples are not to suggest that we can always assess adverse environmental impacts with certainty but that critical historical analysis can allocate responsibility where it belongs.

Placing issues in context, however, is useful not only for theoretical reasons; it also has practical utility. Identifying the social origins and trajectories of environmental problems is a necessary precondition for understanding the dynamics for and against their resolution. The promotion of automobiles in China, for instance, is not simply an accident, but it is intimately involved in the Communist Party's industrialization strategy. To reduce environmental problems to the present may facilitate the promotion of technical solutions, but it also obscures their deep social roots. Policies that do not confront the social sources of environmental problems essentially legitimate the right of key perpetrators to define the agenda. Such policies, therefore, can be very efficient and also very ineffective.

Interactions and Constitutions

But what kind of evidence must a critical IPE use? Accounts that are limited to tracing the placement of particular issues onto the international agenda or that describe the involvement of particular agents but do not give us some sense of the creation of these issues and the variable involvement of stakeholders are not adequate. Critical IPE requires evidence that takes into account both the constitution and the interactions of stakeholders. We are not intending to provide a detailed account of such a historical-relational perspective, nor do we advance here a particular approach within it (for various views as they apply to world politics see Bukharin 1966; Braudel 1980; Wallerstein 1974; Chase-Dunn 1989; Ollman 1993; Cox 1987; Murphy and Tooze 1991; Mittelman 1996a; Burch and Denemark 1997). Our goal is to identify some key elements and indicate how they can inform the IPE of the environment.

Historicizing values and preferences. At the most immediate level, such an approach requires a movement away from essentialist assumptions about values and preferences, and thus problems and solutions (Ellis 1996; Escobar 1999).[2] This is not to say that social entities do not have long-term, deeply held political values and preferences that are internally related to the political economies within which they are constituted, nor that nature should not be valued on its own terms. It is to say, however, that these values and preferences are revealed through theoretical and empirical investigations rather than ahistorical assumptions, such as asserting that states always value an unspecified security or survival, that liberal trade is universally beneficial, or that our knowledge or experience of nature is unmediated by our own sensitivities.

In this sense, a critical political economy of the environment cannot assume that some types of agents are inherently nonenvironmentalist or that they have immutable environmental preferences. For instance, some environmentalist organizations are procapitalist, while others are more critical of capitalism; and their positions may vary depending on the nature of capitalism and the internal trajectory of the organization itself, as the trajectory of and divisions among the German greens have shown. The goal, therefore, should be to investigate the origins, changes, and purpose of their positions vis-a-vis the environment. From such an angle, we will be able to differentiate among policy proposals at the same time that we recognize their promises and limitations.

Historicizing actors and nature.   In addition to avoiding any essentialist assumptions about the desires of agents or the value of nature, a critical IPE of the environment must not reify social entities or nature, both of which vary in time and across time. The recognition that not all states are the same should not come as a surprise; theories of imperialism, long duration, dependency, and even interdependence provide ample evidence of the uneven constitution of states, both internally and comparatively. The same applies to corporations, unions, and any other social forces. Contemporary corporations are different from their nineteenth-century predecessors, and there is a great deal of variation among them at present: some unions have more internal democracy while others have less; some environmental groups are more rank and file while others are associations of professionals. As with values and preferences, it is important to recognize both the differences among various social entities and the parameters within which they vary. Recognizing the ideological variation among environmentalists, for instance, will go a long way in explaining their stands in international environmental politics (see Chapters 2 and 3). Similarly, domestic politics and policy help a great deal in explaining the international environmental preferences of states.

In the same sense, the environment (including nature) is also historical (Cronon 1996a; Miller and Rothman 1997). We are not referring here simply to natural history but also to the intimate connections between human practices and what we consider as the natural state. The move to agriculture has reorganized nature during the last 10,000 years or so; beneath the lush forests of the Yucatan lie impressive cities; "ecological imperialism" has inexorably transformed the interface of local and external species during the last millennium; the parks and wilderness areas that we so value are the product of human engineering. To recognize these realities without denying the inherent values of nature is indeed an important challenge.

Historical contexts.   Lest we give the impression that we are advocating some kind of historical relativism, we argue that a critical IPE of the environment must identify the historical contexts within which social entities operate and which they shape, as they are shaped by them. These are historical totalities in the sense that we can track their creation, rather than essentialist or organismic totalities that are assumed; they are relational because the constitution and interactions of the various entities are contingent upon the social divisions of labor that bring them together.

This is not to say that everything is related to everything else, a common rhetorical device of many environmentalists. Rather, it is to say that we must take into account the implications of *historical* relations for *both* the interactions and constitution of social entities. Such an approach diverges from the structural-functionalist view that cross-border environmental problems militate in favor of cross-border solutions that may be a challenge to the state system. A historical-relational approach seeks to understand the mutual and uneven constitution of actors and nature in order to better understand the interactions within and across these two categories. Thus, it seeks to reconstruct the "who" and the "what" in order to move beyond the atomistic, essentialist, and structural-functionalist assumptions underpinning mainstream IR theories (as well as some less mainstream ones).

To illuminate, it is not simply the case that all stakeholders will evaluate the available options, constrained by their ability to collect and absorb information, and that they will entertain only those options that their capacities permit. It is also the case that what may seem to be options to some are not options for others. In some instances, socialization may be so strong that individuals or groups cannot even conceive that they should at least *consider* different options. More important, and more damaging for atomistic and essentialist views, is the recognition that certain options do not make sense, regardless of what the capacities of the evaluator may be. The rights of nature, for instance, make sense only to those who have a concept of nature.

In short, constitution is more than capacity, a distinction that critical IPE must integrate into its analyses of power relations. Otherwise, atomistic and essentialist arguments about the nature and desires of individuals or groups will continue to dominate, with important implications for the environment as well as other social issues. Take, for instance, the increasing clamor in favor of commodification and privatization. On the one hand, the advocacy of privatization denies that there may be a wide variety of efficient and equitable alternative solutions to collective problems (for various such solutions and proposals see Ostrom 1990; Bowles and Gintis 1998). On the other hand, it justifies the actions of those who benefit from privatization by implying that, deep down, everyone would do the same if they could. The centrality of this kind of thinking in mainstream IR and in everyday life is all too evident.

This sensitivity to historical social contexts allows the contributors to recognize the significance and complexities of instrumental debates but without obscuring the systemic biases in which these debates take place. Thus, there is no assumption here that historical agents have fixed strategic and tactical preferences, although it is clear that their political preferences do shape strategy and tactics. As Chapter 4 suggests, the strategies and tactics of corporations and environmental nongovernmental organizations (ENGOs) in terms of choosing policy arenas depend on the characteristics of those arenas rather than some essential preference for domestic over international politics. In this vein, the use of domestic arenas by corporations, which are also key advocates of cross-border liberalization, makes a great deal of sense and restores agency to understanding contemporary politics. While recognizing these strategic and tactical complexities, however, our collaborators also realize that in order for ENGOs to have a voice at the World Trade Organization (WTO) (Chapter 3), or to participate in voluntary arrangements with transnational corporations (TNCs) (Chapter 5), or to formally shape Dominican, Cuban, or Brazilian environmental politics (Chapters 7 and 8), certain principles must be accepted and internalized.

Bringing in Purpose

The historical-relational perspective outlined above informs the discussion of purpose that follows. Again, rather than provide a comprehensive account of purpose, we focus on what we consider to be key dimensions and indicate how these can apply to environmental politics.

Voice and Choice

One of the issues that has received a great deal of attention in domestic and international environmental politics, and the broader "new social movement" literature, is the impact of ENGOs on deepening participation and constructing a "civil society" that navigates between state and capital (Wapner 1996; Lipschutz with Mayer 1996; Peet and Watts 1996; Brosius 1999). We do not disagree that environmental organizations should be examined in their own terms. But social movements are neither a new phenomenon nor have they always been emancipatory in nature. Environmental politics, therefore, must be investigated and compared without any a priori assumptions about where they belong in the grand scheme of things. Demonizing the state, for instance, precludes us from recognizing that it is frequently a more fluid and contested arena than society.

Equally important, we believe that in order to understand the role of a particular agent or social movement, one must look at both voice and choice (Stevis and Mumme forthcoming). Inclusive participation is not a guarantee of deeper democracy (see Chapters 3, 5, and 8). It is quite possible that every stakeholder will be allowed to participate equally but within very defined limits of choice. For instance, privatization would allow each citizen to participate as a consumer, formally a more direct form of participation than representative democracy. Representative democracy, however, can allow us to decide on whether we want privatization or not. In short, we must investigate the interplay of procedural and substantive rules.

Rules for Relations

A common way to approximate the social purpose of policies (and in fact, whole social formations) is to distinguish between procedural and substantive rules, defining the first as form and the latter as purpose. Such a tactic, useful as it may be analytically, can also lead to an even deeper formalism in assuming that procedural rules are empty of substantive preferences and that substantive rules have the same implications regardless of the power relations between the social entities involved. We argue that one must look at the historical concatenations of procedural and substantive rules. From such a point of view, organizational and administrative rules seek to place an order on even messier historical relations. For instance, criminal activities and offshore banking create divisions of labor in the absence of any rules, certainly public ones. In short, social relations can exist and operate in the absence of rules, but rules are important for their standardization and legitimation in the long run. Moreover, since divisions of labor and associated social relations can be organized through different rules, their determination is routinely a major political issue.[3]

One way to highlight the historical contingency of rules, and its implications for reflecting on social purpose, is to look at property. Private property rights can now be used to protect peasants from expropriation and workers from an old age without pension. On the other hand, modern corporations seek the commodification of property. To the extent that commodification prevails over stable property rights or entitlements (Sen 1981), it becomes a major source of uncertainty and discontent for the poor—even though both rich and poor may use the language of property rights. In other contexts, however, noncommodification could well be the source of oppression. Accordingly, feudal property rights and castes have historically limited the capacity of serfs and "untouchables" to buy themselves out of these situations.

In environmental affairs, either commodification or inalienable property rights could well be used to protect or damage the environment. Taking nature out of the market is not a guarantee of better environmental policies. Rather, we must investigate the purpose and impact of particular rules during particular historical periods. This implies two things: first, that our evidence and generalizations must be grounded in good history; second, that our research of the past must let the past speak as much as possible rather than impose answers veiled as methods (Hardin 1968; for critiques see Ostrom 1990 and Ross 1998).

The contributors to this book recognize this necessary "decentering" of rules. Accordingly, they do not assume that similar terms have the same meaning or implications, regardless of who uses them (see discussion of "sustainable development" in Chapters 2 and 3, and enclosure in Chapter 6, for instance). Most significantly, how-ever, these accounts are not relativist in that the impacts of rules at particular points in time have definite and investigable meanings and implications that are not solely the creation of the agent or of disem-bodied language.

Combining History and Purpose

The connections between history and purpose are evident in our pre-vious discussions. In what follows, we apply those insights to the framing of environmental problems and solutions and to understand-ing managerial environmentalism's bid for hegemony.

Problems and Solutions

Social scientists have long noted that problems fit the solutions as often as solutions fit the problems. As a result, a rigidly temporal examination of the two is inadequate. For instance, as Chapter 9 notes, the emission standards solution implies the acceptance of pri-vate automobiles; Chapter 8 points out that the framing of urban pol-lution problem in the Dominican Republic obscures the role of industrial location and accentuates the impact of the poor. In general, it is our view that unless we subject both problems and solutions to critical analysis, not only will their common political biases go unno-ticed, but important practical shortcomings will also be left unad-dressed. We briefly examine some of the issues that emerge as one looks at the framing of problems and solutions.

It is clearly possible that some problems or solutions are never identified as such. The reasons for this are important. At one extreme, it may be the case that our state of theoretical and practical knowledge does not allow us to recognize a problem and/or a solu-tion (see Chapter 10). While such cases do exist, the pretext of igno-rance is frequently used to mask debates over environmental issues and legitimate antienvironmental practices. It is here that historical analysis can serve us well.

A second reason why we may not be able to identify problems and solutions is that research programs and techniques are biased.

For instance, a research program may make it impossible to ask certain questions about the impacts of pesticides, and our techniques may be inappropriate to answer certain types of questions, even if posed. The role of the physical and natural sciences has been central to environmental politics and policies, as it should be. As a number of analysts have pointed out, however, particular scientific disciplines can ask and answer only limited sets of questions. Moreover, social reasons always select which among these questions science will address. Thus, the social sciences have an important role to play in identifying the social contexts within which the natural and physical sciences operate (Taylor and Buttel 1992; Schrader-Frechette and McCoy 1993; Jasannof 1996; Barbour 1996).

Yet, there is no guarantee that simply turning to the social sciences is enough. Social sciences themselves are subject to problems similar to those of the natural and physical sciences; thus, we also need a critical and reflexive approach to the social sciences. This is clear if we consider a third reason why environmental problems and solutions may never be posed: the weakness of the parties most affected by these problems and solutions. No one can underestimate the reasons for and implications of such silences, a factor that militates in favor of reflexive research and precautionary practices.

While our social and scientific resources may prevent us from even suspecting the existence of an environmental problem, such instances are less important than cases when the nature of the problem and the solution are the subject of dispute, an issue that receives a great deal of attention in this book. This is evident, for instance, in Chapter 10's account of the victory of Newtonian over Aristotelian thinking, in Chapter 6's discussion of the conflicts over the enclosure and commodification of land and knowledge during the last 400 years, and in Chapter 2's account of post–World War II international environmental politics.

In general, it may be the case that the choice to focus on a particular problem—let us say global climate change as opposed to urban sanitation—is evidence of a biased environmental agenda. In our view, however, the ways in which problems and solutions are posed is an even better indicator of bias. Global climate change, for instance, can be cast as a technical problem rather than in terms of reorganizing our ways of being in the world (see Chapter 9); similarly, urban sanitation can be framed either as a problem of broader social priorities or as garbage collection.

Mainstream theorists do recognize that the meanings of terms are contested and variable, but they delineate the range of contestation and variation in ways that marginalize alternative views and narrow the range of the legitimate. Thus, while sustainable development can have various meanings, its sustainability and equity components are lost in increasingly instrumentalist debates over the meaning and operationalization of the term.

In this vein, the posing of problems and solutions takes place at various levels. At the deepest level, the problem/solution–posing process is delineated by longer-term ideational and ideological preferences (see Chapters 3, 6, 9, and 10). At a more strategic level, they have to do with the hegemony of particular discourses (see Chapters 2, 3, 4, 7, and 8) that shape the concepts and aspirations that frame immediate problems and solutions. At the most immediate level, the historical combinations of ideology and discourse facilitate and legitimate certain debates over environmental policies and delegitimate, or make incomprehensible, others.

A number of the chapters in this book do, in fact, deal with these instrumental debates while placing them in their broader contexts. In short, they consider the ways in which the realm of the possible, and consequently the desirable, is constructed. As Chapter 9 points out in analyzing the Long-Range Transboundary Air Pollution (LRTAP) Convention, it is not evident that the environmental problems that the convention has successfully solved are the structural problems that should be addressed. Quite possibly, the convention is the best feasible one given the particular configuration of interests and capacities. Stated differently, the standards that are acceptable to a particular configuration of actors have been turned into standards for all stakeholders. As Chapters 3 and 4 also point out, intergovernmental organizations (IGOs) and corporate elites have accepted that some environmental measures are necessary; in exchange, they expect that such measures will be subordinate to economic liberalization.

The focus on the social construction of problems and solutions is not only a moral and political issue, central as these dimensions are. Dissecting the nature of the problems and the solutions, we suggest, provides superior descriptions, interpretations, and predictions, a goal for much of conventional IPE and IR. The failure of dominant mainstream theories to predict the end of statist socialism in a manner consistent with their assumptions and the paucity of their post facto interpretations is evidence that intellectual hegemony may owe more to ideological preferences and less to intellectual reasons. In addition, the reluctance of some radical theorists to take their analyses of the same cases to their logical conclusions is also evidence of the diffuse hegemony of mainstream thought. Social theories that do not take into account the historicity of actors, preferences, and relations are destined to fail because they have no subject matter. This is a danger that faces, in our view, both essentialist environmentalists and essentialist social analysts.

We would also argue that critical analyses are necessary for more effective policies. Public policy aims at influencing human behavior. Inadequate understandings of who those people are and what kinds of activities are implicated are a recipe for failure, unless the goal of the policy is to actually exterminate or permanently marginalize particular groups and practices (see Chapter 7). Even from the perspective of power, reflexive information is necessary. It is not surprising then that during periods of colonial or quasi-colonial expansion we also witness growth and deep divisions within disciplines, such as anthropology, history, and political science, most likely to provide such information.

The Hegemony of Managerial Environmentalism?

The use of market instruments to achieve environmental goals, as well as the adoption of environmental priorities by liberal alliances, has been the subject of growing debate (Eckersley 1995a). What do these developments mean? Are they evidence of the retreat of the state vis-à-vis the firm and thus of environmental regulation? Or are they evidence of innovative policies that marshal the resources of corporations in the service of the environment? Clearly, the greening of the firm and of many states leaves much to be desired. Yet, it is also clear that many state agencies and many firms are genuinely committed (for a range of reasons) to some environmental standards and policies.[4] A critical approach, in our view, must be able to distinguish between public relations and genuine commitment and elucidate the purpose and limitations of such commitments. While radical analysts will correctly point to the environmental deficiencies of the greening of the firm, they would be mistaken to reject its political implications (see Chapter 5). Moreover, they would also err in suggesting that environmentalists and state agencies that are joining capital in bipartite or tripartite arrangements are falling from grace. As

with other social movements, tactical or rhetorical agreement at particular times cannot be considered as evidence of homogeneity. The
historical record clearly points to the divergent origins and politics of
environmentalism at the societal and state levels.

It is with these provisos in mind that we examine managerial
environmentalism's bid for theoretical and practical hegemony. First,
we must note that managerial environmentalism, as used in this book
and other research, includes both the efforts of corporate managers to
become environmental leaders and efforts by neoliberal governments
to establish policies that assume that firms and markets are the best
arbiters of sound and efficient environmental policies. As such it is a
more laissez-faire version of environmental management (see Luke
1999b; Chapters 2 and 3). Central to both environmental management and managerial environmentalism is a great deal of confidence
in their problem-solving capacities, whether through scientific
resource conservation or socially unregulated market mechanisms.

In this vein, what are the ingredients of managerial environmentalism? How does it differ from related discourses? What alliances
does it facilitate and require? In this chapter, we discuss three ideal
types/discourses—voluntary policies, administrative policies and
regulations, and weak ecological modernization—to better delineate
managerial environmentalism.[5]

Private international policies do, in fact, differ among themselves (Eckersley 1995b; Jacobs 1995; Cutler 1998; Chapter 5).[6] At
one extreme there are totally voluntary policies that may be promoted by capital or states. As Chapter 5 discusses, many of these
policies are bipartite in that they involve capital and ENGOs.
Somewhere in the middle are quasi-voluntary policies, such as those
of the International Organization for Standardization (ISO) (Clapp
1998), as well as various policies related to labor (Harvey et al.
1998). What makes them quasi-voluntary is the level of their formal-
ization and the mutual expectations that they bring forth. Both of
these private types of policies should be distinguished from policies
that involve substantial amounts of privatization but fall within goals
shaped by public policy. In short, it is one thing for corporations to
use trading permits of their choosing and another thing to be allowed
to choose within definite parameters. A formalistic view of privatization, therefore, can bundle together a wide variety of superficially
similar policies or policy proposals (Meier 1995; Bowles and Gintis
1998).

In general, many sectors of capital have been in favor of voluntaristic policies of the first two types, while ENGOs have taken a somewhat more cautious approach. Credible managerialist alliances require the participation of ENGOs or green parties and of state environmental agencies. Their participation, in turn, must be purchased with something more than purely voluntary or quasi-voluntary arrangements.[7] Although there are groups that have joined voluntary arrangements, these are not likely to have broad and long-lasting impacts (see Chapter 5).

In short, environmental agencies and ENGOs that join in managerial alliances are not simply dupes but do exercise countervailing pressures that force some business elites (for various reasons) to adopt some environmental priorities. These elites, in turn, exert pressure from within capital. Pressure from other stakeholders is well known; pressure emanating from within capital may be less well known. For one, there may be enlightened elites who realize that some environmental priorities and practices are desirable. Second, corporations may want stronger, if selective, public regulation in order to minimize their legal exposure (see Chapters 3 and 4; Streeck 1998). Third, sectors of capital from one country or components from within a sector may call for stronger regulation in order to prevent perceived unfair competition (Levêque 1996; Vogel 1995). In short, extreme voluntarism does not provide the foundations for a hegemonic managerialist alliance, partly due to external pressures and partly due to internal pressures.

This brings us to administrative policies and regulations (see Paehlke and Torgerson 1990). Contrary to hyperliberal mythology, as we have noted above, capital is not opposed to all binding public policies but only to certain *types* of binding policies (Streeck 1998; Chapter 4). Thus, we should not simply distinguish between binding or enforceable policies and soft, nonbinding policies. As Chapters 8 and 9 point out, it is important to examine what the goals of the policy are and who is cast as the responsible party. Binding and effective policies may aim at regulating fundamentally unsound practices. Strong clean water laws for cities built in arid environments are an example of sound policies serving an unsound pattern of growth.

What is important for our purposes here are the reasons behind binding and relatively effective environmental policies. In some cases, the reasons may be based on some general commitment to improving the environment because of the impacts of various practices on nature and people; in others, the impetus may be to correct market imperfections. While this "trading up" may improve the environment in some ways, the limits to such improvement are determined by the comfort zones of particular social agents (Vogel 1995).

For various reasons, then, there are many domestic and international policies that, while not optimal by various reasonable standards, are quite far-reaching in their environmental and social implications. Environmentally they have modified popular and policy discourses to include options hitherto marginalized. Socially, they have reorganized the state and the political economy of sectors, regions, and countries. In short, there are now social forces constituted by those practices. To assume that the onslaught of neoliberal capitalism will simply wipe them out is to reify its power. A critical IPE of the environment, therefore, is not simply one that points to the attacks emanating from neoliberal capital and its state allies but also to the capacities of the social forces they are attacking and whose allegiance they need.

A solution to this conundrum is offered by weak ecological modernization (Weale 1992; Hajer 1995; Christof 1996). The strong version seeks to radically reshape the way and the degree to which we produce and consume things. The weak version seeks to improve environmental policies by modifying what we produce and consume but not who decides what and how much. In the United States, for instance, appliance manufacturers have become somewhat more environmentally sensitive over the last twenty-five years. Yet, because houses have concurrently grown larger, energy consumption is now higher per capita than it was in the early 1970s.

The basic problem with weak ecological modernization is that it is also predicated on the comfort zone of particular agents. Corporations will reform to the degree that they remain competitive and will push for reform to avoid unfair competition. Yet, weak ecological modernization does allow enlightened corporate and state elites to gain the high ground vis-à-vis their more inflexible colleagues and facilitates collaboration with environmentalists and state agencies.

The basic characteristic of managerial environmentalism, therefore, is not total disregard for the environment or a doctrinaire adoption of voluntary policies or rejection of state policies. Rather, the measure of its success is the legitimation of environmental priorities that allow capital structural autonomy and flexibility in exchange for limited instrumental oversight. Stated otherwise, the measure of its success is the degree to which it renders environmental priorities heteronomous—that is, conditioned by and subordinate to nonenvironmental priorities. This, of course, is not a new goal, as has been demonstrated in areas such as work, human rights, and leisure, to name a few.

The Limits of Managerial Environmentalism

The proliferation of hyperliberalism and various voluntaristic arrangements in recent times has served to exaggerate the capacities and prospects of capital. As noted in Chapter 4, we should not underestimate these capacities and their implications. It is important to realize, however, that capital must also make history under circumstances not entirely of its own making. The hegemony of managerial environmentalism is predicated on its ability to maintain alliances among important constituencies, each with its own interests and resources. It will remain hegemonic only to the degree that it can pay the costs of hegemony—that is, some form of environmental improvement. Such improvements could be the result of a combination of allocative environmental regulation and weak ecological modernization.

Credible managerial environmentalist alliances cannot go back to some ideal laissez-faire vision. They have to be broad enough to attract various environmentalists, state agencies, and other social forces. What makes this alliance hegemonic is that it legitimates the primacy of a reformed capitalism. That much we can assert; what the precise political balance will be depends on the capacities and tactics of the various participants. In any event, creating a hegemonic alliance requires partners. While from an unreflexive point of view these partners may appear to be unethical or wrong, in reality each has its own priorities and will not join the alliance unless they are given a stake in it.

Critical environmentalists can investigate the implications of such politics for people and the environment and point to the ways that they create new obstacles for the emancipation of either. However, dismissing the ability of such arrangements to reform the world in directions that legitimate environmental management is dangerous. Thus, a critical IPE of the environment needs a language and a politics that is neither essentialist nor maximalist and that allows for resistance *and* "real utopias." Most important, of course, a critical IPE of the environment needs critical and organized environmentalists who reflect on the history and purpose of environmental politics, including their own.

Notes

1. This provides us with an opportunity to take stock, if in a different fashion, of the state of international environmental politics a bit more than ten years after our first overview of the subject (Stevis et al. 2000).

2. Essentialist views assign certain immanent and immutable characteristics to agents or subjects. When essentialism is applied to others, it is often referred to as orientalism (Said 1979). As Laferrière suggests in Chapter 10, we do not think that all of deep ecology can be subjected to the above criticism. Further, we believe that orientalism can be a problem both with some intrinsic value and some instrumental value approaches. For instance, instrumentalist approaches that see nature as a museum are as orientalist as intrinsic value approaches that portray nature as a quasi-religious entity.

3. Our use of the concept of rules here is narrower than that of rules-constructivists (see Burch and Denemark 1997). The interplay of relations and rules is an issue worth additional investigation on its own.

4. We believe that many state policies are genuine improvements. The endangered species act, standing for citizens, and the German precautionary principle are examples of strong environmental policies. We recognize that state policies are contested and often contradictory. We do not think, therefore, that we can use the same generalizations for states as we do for firms.

5. We must note here that managerial environmentalism as well as the three variants that we are dealing with cover a limited range of possible options.

6. The private-public distinction is used heuristically. From a critical perspective, the mutual constitution and interplay of state and nonstate forces vary historically. Neither the sources nor impacts of social acts are ever wholly within the private or public sphere.

7. The pressure for long-term, nonvoluntaristic arrangements also comes from business in its quest for enforceable standardization.

Acronyms

AIREN	Asociación Impresarial Región Norte (Businessmen's Association for the Northern Region)
APEDI	Asociación para el Desarrollo, Inc. (Development Association, Santiago)
BP	British Petroleum Corporation
CAN	Climate Action Network
CEPAL	Comisión Economíca para América Latina y el Caribe (Economic Commission for Latin America and the Caribbean)
CERES	Coalition for Environmentally Responsible Economies
CFCs	chlorofluorocarbons
CITMA	Ministerio de Ciencia, Tecnología y Medio Ambiente (Ministry of Science, Technology, and the Environment)
CMEA	Council for Mutual Economic Assistance
CNSE	Comisión Nacional para el Saneamiento Ecológico (National Commission for Ecological Sanitation)
CONORDEN	Consejo de Ordenamiento (Council for the Orderly Development of Santiago)
CORAASAN	Corporación de Acueducto y Alcantarillado de Santiago (Water and Sewer Corporation of Santiago)
CSCE	Conference on Security and Cooperation in Europe
CSIR	Council of Scientific and Industrial Research (India)
CTE	Committee on Trade and the Environment (WTO)
EDF	Environmental Defense Fund
ENGO	environmental nongovernmental organization
EPO	European Patent Office
FAO	Food and Agriculture Organization

FCCC	Framework Convention on Climate Change (UN)
FOE	Friends of the Earth
FSC	Forestry Stewardship Council
GATT	General Agreement on Tariffs and Trade
GCC	Global Climate Coalition
GCMs	general circulation models
GDP	gross domestic product
GTA	Grupo de Trabalho Amazônico/Amigos da Terra Internacional (Amazonian Working Group/Friends of the Earth International)
GTZ	Gesellschaft für Technische Zusammenarbeit (Organization for Technical Assistance, Germany)
IBAMA	Instituto Brasileiro do Meio Ambiente e Recursos Renovàveis (Brazilian Institute for the Environment and Renewable Resources)
IBEAC	Imperial British East Africa Company
ICC	International Chamber of Commerce
ICI	Imperial Chemical Industries
ICME	International Council on Metals and the Environment
IDB	Inter-American Development Bank
IFAP	International Federation of Agricultural Producers
IFC	International Finance Corporation
IFOAM	International Federation of Organic Agriculture Movements
IGO	intergovernmental organization
IISD	International Institute for Sustainable Development
ILO	International Labour Organization
IMF	International Monetary Fund
INDRHI	Instituto Nacional de Recursos Hidráulicos (National Institute for Water Resources, Dominican Republic)
IO	international organization
IPCC	Intergovernmental Panel on Climate Change
IPE	international political economy
IR	international relations
ISA	Instituto Superior de Agricultura (Advanced Institute for Agricultural Studies)
ISI	import substitution industrialization
ISO	International Organization for Standardization

ITC	International Technical Conference
ITTO	International Tropical Timber Organization
IUCN	International Union for the Conservation of Nature
IUPN	International Union for the Protection of Nature
LRTAP	Long-Range Transboundary Air Pollution, Convention on
MAI	Multilateral Agreement on Investment
MEAs	multilateral environmental agreements
MNC	multinational corporation
NGO	nongovernmental organization
NIEO	new international economic order
NO_x	nitrogen oxide
OECD	Organization for Economic Cooperation and Development
OPEC	Organization of Petroleum Exporting Countries
PAC	Political Action Committee
PANAFLORO	Plano Agropecuário e Florestal da Amazônia (Agriculture, Cattle, and Forestry Plan of Amazonia)
PCB	polychlorinated biphynol
PPM	process and production method
PPG7	Pilot Program for the Tropical Forests of Brazil
PV	photovoltaic
PVC	polyvinyl chloride
RAFI	Rural Advancement Foundation International
SCOPE	Scientific Committee on Problems of the Environment
SO_2	sulfur dioxide
TNC	transnational corporation
TREMs	Trade-Related Environmental Measures
TRIPs	Trade-Related Aspects of Intellectual Property Rights (WTO)
TVA	Tennessee Valley Authority
UNCED	United Nations Conference on Environment and Development
UNCHE	United Nations Conference on the Human Environment
UNCHS	United Nations Centre for Human Settlements
UNCTAD	United Nations Conference on Trade and Development

UNDP	United Nations Development Programme
UNECE	United Nations Economic Commission for Europe
UNEP	United Nations Environment Programme
UNESCO	United Nations Educational, Scientific, and Cultural Organization
UNSCCUR	United Nations Scientific Conference on the Conservation and Utilization of Resources
USAID	U.S. Agency for International Development
USCIB	U.S. Council for International Business
VOC	volatile organic compound
WBCSD	World Business Council for Sustainable Development
WCED	World Commission on Environment and Development
WCS	World Conservation Strategy
WEFA	Wharton Economic Forecasting Associates
WHO	World Health Organization
WTO	World Trade Organization
WWF	World Wide Fund for Nature/World Wildlife Fund

Bibliography

Accu-Weather. (1994). "Changing Weather: Facts and Fallacies About Climate Change and Weather Extremes." State College, PA: Accu-Weather, Inc.

Adams, W., ed. (1990). *Green Development: Environment and Sustainability in the Third World.* New York: Routledge.

Agreement on Trade-Related Aspects of Intellectual Property Rights, Including Trade in Counterfeit Goods, Dec. 15, 1993. (1994). *International Legal Materials* 33(1): 81–111.

Amin, Samir. (1977). *Imperialism and Unequal Development.* New York: Monthly Review.

Aoki, Keith. (1998). "Neocolonialism, Anticommons Property, and Biopiracy in the (Not-So-Brave) New World Order of International Intellectual Property Protection." *Indiana Journal of Global Legal Studies* 6(1): 1–58.

Appelbaum, Richard P., and Jeffrey Henderson. (1995). "The Hinge of History: Turbulence and Transformation in the World Economy." *Competition and Change* 1(1): 1–12.

Arden-Clarke, Charles. (1996a). *The WTO Committee on Trade and the Environment: Is It Serious?* Gland, Switzerland: WWF International.

———. (1996b). *PPMs and Globalization.* Gland, Switzerland: WWF International.

Audley, John. (1997). *Green Politics and Global Trade: NAFTA and the Future of Environmental Politics.* Washington, DC: Georgetown University Press.

Bachrach, Peter, and Morton S. Baratz. (1963). "Two Faces of Power." *American Political Science Review* 56(4): 947–952.

Balandier, Georges. (1971). *Sens et Puissance.* Paris: Presses Universitaires de France.

Barbour, Michael. (1996). "Ecological Fragmentation in the Fifties." In William Cronon, ed., *Uncommon Ground: Rethinking the Human Place in Nature.* New York: W.W. Norton, pp. 233–255.

Barnet, Richard J., and John Cavanagh. (1994). *Global Dreams: Imperial Corporations and the New World Order.* New York: Simon and Schuster.

Barraclough, Solon. (Forthcoming). "Protecting Social Achievements During Economic Crisis in Cuba." In D. Ghai, ed., *Social Development and Public Policy: A Study of Some Successful Experiences.* London: Macmillan.

Barrow, Clyde W. (1993). *Critical Theories of the State.* Madison: University of Wisconsin Press.

Bartlett, Robert, Priya Kurian, and Madhu Malik, eds. (1995). *International Organizations and Environmental Policy.* Westport, Conn.: Greenwood Press.

Bayart, Jean-François. (1989). *L'État en Afrique: La Politique du Ventre.* Paris: Fayard.

Beck, Ulrich. (1992). *Risk Society: Towards a New Modernity.* London: Sage.

———. (1996). "Risk Society and the Provident State." In S. Lash, B. Szerzynski, and B. Wynne, eds., *Risk, Environment and Modernity: Towards a New Ecology.* London: Sage, pp. 27–43.

Beckerman, Wilfred. (1996). *Through Green-Colored Glasses: Environmentalism Reconsidered.* Washington, D.C.: Cato Institute.

Beder, Sharon. (1997). *Global Spin: The Corporate Assault on Environmentalism.* Melbourne: Scribe Publications.

Benedick, Richard E. (1991). *Ozone Diplomacy.* Cambridge: Harvard University Press.

Benjamin-Alvarado, Jonathan. (2000). *Power to the People: Energy and the Cuban Nuclear Program.* New York: Routledge.

Berkes, F., D. Feeny, B. J. McCay, and J. M. Acheson. (1989). "The Benefit of the Commons." *Nature* 340 (July 13): 91–93.

Berman, Bruce. (1990). *Control and Crisis in Colonial Kenya: The Dialectic of Domination.* London: James Currey.

Bernard, Mitchell. (1997). "Ecology, Political Economy and the Counter-Movement: Karl Polanyi and the Second Great Transformation." In Stephen Gill and James H. Mittelman, eds., *Innovation and Transformation in International Studies.* Cambridge: Cambridge University Press, pp. 75–89.

Biehl, Janet. (1991). *Finding Our Way: Rethinking Ecofeminist Politics.* Montreal: Black Rose.

———. (1998). *The Politics of Social Ecology: Libertarian Municipalism.* Montreal: Black Rose.

Biersack, Aletta, ed. (1999). Special Issue: Ecologies for Tomorrow: Reading Rappaport Today. *American Anthropologist* 101(1).

Blowers, Andrew. (1997). "Environmental Policy: Ecological Modernization or the Risk Society?" *Urban Studies* 34 (5–6): 845–871.

Boardman, Robert. (1981). *International Organization and the Conservation of Nature.* Bloomington: Indiana University Press.

Bodley, John H. (1982). *Victims of Progress.* Palo Alto, CA: Mayfield.

Boehmer-Christiansen, Sonja. (1994a). "Global Climate Protection Policy: The Limits of Scientific Advice: Part 1." *Global Environmental Change* 4(2): 140–159.

———. (1994b). "Global Climate Protection Policy: The Limits of Scientific Advice: Part 2." *Global Environmental Change* 4(3): 185–200.

Boehmer-Christiansen, Sonja, and Jim Skea. (1991). *Acid Politics: Environmental and Energy Politics in Britain and Germany.* London: Belhaven Press.

Bookchin, Murray. (1991 [1980]). *Toward an Ecological Society.* Montreal: Black Rose.

———. (1991a). *The Ecology of Freedom: The Emergence and Dissolution of Hierarchy,* rev. ed. Montreal: Black Rose.

———. (1992). *Urbanization Without Cities: The Rise and Decline of Citizenship.* Montreal: Black Rose.

Bowles, Samuel, and Herbert Gintis. (1998). *Recasting Egalitarianism: New Rules for Communitities, States and Markets.* Edited by Eric Olin Wright. London: Verso.

Boyle, Stewart. (1998). "Early Birds and Ostriches." *Energy Economist* (May): 12–17.

Braudel, Fernand. (1969). *Écrits sur l'Histoire.* Paris: Flammarion.

———. (1980). *On History.* Translated by Sarah Mathews. Chicago: University of Chicago Press.

Brecher, Jeremy, and Tim Costello. (1998). *Global Village or Global Pillage: Economic Reconstruction from the Bottom Up.* Boston, MA: South End Press.

Brenton, Tony. (1994). *The Greening of Machiavelli.* London: Royal Institute of International Affairs.

Bresser Pereira, Luiz Carlos. (1996). *Economic Crisis and State Reform in Brazil: Toward a New Interpretation of Latin America.* Boulder, Colo.: Lynne Rienner.

Brett, E. A. (1973). *Colonialism and Underdevelopment in East Africa: The Politics of Economic Change, 1919–1939.* New York: NOK Publishers.

Bridges Weekly Trade Digest. (1998). "Clinton Endorses Call for High-Level WTO Meeting on Trade-Environment and Calls for WTO Openness," 18 May.

Brosius, J. Peter. (1999). "Green Dots, Pink Hearts: Displacing Politics from the Malaysian Rain Forest." In Aletta Biersack, ed., Ecologies for Tomorrow: Reading Rappaport Today. *American Anthropologist* 101(1): 36–57.

Brown, Lester, et al. (1996). *State of the World 1996.* London: Earthscan.

Browne, John. (1997). "Climate Change." Text of speech given at Stanford University, 19 May.

Buchholz, Rogene A. (1993). *Principles of Environmental Management: The Greening of Business.* Englewood Cliffs, NJ: Prentice Hall.

Bukharin, Nikolai. (1966 [1915]). *Imperialism and World Economy.* New York: Howard Fertig.

Bullard, Robert D. (1990). *Dumping in Dixie: Race, Class, and Environmental Quality.* Boulder: Westview.

Burch, Kurt, and Robert Denemark, eds. (1997). *Constituting International Political Economy.* Vol. 10 of *IPE Yearbook.* Boulder: Lynne Rienner.

Buttel, F. H. (2000). "World Society, the Nation-State, and Environmental Protection." *American Sociological Review* 65: 117–121.

Caldwell, Lynton K. (1988). "Beyond Environmental Diplomacy: The

Changing Institutional Structure of International Cooperation." In J. Carroll, ed., *International Environmental Diplomacy: The Management and Resolution of Transfrontier Environmental Problems.* Cambridge: Cambridge University Press, pp. 13–27.

———. (1996). *International Environmental Policy,* 3d ed. Durham and London: Duke University Press.

Callon, Michel. (1998). *The Laws of the Markets.* Oxford: Blackwell.

Camilleri, Joseph. (1996). "Impoverishment and the National State." In F. Osler Hampson and J. Reppy, eds., *Earthly Goods: Environmental Change and Social Justice.* Ithaca: Cornell University Press, pp. 122–153.

Capra, Fritjof. (1991). *The Tao of Physics.* Boston: Shambhala.

Cardoso, Fernando Henrique. (1977). "The Consumption of Dependency Theory in the United States." *Latin American Research Review* 12 (3): 7–24.

———. (1995). *Mãos à Obra Brasil: Propostas de Governo Fernando Henrique.* Brasilia: n.p.

Carnoy, Martin. (1984). *The State and Political Theory.* Princeton: Princeton University Press.

———. (1993). "Multinationals in the Changing World Economy: Whither the Nation-State?" In Martin Carnoy, Manuel Castells, Stephen Cohen, and Fernando Cardoso, eds., *The New Global Economy in the Information Age.* University Park: Pennsylvania State University Press, pp. 45–96.

Carranza Valdés, Julio, Luis Gutiérrez Urdaneta, and Pedro Monreal González. (1996). *Cuba: Restructuring the Economy—A Contribution to the Debate.* London: University of London, Institute for Latin American Studies.

Carrasco, Domingo, Víctor Vásquez, José Payero, and Kevin Murphy. (1993). *El Río Yaque del Norte: Posibles Causas y Consecuencias de su Deterioro.* Santiago, Dominican Republic: Instituto Superior de Agricultura, Estudio de Caso.

Carson, Rachel. (1962). *Silent Spring.* Boston: Houghton Mifflin.

Castells, Manuel. (1997). *The Information Age: Economy, Society and Culture.* Vol. 2, *The Power of Identity.* Malden, MA: Blackwell.

Castillo, Fausto. (1996). *Tratamiento de Aguas Negras en la Ciudad de Santiago.* Manuscript. Santiago, Dominican Republic.

Caulkin, Simon. (1997). "Amnesty and WWF Take a Crack at Shell." *The Observer,* 11 May.

Ceara Hatton, Miguel. (1996). "De Reactivación Desordenada Hacia el Ajuste con Liberalización y Apertura (1987–1990 y 1991–1992)." In E. Betances and H. A. Spalding, Jr., eds., *The Dominican Republic Today: Realities and Perspectives.* New York: Bildner Center for Western Hemispheric Studies, pp. 33–73.

CEPAL (Comisión Económica para América Latina y el Caribe). (1997). *La Economía Cubana: Reformas Estructurales Y Desempeño en los Noventas.* Mexico City: CEPAL.

Cerny, Philip. (1990). *The Changing Architecture of Politics: Structure, Agency and the Future of the State*. London: Sage.

Chambers, J. D. (1953). "Enclosure and Labour Supply in the Industrial Revolution." *The Economic History Review*, second series, 5(3): 319–343.

Chantada, Amparo. (1991). "Medio Ambiente, Crisis y Desarrollo: Reflexión en Torno a los Ríos Ozama y Isabela." *Estudios Sociales* 24(83): 5–36.

————. (1996) "Medio Ambiente, Crisis y Desarrollo: Reflexiones en Torno a los Ríos Ozama y Isabellha." In A. Selman, ed., *Antología Urbana de Ciudad Alternativa*. Santo Domingo: Ciudad Alternativa, pp. 149–181.

Chase-Dunn, Christopher. (1989). *Global Formation: Structures of the World-Economy*. Cambridge, MA: Blackwell.

Chasek, Pamela, ed. (2000). *The Global Environment in the Twenty-First Century: Prospects for International Cooperation*. Tokyo: United Nations University Press.

Chatterjee, Pratap. (1997). "Marching to a New Mantra." *The Guardian*, 14 May.

Chatterjee, Pratap, and Matthias Finger. (1994). *The Earth Brokers: Power, Politics, and World Development*. New York and London: Routledge.

Christoff, Peter. (1996). "Ecological Modernization, Ecological Modernities." *Environmental Politics* 5(3): 476–500.

CITMA (Ministerio de Ciencia, Tecnología y Medio Ambiente). (1995). *Cuba: Medio Ambiente y Desarrollo*. Havana: Centro de Información, Divulgación y Educación Ambiental (CIDEA), Agencia de Medio Ambiente. (Published in collaboration with World Wide Fund for Nature)

Clapp, Jennifer. (1997). "Threats to the Environment in an Era of Globalization: An End to State Sovereignty?" In T. Schrecker, ed., *Surviving Globalism: The Social and Environmental Challenges*. London: Macmillan, pp. 123–140.

————. (1998). "The Privatization of Global Governance: ISO 14000 and the Developing World." *Global Governance* 4(3): 295–316.

Claussen, Eileen. (1999). Personal interview, 3 February.

Clegg, Stewart. (1989). *Frameworks of Power*. London: Sage.

Cobb, J. Michael, Boris Oxmen, Milagros Nanita-Kennett, and George E. Peterson. (1991). "Dominican Republic Environmental Strategy." Report prepared for USAID mission in Santo Domingo and Regional Housing and Urban Development Office for the Caribbean, Jamaica. Washington, DC: Urban Institute.

Cobb, Roger W., and Marc Howard Ross. (1997). "Agenda Setting and the Denial of Agenda Access: Key Concepts." In Roger W. Cobb and Marc Howard Ross, eds., *Cultural Strategies of Agenda Denial: Avoidance, Attack and Redefinition*. Lawrence: University of Kansas Press, pp. 3–24.

Cobbett, William. (1912). *Rural Rides*. Vol. 2. London: Everyman.

Collis, David S. (1995). "Environmental Implications of Cuba's Economic

Crisis." Cuba Briefing Paper No. 8. The Cuba Project, Center for Latin American Studies, Georgetown University, Washington, DC.

Commoner, Barry. (1971). *The Closing Circle: Nature, Man and Technology.* New York: Knopf.

Conca, Ken. (1993). "Environmental Change and the Deep Structure of World Politics." In Ronnie D. Lipschutz and Ken Conca, eds., *The State and Social Power in Global Environmental Politics.* New York: Columbia University Press, pp. 306–326.

Consejo Nacional de Zonas Francas de Exportación. (1998). *Informe Estadístico 1997: Sector de Zonas Francas.* Santo Domingo: Departamento de Información y Estadísticas.

Coombe, Rosemary J. (1998). "Intellectual Property, Human Rights & Sovereignty: New Dilemmas in International Law Posed by the Recognition of Indigenous Knowledge and the Conservation of Biodiversity." *Indiana Journal of Global Legal Studies* 6(1): 59–115.

Cordani, Umberto Giuseppe, Jacques Marcovitch, and Eneas Salati, eds. (1997). *Rio 92 Cinco Anos Depois. Avaliaçao das Ações Brasileiras em Direção ao Desenvolvimento Sustentável Após a Rio–92.* São Paulo: Alfagraphics.

Corporate Europe Observer. (1998). "Is Business Leaving a Sinking MAI?" Issue 2 (October). Amsterdam: Corporate Europe Observatory.

Corporate Watch. (n.d.).

Council on Environmental Quality and the Department of State. (1980). *Global 2000 Report to the President: Entering the Twenty-First Century.* Washington, DC: Government Printing Office.

Cox, Robert W. (1986 [1981]). "Social Forces, States and World Orders: Beyond International Relations Theory." In Robert Keohane, ed., *Neorealism and Its Critics.* New York: Columbia University Press, pp. 200–254.

———. (1987). *Production, Power and World Order: Social Forces in the Making of History.* New York: Columbia University Press.

———. (1993). "Gramsci, Hegemony and International Relations: An Essay in Method." In Stephen Gill, ed., *Gramsci, Historical Materialism and International Relations.* Cambridge: Cambridge University Press, pp. 49–66.

———. (1996a [1979]). "Ideologies and the New International Economic Order: Reflections on Some Recent Literature." In Robert W. Cox with Timothy J. Sinclair, eds., *Approaches to World Order.* Cambridge: Cambridge University Press, pp. 376–419.

———. (1996b [1981]). "Social Forces, States, and World Orders." In Robert W. Cox with Timothy J. Sinclair, eds., *Approaches to World Order.* Cambridge: Cambridge University Press, pp. 85–123.

———. (1996c [1992]). " Multilateralism and World Order." In Robert Cox with Timothy Sinclair, eds., *Approaches to World Order.* Cambridge: Cambridge University Press, pp. 494–523.

———. (1996d). "A Perspective on Globalization." In James Mittleman, ed., *Globalization: Reflections.* Vol. 9 of *IPE Yearbook.* Boulder, Colo.: Lynne Rienners, pp. 21–30.

————. (1997). "An Alternative Approach to Multilateralism for the Twenty-first Century." *Global Governance* 3(1): 103–116.

————. (1999). "Civil Society at the Turn of the Millennium: Prospects for an Alternative World Order." *Review of International Studies* 25 (1): 3–28.

Coyula, Mario. (1996). "The Neighborhood as Workshop." *Latin American Perspectives* 23(4): 90–103.

Crespo, Samyra, and Pedro Leitão. (1993). *O Que o Brasileiro Pensa da Ecologia.* Rio de Janeiro: MAST/CNPq, CETEM, ISER.

Cronon, William, ed. (1996a [1995]). *Uncommon Ground: Rethinking the Human Place in Nature.* New York: W.W. Norton.

————. (1996b [1995]). "Introduction: In Search of Nature." In William Cronon, ed., *Uncommon Ground: Rethinking the Human Place in Nature.* New York: W.W. Norton, pp. 23–56.

Crumley, Carole, ed. (1994). *Historical Ecology: Cultural Ecology and Changing Landscapes.* Santa Fe, NM: School of American Research Press.

Crumpton, A. C. (2000). "Review of The Global Environment." *Science, Technology and Human Values* 25: 120–122.

Cruz, Hernández, Maria Caridad, and Concepción Batista Medina. (1997). "Proyecto del Parque Metropolitano de la Habana: Retos y Riesgos Ambientales." Paper presented at the workshop "The Future of the Latin American City," Ithaca, NY, 7–10 July.

Curtler, William Henry Ricketts. (1920). *The Enclosure and Redistribution of Our Land.* Oxford: Clarendon Press.

Cushman, John H. (1998). "New Policy Center Seeks to Steer the Debate on Climate Change." *New York Times,* 8 May.

Cutler, Claire. (1995). "Global Capitalism and Liberal Myths: Dispute Settlement in Private International Trade Relations." *Millennium* 24(3): 377–397.

————. (1998). "Locating 'Authority' in the Global Political Economy." *International Studies Quarterly* 43(1): 59–81.

Dalby, Simon. (1992). "Security, Modernity, Ecology: The Dilemmas of Post–Cold War Security Discourse." *Alternatives* 17: 95–134.

Daly, Herman E. (1998). "Sustainable Growth: An Impossibility Theorem." In John S. Dryzek and David Schlosberg, eds., *Debating the Earth: The Environmental Politics Reader.* New York: Oxford University Press, pp. 285–289.

Daly, Herman E., and James Cobb. (1990). *For the Common Good: Redirecting the Economy Towards Community, the Environment and a Sustainable Future.* London: Green Print.

Davis, Robert E. (1996). *Global Warming and Extreme Weather: Fact vs. Fiction.* Washington DC: Global Climate Coalition.

Dawkins, K., and S. Suppan. (1996). *Sterile Fields: The Impact of Intellectual Property Rights and Trade on Biodiversity and Food Security.* Minneapolis: Institute for Agriculture and Trade Policy.

de Campos Mello, Valérie. (1996). "Globalização e Desenvolvimento

Sustentável: O Caso da Amazônia Brasileira." *Contexto Internacional* 18(2): 291–328.

———. (1997) *Economy, Ecology and the State: Globalization and Sustainable Development in Brazil.* Ph.D. diss., European University Institute, Florence.

Derby, Lauren. (1998). "The City Rises: The Making of Ciudad Trujillo." Paper presented at the Twenty-first International Congress of the Latin American Studies Association, Chicago, September.

Devall, Bill, and George Sessions. (1985). *Deep Ecology: Living as if Nature Mattered.* Salt Lake City: Peregrine Smith.

Di Chiro, Giovanna. (1996). "Nature as Community: The Convergence of Environmental and Social Justice." In William Cronon, ed., *Uncommon Ground: Rethinking the Human Place in Nature.* New York: W.W. Norton, pp. 298–320.

Dickson, Lisa, and Alistair McCulloch. (1996). "Shell, the Brent Spar and Greenpeace: A Doomed Tryst?" *Environmental Politics* 5(1): 122–129.

Dilley, Marjorie Ruth. (1966). *British Policy in Kenya Colony.* New York: Barnes and Noble.

Dobbs, Betty Jo Teeter, and Margaret C. Jacob. (1995). *Newton and the Culture of Newtonianism.* Atlantic Highlands, NJ: Humanities Press.

Dobson, Andrew. (1990). *Green Political Thought.* London: Routledge.

———. (1995). *Green Political Thought,* 2d ed. London: Routledge.

———. (1996). "Environmental Sustainabilities: An Analysis and a Typology." *Environmental Politics* 5(3): 401–428.

Dodds, Felix, ed. (1997). *The Way Forward: Beyond Agenda 21.* London: Earthscan.

Doran, Peter. (1995). "Earth, Power, Knowledge: Towards a Critical Global Environmental Politics." In John Macmillan and Andrew Linklater, eds., *Boundaries in Question: New Directions in International Relations.* London and New York: Pinter, pp. 193–211.

Dosi, Giovanni, Keith Pavitt, and Luc Soete. (1991). *The Economics of Technical Change and International Trade.* Hemel Hempstead, UK: Harvester Wheatsheaf.

Dougherty, Carter. (1998). "U.S. Poised to Seek Extension of Deadline for OECD Investment Pact." *Inside U.S. Trade,* 13 February.

Drakakis-Smith, David. (1995). "Third World Cities: Sustainable Urban Development, I." *Urban Studies* 32 (4–5): 659–677.

———. (1996). "Third World Cities: Sustainable Urban Development, II— Population, Labor and Poverty." *Urban Studies* 33 (4–5): 673–701.

———. (1997). "Third World Cities: Sustainable Urban Development, III— Basic Needs and Human Rights." *Urban Studies* 34 (5–6): 797–823.

Drohan, Madelaine. (1998). "How the Net Killed the MAI: Grassroots Groups Used Their Own Globalization to Derail Deal." *Toronto Globe and Mail,* 29 April.

Dryzek, John S. (1997). *The Politics of the Earth: Environmental Discourses.* New York: Oxford University Press.

Dubash, Navroz K., and Michael Oppenheimer. (1992). "Modifying the

Mandate of Existing Institutions: NGOs." In I. Mintzer ed., *Confronting Climate Change: Risks, Implications and Responses.* Cambridge: Cambridge University Press, pp. 265–281.

Dunlap, R. E., and W. R. Catton, Jr. (1994). "Struggling with Human Exemptionalism." *The American Sociologist* 25: 5–30.

Easterbrook, Gregg. (1994). "Forget PCB's, Radon, Alar." *New York Times Magazine,* 11 September, pp. 60–63.

Eckersley, Robyn. (1992). *Environmentalism and Political Theory.* Albany, NY: SUNY Press.

———, ed. (1995a). *Markets, the State, and the Environment: Towards Integration.* South Melbourne: Macmillan Education Australia.

———. (1995b). "Markets, the State and the Environment: An Overview. In Robyn Eckersley, ed., *Markets, the State, and the Environment: Towards Integration.* South Melbourne: Macmillan Education Australia, pp. 7–45.

The Ecologist. (1992). "Development as Enclosure," 22(4): 131–147.

———. (1997). "Thailand Threatened Over Intellectual Property Law," 27(3): C3

The Economist. (1992a). "Let Them Eat Pollution," 8 February, p. 66.

———. (1992b). "Pollution and the Poor: Why 'Clean Development' at any Price is a Curse on the Third World," 15 February, p. 18.

———. (1995). "Multinationals and Their Morals," 12 December, p. 18.

———. (1996). "MacWorld," 29 June, pp. 77–78.

Edwards, Paul H., and Myanna H. Lahsen. (1999). "Climate Science and Politics in the United States." Prepared for P. Edwards and C. Miller, eds., *Planetary Management and Political Culture: National Perspectives on Climate Science and Policy.* Unpublished manuscript.

Ehrlich, Paul. (1968). *The Population Bomb.* New York: Ballantine Books.

Ellis, Jeffrey. (1996). "On the Search for a Root Cause: Essentialist Tendencies in Environmental Discourse." In William Cronon, ed., *Uncommon Ground: Rethinking the Human Place in Nature,* New York: W.W. Norton, pp. 256–268.

Elliott, Loraine. (1998). *The Global Politics of the Environment.* London: MacMillan Press.

Erlam, Keith, and Ludolf Plass. (1996). *Trade and Environment: A Business Perspective.* Geneva: World Business Council for Sustainable Development.

Escobar, Arturo. (1995). *Encountering Development: The Making and Unmaking of the Third World.* Princeton: Princeton University Press.

———. (1999). "After Nature: Steps to an Anti-Essentialist Political Ecology." *Current Anthropology* 40(1): 1–30.

Espinal, Rosario. (1998). "Business and Politics in the Dominican Republic." In F. Durand and E. Silva, eds., *Organized Business, Economic Change, and Democracy in Latin America.* Coral Gables, FL: North-South Center Press, pp. 99–121.

Esty, Daniel. (1994). *Greening the GATT: Trade, Environment, and the Future.* Washington, D.C.: Institute for International Economics.

Ethical Consumer Magazine. (1997/1998). Special Issue: Ethical Consumerism. January.

European Commission. (1998). "WTO New Round: Trade and Investment." Brussels: European Commission.

Ewing, K. P., and R. Tarasofsky. (1996). *The "Trade and Environment" Agenda: Survey of Major Issues and Proposals—from Marrakesh to Singapore.* Bonn and Gland: IUCN.

Fabig, Heike, and Richard Boele. (1999). "The Changing Nature of NGO Activity in a Globalising World: Pushing the Corporate Responsibility Agenda." *IDS Bulletin* 3(3): 58–67.

Fagerberg, J. (1988). "International Competitiveness." *Economic Journal* 98: 355–374.

Feinsilver, Julie. (1993). *Healing the Masses: Cuban Health Politics at Home and Abroad.* Berkeley: University of California Press.

Fischer, Kurt, and Johan Schot, eds. (1993). *Environmental Strategies for Industry.* Washington, DC: Island Press.

Fischer, Stanley. (1997). "Capital Account Liberalization and the Role of the IMF." Text of speech given at IMF Seminar on Asia and the IMF, Washington, DC, September.

Fitzsimmons, M., and D. Goodman. (1998). "Incorporating Nature: Environmental Narratives and the Reproduction of Food." In B. Braun and N. Castree, eds., *Remaking Reality: Nature at the Millennium.* London: Routledge, pp. 194–220.

FOE (Friends of the Earth). (1996). *A Call to Close the Committee on Trade and Environment.* Amsterdam: Friends of the Earth International.

Ford, Lucy. (1999). "Social Movements and the Globalization of Environmental Governance." *IDS Bulletin* 30(3): 68–74.

Foster, John Bellamy. (1994). *The Vulnerable Planet.* New York: Monthly Review Press.

———. (1999). "Marx's Theory of Metabolic Rift: Classical Foundations for Environmental Sociology." *American Journal of Sociology* 105: 366–405.

Foucault, Michel. (1980). *The History of Sexuality.* Vol. 1, *An Introduction.* New York: Vintage.

———. (1991). *The Foucault Effect: Studies in Governmentality.* Edited by Graham Burchell, Colin Gordon, and Peter Miller. Chicago: University of Chicago Press.

Frank, D. J., A. Hironka, and E. Shofer. (2000). "The Nation-State and the Natural Environment, 1900–1995." *American Sociological Review* 65: 96–116.

Fukuyama, Francis. (1992). *The End of History and the Last Man.* New York: Free Press.

García Canclini, Néstor. (1995). *Hybrid Cultures: Strategies for Entering and Leaving Modernity.* Minneapolis: University of Minnesota Press.

Garrido, Emigdio O., Luis Ozuna, Leonel Mera, and León Omledo. (1997).

"Teoría y Práctica de la Gestión Ambiental." Manuscript, Center for Urban and Regional Studies, Pontificia Universidad Católica Madre y Maestra, Santiago, DR.

GATT (General Agreement on Tariffs and Trade). (1994). *The Results of the Uruguay Round of Multilateral Trade Negotiations: The Legal Text.* UTN.TNC/45 (Min). Geneva: GATT.

Gazeta Mercantil. (1997a). "Meio Ambiente: População à Frente do Governo," 10 March.

———. (1997b). "Brasil Anda Devagar Depois da Rio 93," 12 March.

GCC (Global Climate Coalition). (1995). Press release.

Gehring, Thomas. (1994). *Dynamic International Regimes: Institutions for International Environmental Governance.* Vol. 5. Frankfurt/Main: Peter Lang Europaeischer Verlag der Wissenschaften.

Gelbspan, Ross. (1997). *The Heat Is On.* Reading, MA: Addison Wesley.

George, Jim. (1994). *Discourses of Global Politics: A Critical (Re)Introduction to International Relations.* Boulder: Lynne Rienner.

Germain, Randall D., and Michael Kenny. (1998). "Engaging Gramsci: International Relations Theory and the New Gramscians." *Review of International Studies* 24: 3–21.

Getz, Kathleen A. (1993). "Selecting Corporate Political Tactics." In B. M. Mitnick, ed., *Corporate Political Agency.* Newbury Park, CA: Sage, pp. 242–273.

Gill, Stephen. (1990). *American Hegemony and the Trilateral Commission.* Cambridge: Cambridge University Press.

———. (1995). "Theorising the Interregnum: The Double Movement and Global Politics in the 1990s." In B. Hettne, ed., *International Political Economy: Understanding Global Disorder.* London: Zed Books, pp. 65–99.

Gill, Stephen and David Law. (1993). "Global Hegemony and the Structural Power of Capital." In Stephen Gill, ed., *Gramsci, Historical Materialism and International Relations.* Cambridge: Cambridge University Press, pp. 93–124.

Gills, Barry. (1997). "Globalisation and the Politics of Resistance." *New Political Economy* 2(1): 11–15.

Gilpin, Robert. (1987). *The Political Economy of International Relations.* Princeton: Princeton University Press.

Glasbergen, Pieter, ed. (1998). *Cooperative Environmental Governance.* Dordrecht, Netherlands: Kluwer Academic Publishers.

Glover, Dominic. (1999). "Defending Communities: Local Exchange Trading Systems from an Environmental Perspective." *IDS Bulletin* 30(3): 75–82.

Goldfrank, Walter, David Goodman, and Andrew Szasz, eds. (1999). *Ecology and the World-System.* Westport, CT: Greenwood Press.

Goldsmith, Edward. (1997a). "Scientific Superstitions: The Cult of Randomness and the Taboo on Teleology." *The Ecologist* 27(5): 196–201.

————. (1997b). "Can the Environment Survive the Global Economy?" *The Ecologist* 27(6): 242–248.

Golley, Frank Benjamin. (1993). *A History of the Ecosystem Concept in Ecology: More Than the Sum of the Parts.* New Haven: Yale University Press.

Gonner, E. C. K. (1966). *Common Land and Inclosure.* London: Frank Cass.

Gonzales, A. T. (1996). *Expert Panel on Trade and Sustainable Development: Report of First Meeting.* Gland, Switzerland: WWF International.

Gordon David. (1988). "The Global Economy: New Edifice or Crumbling Foundations?" *New Left Review* 168: 24–64.

Gorelick, Stephen. (1997). "Big Mac Attacks: Lessons from the Burger Wars." *The Ecologist* 27(5).

Gorz André. (1980). *Ecology as Politics.* London: Pluto.

Gottlieb, Robert. (1993). *Forcing the Spring: The Transformation of the American Environmental Movement.* Washington, DC: Island Press.

Gramsci, Antonio. (1971). *Selections from the Prison Notebooks.* Edited by Quintin Hoare and Geoffrey Nowell-Smith. New York: International Publishers.

Greenline (magazine). (1997). "Environmental Rights and Resistance in Nigeria," 146: 13.

Grove, Richard. (1995). *Green Imperialism: Colonial Expansion, Tropical Edens and the Origins of Environmentalism, 1600–1860.* New York: Cambridge University Press.

GTA (Grupo de Trabalho Amazônico)/Amigos da Terra Internacional. (1996). *Políticas Públicas Coerentes para uma Amazônia Sustentável. O Desafio da Inovação e o Programa Piloto.* Brasília and São Paulo: GTA.

Gudeman, Stephen. (1996). "Sketches, Qualms, and Other Thoughts on Intellectual Property Rights." In Stephen B. Brush and Doreen Stabinsky, eds., *Valuing Local Knowledge.* Washington, DC: Island Press, pp. 102–121.

Guevara, Ernesto (Che). (1968). "Man and Socialism in Cuba." In *Venceremos: The Speeches and Writings of Ernesto Che Guevara.* New York: Macmillan, pp. 387–400.

Guimarães, Roberto P. (1991a). *The Ecopolitics of Development in the Third World.* Boulder: Lynne Rienner.

————. (1991b). "Bureaucracy and Ecopolitics in the Third World: Environmental Policy Formation in Brazil." *International Sociology* 6(1): 73–96.

Haas, Ernst. (1991). *When Knowledge Is Power.* Los Angeles: University of California Press.

Haas, Peter M. (1990). *Saving the Mediterranean: The Politics of International Environmental Cooperation.* New York: Columbia University Press.

————. (1992). "Introduction: Epistemic Communities and International Policy Coordination." *International Organization* 46(1):1–35.

Haas, Peter M., Robert Keohane, and Marc Levy, eds. (1993). *Institutions for the Earth: Sources of Effective Environmental Protection.* Cambridge: MIT Press.

Hajer, Maarten A. (1995). *The Politics of Environmental Discourse: Ecological Modernization and the Policy Process.* Oxford: Clarendon Press.

Hamberg, Jill. (1998). "Revolutionary Cuba's Spatial Policies: Successes and Challenges." Paper presented at the Twenty-first International Congress of the Latin American Studies Association, Chicago, September.

Hampson, Fen Osler, and Judith Reppy, eds. (1996). *Earthly Goods: Environmental Change and Social Justice.* Ithaca: Cornell University Press.

Hardin, Garrett. (1968). "The Tragedy of the Commons." *Science* 162(13 December): 1243–1248.

Hardoy, Jorge, and David Satterthwaite. (1991). "Environmental Problems of Third World Cities." *Public Administration and Development* 11(4): 341–361.

Harvey, David. (1996). *Justice, Nature and the Geography of Difference.* Malden, MA: Blackwell.

Harvey, Pharis, Terry Collingsworth, and Bama Arthreya. (1998). *Developing Effective Mechanisms for Implementing Labor Rights in the Global Economy.* Washington, DC: International Labor Rights Fund. Discussion Draft available on ILRF's website: http://www.laborrights.org/ilrf.html.

Haufler, Virginia. (1995). "Crossing the Boundary Between Public and Private." In V. Rittberger, ed., *Regime Theory and International Relations.* Oxford: Clarendon Press, pp. 94–112.

———. (1997). "Private Sector International Regimes: An Assessment." Paper presented at the Warwick University conference "Non-state Actors and Authority in the Global System," October/November.

Hayward, Tim. (1994). *Ecological Thought: An Introduction.* Cambridge: Polity.

Heilbroner, Robert L. (1985). *The Nature and Logic of Capitalism.* London: Norton.

Held, D., and A. McGrew. (1994). "Globalization and the Liberal Democratic State." In Y. Sakamoto, ed., *Global Transformation: Challenges to the State System.* Tokyo: United Nations University, pp. 57–84.

Helleiner, Eric. (1996). "International Political Economy and the Greens." *New Political Economy* 1(1): 59–77.

———. (1997). "Braudelian Reflections on Economic Globalisation: The Historian as Pioneer." In S. Gill and J. H. Mittelman, eds., *Innovation and Transformation in International Studies.* Cambridge: Cambridge University Press, pp. 90–104.

Hernández, José Miguel. (1997). "La Cooperación Publico-Privada en la Gestion Ambiental: El Caso de Santiago de los Caballeros." Paper presented at the workshop "The Future of the Latin American City," Ithaca, New York, 7–10 July.

Herz, John. (1951). *Political Realism and Political Idealism*. Chicago: University of Chicago Press.

Hindustan Times. (1998). "Neem Goes Global!" *Hindustan Times Sunday Magazine*, 18 October. From *Hindustan Times* website: http://www.hindustantimes.com/nonfram/181098/SUN06.htm.

Hirst, Paul, and Grahame Thompson. (1996). *Globalization in Question*. Malden, MA: Blackwell.

Hobbes, Thomas. (1985 [1651]). *Leviathan*. London: Penguin Books.

Hoedeman, Olivier, Belen Balanya, Adam Ma'Anit, and Erik Wesselius. (1998). "MAIgalomania: The New Corporate Agenda." *The Ecologist* 28(3): 154–161.

Hoffman, Andrew. (1996). "Trends in Corporate Environmentalism: The Chemical and Petroleum Industries: 1960–1993." *Society and Natural Resources* 9: 47–64.

Homer-Dixon, Thomas. (1994). "Environmental Scarcities and Violent Conflict: Evidence From Cases." *International Security* 19: 4–40.

Hopkinson, N. (1995). *The Future World Trade Organisation Agenda*. London: HMSO.

Humphreys, David. (1997). "Environmental Accountability and Transnational Corporations." Paper presented to the International Academic conference "Environmental Justice: Global Ethics for the 21st Century," University of Melbourne, Victoria, Australia, October.

Hurrell, Andrew. (1992). "The International Politics of Amazonian Deforestation." In Andrew Hurrell and Benedict Kingsbury, eds., *The International Politics of the Environment: Actors, Interests and Institutions*. Oxford: Clarendon Press, pp. 398–429.

Hurrell, Andrew, and Benedict Kingsbury, eds. (1992). *The International Politics of the Environment: Actors, Interests and Institutions*. Oxford: Clarendon Press.

ICC (International Chamber of Commerce). (1996). *Trade Measures for Environmental Purposes*. Paris: ICC Commission on International Trade and Investment Policy and the Commission on Environment.

———. (1998). *World Business Priorities for the Second Ministerial Conference of the World Trade Organization*. Paris: ICC Commission on International Trade and Investment Policy.

———. (1999). *World Business Priorities for a New Round of Multilateral Trade Negotiations*. Paris: ICC Commission on International Trade and Investment Policy.

ICC Business World. (1998). "Business States Its Views on OECD Investment Agreement." Paris, ICC, 16 January.

ICIDI (Independent Commission On International Development Issues). (1980). *North-South: A Programme for Survival*. London: Pan Books.

ICME (International Council on Metals and the Environment). (1996). *Newsletter* 4(4).

IFOAM (International Federation of Organic Agriculture Movements).

(1997). "Good News in Two IFOAM Actions on Genetic Engineering." Press release dated 8 December: http://ecoweb.dk/ifoam/gmo/ pr971208.htm.

IFAP (International Federation of Agricutural Producers). (1996). *Trade and Environment: A Farmer's Perspective.* Paris: IFAP.

IISD (International Institute for Sustainable Development). (1996a). *The World Trade Organization and Sustainable Development: An Independent Assessment Summary.* Winnipeg: IISD.

——. (1996b). *Global Green Standards.* Winnipeg: IISD.

Ikwue, A., and Jim Skea. (1996). "Business and the Genesis of the European Community Carbon Tax Proposal." In R. Welford and R. Starkey, eds., *Earthscan Reader in Business and the Environment.* London: Earthscan, pp. 227–251.

INDRHI (Instituto Nacional de Recursos Hidráulicos) and Gesellshaft für Technishe Zusammenarbeit. (1993). *"Proyecto "Fortalecimiento del INDRHI en Atividades Hidrológicas'."* Informe No. 74.

Inside U.S. Trade. (1998). "OECD Members Likely to Water Down Plans for Investment Pact," 30 October.

ISA (Instituto Superior de Agricultura). (1996). "Proyecto de Recuperación y Manejo de la Cuenca del Río Yaque del Norte. Subproyecto Manejo de Calidad de Agua en la Cuenca del Río Yaque del Norte." Santiago, Dominican Republic.

Itzigsohn, José Miguel. (1997). "The Dominican Republic: Politico-Economic Transformation, Employment, and Poverty." In R. Tardanico and R. Menjívar Larín, eds., *Global Restructuring, Employment, and Social Inequality in Urban Latin America.* Miami: North-South Center Press, pp. 47–72.

Jacobs, Michael. (1995). "Sustainability and the Market: A Typology of Environmental Economics." In Robyn Eckersley, ed., *Markets, the State and the Environment.* South Melbourne: Macmillan Education Australia, pp. 46–70.

Jakobeit, Cord. (1998). "Wirksamkeit in der Internationalen Umweltpolitik." *Zeitschrift für Internationale Beziehungen* 5 (2): 345–366.

Jameson, Fredric. (1991). *Postmodernism, or the Cultural Logic of Late Capitalism.* Durham and London: Duke University Press.

Jasannof, Sheila. (1996). "Science and Norms." In Fen Osler Hampson and Judith Reppy, eds., *Earthly Goods: Environmental Change and Social Justice.* Ithaca: Cornell University Press, pp. 173–197.

Joint NGO Statement on the Multilateral Agreement on Investment. (1997). Paris.

Joint NGO Statement on Issues and Proposals for the WTO Ministerial Conference. (1996). Mimeo.

Kamieniecki, Sheldon, ed. (1993). *Environmental Politics in the International Arena: Movements, Parties, Organizations, and Policy.* Albany: SUNY Press.

Katzenstein, P. J., R. O. Keohane, and S. D. Krasner. (1998). "International

Organization and the Study of World Politics." *International Organization* 52 (4): 645–685.

Kay, David A., and Harold K. Jacobson, eds. (1983). *Environmental Protection: The International Dimension.* Totowa, NJ: Allanheld, Osmun.

Keohane, Robert. (1984). *After Hegemony: Cooperation and Discord in the World Political Economy.* Princeton: Princeton University Press.

———. (1989). *International Institutions and State Power.* Boulder: Westview.

Khor, Martin. (1998). "A Worldwide Fight Against Biopiracy and Patents on Life." At Third World Network website: http://www.twnside.org.sg/souths/twn/title/pat-ch.htm, accessed 11/16/98.

Kirkby, John, Phil O'Keefe, and Lloyd Timberlake. (1995). "Sustainable Development: An Introduction." In John Kirby et al., eds., *The Earthscan Reader in Sustainable Development.* London: Earthscan, pp. 1–14.

Kitching, Gavin. (1980). *Class and Economic Change in Kenya: The Making of an African Petite-Bourgeoisie.* New Haven: Yale University Press.

Korten, David C. (1995). *When Corporations Rule the World.* West Hartford, CT: Kumarian Press.

Krasner, Stephen. (1985). *Structural Conflict: The Third World Against Global Liberalism.* Berkeley: University of California Press.

Kütting, Gabriela. (1998). "The Critical Loads Approach and IR: Effective International Environmental Policy-Making?" *International Environmental Affairs* 10(2): 98–112.

Laferrière, Eric. (1995). *The Failure of Peace: An Ecological Critique of International Relations Theory.* Ph.D. diss., McGill University.

———. (1996). "Emancipating International Relations Theory: An Ecological Perspective." *Millennium* 25(1): 53–75.

Laferrière, Eric and Peter J. Stoett. (1999). *International Relations Theory and Ecological Thought: Towards a Synthesis.* London and New York: Routledge.

Lele, U., et al. (2000). *Forests in the Balance: Challenges of Conservation with Development: An Evaluation of Brazil's Forest Development and World Bank Assistance.* Washington, DC: World Bank, Operations Evaluation Department.

Leontieff, Wassily, Ann P. Carter, and Peter Petri. (1977). *The Future of the World Economy.* New York: Oxford University Press.

Leopold, Aldo. (1966 [1949]). *A Sand County Almanac.* New York: Ballantine.

Levêque, François. (1996). *Environmental Policy in Europe: Industry, Competition and the Policy Process.* Cheltenham, England: Edward Elgar.

Levy, David L. (1997). "Environmental Management as Political Sustainability." *Organization and Environment* 10(2): 126–147.

Levy, David L., and Daniel Egan. (1998). "Capital Contests: National and

Transnational Channels of Corporate Influence on the Climate Change Negotiations." *Politics and Society* 26(3): 337–361.

Levy, Marc. (1993). "Political Science and the Question of Effectiveness of International Environmental Institutions." *International Challenges* 13: 17–35.

Levy, Marc, Oran Young, and Michael Zürn. (1994). *The Study of International Regimes*. IIASA Working Paper. Laxenburg, Austria, pp. 94–113.

Lewis, Martin W. (1992). *Green Delusions: An Environmentalist Critique of Radical Environmentalism*. Durham and London: Duke University Press.

Lewis , William. (1997). "Shell to Face Shareholder Vote on Ethics." *Financial Times*, 12 April.

Lipschutz Ronnie, and Ken Conca, eds. (1993a). *The State and Social Power in Global Environmental Politics*. New York: Columbia University Press.

———. (1993b). "A Tale of Two Forests." In Ronnie Lipschutz and Ken Conca, eds., *The State and Social Power in Global Environmental Politics*. New York: Columbia University Press, pp. 1–18.

Lipschutz, Ronnie, with Judith Mayer. (1996). *Global Civil Society and Global Environmental Governance: The Politics of Nature from People to Planet*. Albany, NY: SUNY Press.

Lipscomb, J. F. (1974) *White Africans*. Westport, CT: Greenwood Press.

Litfin, Karen, ed. (1998). *The Greening of Sovereignty in World Politics*. Cambridge, MA.: MIT Press.

Locke, John. (1988). *Two Treatises of Government*. Edited by Peter Laslett. Cambridge: Cambridge University Press.

Lofchie, Michael F. (1989). *The Policy Factor: Agricultural Performance in Kenya and Tanzania*. Boulder: Lynne Rienner.

Lok Swaasthya Parampara Samvardhan Samithi. *Neem: A User's Manual.* "A Case History of Biopiracy." At the Health Education Library for People website: http://www.healthlibrary.com/reading/neem/chap10.htm.

Long, F. J., and J. Arnold. (1995). *The Power of Environmental Partnerships*. Management Institute for Environment and Business. Fort Worth: Dryden Press.

Lovelock, James. (1979). *Gaia: A New Look at Life on Earth*. Oxford: Oxford University Press.

Low, Nicholas, and Brendan Gleeson. (1998). *Justice, Society and Nature: An Exploration of Political Ecology*. London and New York: Routledge.

Luke, Timothy. (1997). *Ecocritique: Contesting the Politics of Nature, Economy and Culture*. Minneapolis: University of Minnesota Press.

———. (1999a). *Capitalism, Democracy, and Ecology: Departing from Marx*. Urbana: University of Illinois Press.

———. (1999b). "Eco-Managerialism: Environmenal Studies as a Power/Knowledge Formation." In Frank Fischer and Maarten Hajer, eds.,

Living with Nature: Environmental Politics as Cultural Discourse. New York: Oxford University Press, pp. 103–120.

Lukes, Steven. (1974). *Power—A Radical View.* London: Macmillan.

Lupton, Malcom, and Tony Wolfson. (1994). "Low-Income Housing, the Environment and Mining on the Witwatersrand, South Africa." In H. Main and S. W. Williams, eds., *Environment and Housing in Third World Cities.* Chichester, UK: J. Wiley and Sons, pp. 107–124.

Lynch, Barbara. (1993). "The Garden and the Sea: U.S. Latino Environmental Discourses and Mainstream Environmentalism." *Social Problems* 40 (February): 108–124.

Macdonald, Gordon J., and Marc A. Stern. (1997). "Environmental Politics and Policy in Latin America." In Gordon J. Macdonald, Daniel L. Nielsen, and Marc A. Stern, eds., *Latin American Environmental Policy in International Perspective.* Boulder and Oxford: Westview, pp. 1–11.

Macnaghten, P., and J. Urry. (1998). *Contested Natures.* London: Sage.

Marinetto, Michael. (1998). "The Shareholders Strike Back—Issues in the Research of Shareholder Activism." *Environmental Politics* 7(3): 125–133.

Marsh, George Perkins. (1965 [1864]). *Man and Nature.* Cambridge: Harvard University Press.

Marx, Karl. (1906 [1859]). *Capital: A Critique of Political Economy.* New York: Charles H. Kerr.

May, Christopher. (1998). "Novelty or Business as Usual? The Information Society and the Global Political Economy." Paper presented at the International Studies Association Annual Conference, Minneapolis, March.

Mayer-Tasch, P. (1986). *Die Luft hat keine Grenzen.* Frankfurt/Main: Fischer Verlag.

McCormick, John. (1989). *Reclaiming Paradise: The Global Environmental Movement.* Bloomington: Indiana University Press.

McGranahan, Gordon, Jacob Songsore, and Marianne Kjellén. (1995). "Sustainability, Poverty and Urban Environmental Transitions." In C. Pugh, ed., *Sustainability, the Environment and Urbanization,* London: Earthscan, pp. 103–33.

McGrew, Anthony. (1991). "The Political Dynamics of the New Environmentalism." In Denis Smith, ed., *Business and the New Environment: Implications of the New Environmentalism.* Nottingham, UK: Paul Chapman Publishing, pp. 12–26.

McMichael, P. (1990). "Incorporating Comparison Within a World-Historical Perspective: An Alternative Comparative Method." *American Sociological Review* 55: 385–397.

Meadows, Donella H., Dennis L. Meadows, Jorgen Randers, and William W. Behrens III. (1972). *The Limits to Growth.* New York: Signet.

Meier, Kenneth. (1995). "Myths of Regulation and Consumer Protection." In Kenneth Meier and E. Thomas Garman, eds., *Regulation and Consumer Protection,* 2d ed., Houston: Dame Publications, pp. 1–9.

Merchant, Carolyn. (1980). *The Death of Nature: Women, Ecology, and the Scientific Revolution.* New York: Harper and Row.

Miller, Char, and Hal Rothman, eds. (1997). *Out of the Woods: Essays in Environmental History.* Pittsburgh: University of Pittsburgh Press.

Miller, Marian A. L. (1995). *The Third World in Global Environmental Politics.* Boulder: Lynne Rienner.

Mitchell, Christopher. (1997). "Urban Elections in the Dominican Republic, 1962–1994." Paper presented at the international congress "La República Dominicana en Umbral del Siglo XXI," Santo Domingo, July.

Mitchell, John. (1997). *Companies in a World of Conflict.* London: RIIA/Earthscan.

Mittelman, James H., ed. (1996a). *Globalization: Critical Reflections.* Vol. 9 of *IPE Yearbook.* Boulder: Lynne Rienner.

Mittelman, James H. (1996b). "How Does Globalization Really Work?" In J. H. Mittelman, ed., *Globalization: Critical Reflections, vol. 9 of IPE Yearbook.* Boulder: Lynne Rienner, pp. 229–241.

———. (1998a). "Coxian Historicism as an Alternative Perspective in International Studies." *Alternatives* 23(1): 63–92.

———. (1998b). "Globalization and Environmental Resistance Politics." *Third World Quarterly* 19(5): 847–872.

Mol, A. P. J. (1995). *The Refinement of Production.* Utrecht: Van Arkel.

———. (1997). "Ecological Modernization: Industrial Transformation and Environmental Reform." In M. Redclift and G. Woodgate, eds., *The International Handbook of Environmental Sociology.* Cheltenham, UK: Edward Elgar, pp. 138–149.

Mol, A. P. J., and G. Spaargaren. (2000). "Ecological Modernization Theory in Debate: A Review." *Environmental Politics* 9(1): 17–49.

Montané, Jesús. (1995). *Clausura de la Mesa Redonda Internacional Río Almendares S.O.S.* Havana: Parque Metropolitano.

Montgomery, David, and Charles River Associates. (1995). "Toward an Economically Rational Response to the Berlin Mandate." Washington, DC: Charles River Associates.

Morse, Edward L. (1976). *Modernization and the Transformation of International Relations.* New York: Free Press.

Muchlinski, P. (1999). "A Brief History of Business Regulation." In S. Picciotto and R. Mayne, eds., *Regulating International Business: Beyond Liberalization.* Basingstoke, UK: Macmillan and Oxfam, pp. 47–60.

Mungeam, G. H. (1966). *British Rule in Kenya, 1895–1912.* Oxford: Clarendon Press.

Murphy, Craig N. (1994). *International Organization and Industrial Change.* Oxford: Oxford University Press.

Murphy, Craig N., and Roger Tooze, eds. (1991). *The New International Political Economy.* Volume 6 of *IPE Yearbook.* Boulder: Lynne Rienner.

Murphy, David F., and John Bendell. (1997). *In the Company of Partners.* Bristol: Polity Press.

Murphy, Raymond (1994) *Rationality and Nature*. Boulder: Westview.

———. (1997). *Sociology and Nature: Social Action in Progress*. Boulder: Westview.

Naess, Arne. (1972). "The Shallow and the Deep, Long-Range Ecology Movement: A Summary." *Inquiry* 16: 95–100.

———. (1989). *Ecology, Community and Lifestyle*. Translated and edited by D. Rothenberg. Cambridge: Cambridge University Press.

Nash, Gerald, and Gifford Pinchot. (1967). *The Fight for Conservation*. Seattle and London: University of Washington Press.

National Academy of Engineering. (1989). *Technology and Environment*. Washington, DC: National Research Council.

Negroponte, Nicholas. (1995). *Being Digital*. New York: Knopf.

Neufeld, Mark. (1995). *The Restructuring of International Relations Theory*. Cambridge: Cambridge University Press.

Newell, Peter, and Matthew Paterson. (1998). "Climate for Business: Global Warming, the State and Capital." *Review of International Political Economy* 5(4): 679–704.

Nitzan, Jonathan. (1998). "Differential Accumulation: Towards a New Political Economy of Capital." *Review of International Political Economy* 5(2): 169–216.

Núñez, Ricardo. (1997). *El Suelo Urbano Como Factor de Inclusión Económica y Social*. Cambridge, MA: Lincoln Institute of Land Policy.

O Estado de São Paolo (1997).

O'Connor, James. (1988). "Prospectus: Capitalism, Nature, Socialism." *Capitalism, Nature, Socialism* 1: 1–6.

———. (1998). *Natural Causes: Essays in Ecological Marxism*. New York: Guilford Press.

OECD (Organization for Economic Cooperation and Development). (1993a). *Trade and Environment*. Paris: OECD.

———. (1993b). *Report on Trade and Environment to the OECD Council at Ministerial Level*. Paris: OECD.

———. (1997a). *Australia: Revised Schedule of Preliminary Reservations*. Paris: OECD.

———. (1997b). *Canada: Revised Draft Reservations*. Paris: OECD.

———. (1997c). *The OECD Guidelines for Multinational Enterprises*. Paris: OECD.

———. (1997d). "OECD Policy Brief," No. 2. Paris: OECD.

———. (1997e). "Report by the MAI Negotiating Group." Paris: OECD.

———. (1997f). *Symposium on the MAI*, 20 October 1997, Cairo. Paris: OECD.

———. (1998a). *The MAI Negotiating Text*. Paris: OECD.

———. (1998b). *Commentary to the MAI Negotiating Text*. Paris: OECD.

Ohmae, Kenichi. (1990). *The Borderless World*. London: Collins.

Ollman, Bertell. (1993). *Dialectical Investigations*. London and New York: Routledge.

Olpadwala, Porus, and William Goldsmith. (1992). "The Sustainability of Privilege: Reflections on the Environment, the Third World City, and Poverty." *World Development* 20 (4): 627–640.

Ophuls, William. (1974). *Ecology and the Politics of Scarcity.* San Francisco: W. H. Freeman.

Ostrom, Elinor. (1990). *Governing the Commons: The Evolution of Institutions for Collective Action.* Cambridge: Cambridge University Press.

Ozone Action. (1996). *Distorting the Debate: A Case Study of Corporate Greenwashing.* Washington, DC: Ozone Action.

Pádua, José Augusto. (1991). "O Nascimento da Política Verde no Brasil: Fatores Exógenos e Endógenos." In Héctor Leis, ed., *Ecologia e Política Mundial.* Rio de Janeiro: Fase/Vozes and AIRI/PUC/RIO, pp. 135–161.

Paehlke, Robert, and Douglas Torgerson, eds. (1990). *Managing Leviathan: Environmental Politics and the Administrative State.* Petersborough, Ont.: Bradview Press.

Paniagua Pascual, Maria. (1998). *Environmental Discourses and Collective Action in the Dominican Republic.* Master's thesis, Cornell University.

Panitch, Leo. (1996). "Rethinking the Role of the State." In J. H. Mittelman, ed., *Globalization: Critical Perspectives.* Vol. 9 of *IPE Yearbook.* Boulder: Lynne Rienner, pp. 83–113.

Patel, Surendra J. (1996). "Can the Intellectual Property Rights System Serve the Interests of Indigenous Knowledge?" In Stephen B. Brush and Doreen Stabinsky, eds., *Valuing Local Knowledge.* Washington, DC: Island Press, pp. 305–322.

Paterson, Matthew. (1995). "Radicalising Regimes? Ecology and the Critique of IR Theory." In J. MacMillan and A. Linklater, eds., *Boundaries in Question.* London: Pinter.

———. (1996). "Green Politics." In Scott Burchill and Andrew Linklater, eds., *Theories of International Relations.* Houndmills and London: Macmillan, pp. 252–274.

Peet, Richard, and Michael Watts. (1996). *Liberation Ecologies: Environment, Development, Social Movements.* London and New York: Routledge.

Pepper, David. (1993). *Eco-Socialism: From Deep Ecology to Social Justice.* London: Routledge.

———. (1996). *Modern Environmentalism.* London: Routledge.

Peralta, Emilio, and Guillermo Fulcar. (1994). *Propuesta General, primer borrador. Ordenamiento y Manejo Integral de la Cuenca del Río Yaque del Norte.* Presentado a Junta Directiva de APEDI (Asociación para el Desarrollo, Inc.), June, Santiago, D.R.

Pérez, César. (1996). "Urbanización y Municipio en Santo Domingo." Manuscript. Instituto Tecnológico de Santo Domingo.

Pérez, Louis A., Jr. (1997). *Cuba and the United States: Ties of Singular Intimacy,* 2d ed. Athens: University of Georgia Press.

Pickering, Kevin T., and Lewis A. Owen. (1994). *An Introduction to Global Environmental Issues.* London and New York: Routledge.

Pirages, Dennis. (1978). *The New Context for International Relations: Global Ecopolitics.* N. Scituate, MA.: Duxbury Press.

Piven, Frances Fox, and Richard A. Cloward. (1997). *The Breaking of the American Social Compact.* New York: The New Press.

Platner, James. (1997). Defining Action Alternatives for Addressing Occupational and Environmental Health Hazards. Paper prepared for the 2nd Annual Conference on the Future of the Latin American City, 7–9 July.

Plumwood, Val. (1986). "Ecofeminism: An Overview and Discussion of Positions and Arguments." *Australian Journal of Philosophy* 64: 120–138.

———. (1993). *Feminism and the Mastery of Nature.* London: Routledge.

Polanyi, Karl. (1957 [1944]). *The Great Transformation: Political and Economic Origins of Our Time.* Boston: Beacon Press.

Ponton, Martin. (1995). *Le Choix d'un Système de Gestion des Déchets Domestiques Urbains: Le Cas de Santiago de los Caballeros en République Dominicaine.* Master's thesis, University of Sherbrooke.

Prashad, Vijay. (1994). "Contract Labor: The Latest Stage of Illiberal Capitalism." *Monthly Review* 46(5): 19–26.

Princen, Thomas, and Matthias Finger, with contributions by Jack Manno and Margaret L. Clark. (1994). *Environmental NGOs in World Politics.* London: Routledge.

Rackham, O. (1986). *The History of the Countryside.* London: Dent.

RAFI (Rural Advancement Foundation International). (1998). "Out of Control: Northern Patent Systems Threaten Food Security, Human Dignity, and Are Predatory on the South's Resources and Knowledge." At the RAFI website: http://www.rafi.ca/misc/outofcontrol.html.

Raj, R. Dev. (1998). "Trade-India: Sifting 'Basmati' Grain from Patents Chaff." *Interpress Service World News.* Report dated 17 March: http://www.oneworld.org/ips2/mar98/basmati.html.

Redclift, Michael. (1987). *Sustainable Development: Exploring the Contradictions.* London and New York: Routledge.

Rede Verde de Informações Ambientais. (1998). 25/98, 14 October.

Rediff Business Bureau. (1998). "India to Comply with WTO Ruling in Patent Cases, 'Fulfil Obligations.'" At Rediff Business Bureau website: http://www.redifindia.com/business/1998/sep/17wto.htm.

Reich, Michael. (1994). "Toxic Politics and Pollution Victims in the Third World." In Sheila Jasanoff, ed., *Learning from Disaster.* Philadelphia: University of Pennsylvania Press, pp. 181–203.

Reiterer, M. (n.d.). *Liberalising World Trade and Prospects for the Singapore Ministerial Meetings Trade and the Environment.* Mimeo.

Remfry and Sagar. (1998). *Letter from India.* Issue 7 (October). At http://www.remfry.com/letter.htm.

———. (1999). *Letter from India.* Issue 8 (April). At http://www.remfry.com/letter.htm.

Repetto, Robert, and Duncan Austin. (1997). *The Costs of Climate Protection: A Guide for the Perplexed.* Washington, DC: World Resources Institute.

Reyes Castro, Fernando, and Atahualpa Domínguez U. (1993). *"Zonas Francas Industriales en la República Dominicana: Su Impacto Económico y Social."* Documento de Trabajo No. 73. Geneva: Programa de Empresas Multinacionales, International Labour Office.

Rich, Bruce. (1994). *Mortgaging the Earth*. Boston: Beacon Press.

Rifkin, Jeremy. (1991). *Biosphere Politics*. New York: Crown.

Rikhardsson, P., and R. Welford. (1997). "Clouding the Crisis: The Construction of Corporate Environmental Management." In R. Welford, ed., *Hijacking Environmentalism: Corporate Responses to Sustainable Development*. London: Earthscan, pp. 40–62.

Ritzer, George. (1993). *The McDonaldization of Society*. London: Pine Forge Press.

Robinson, William. (1996a). "Globalization: Nine Theses on Our Epoch." *Race and Class* 38(2): 13–31.

———. (1996b) *Promoting Polyarchy: Globalization, US Intervention, and Hegemony*. New York: Cambridge University Press.

———. (1998). "Beyond Nation-State Paradigms: Globalization, Sociology, and the Challenge of Transnational Studies." *Sociological Forum* 13(4): 561–594.

Rochefort, David A., and Roger W. Cobb. (1993). "Problem Definition, Agenda Access, and Policy Choice." *Policy Studies Journal* 21(1): 56–71.

Rodman, Kenneth. (1997). "Think Globally, Sanction Locally: Non-state Actors, Multinational Corporations, and Human Rights." Paper presented at Warwick University conference "Non-state Actors and Authority in the Global System," October/November.

———. (1998). "Think Globally, Punish Locally: Non-state Actors, MNCs and Human Rights Sanctions." *Ethics and International Affairs* 12: 19–42.

Rodríguez, R., F. Saguez, and R. E. Yunén. (1993). "Diagnóstico General de los Problemas Ambientales en la Ciudad de Santiago." Programa de las Naciones Unidas para el Desarrollo. Proyecto Manejo Ambiental Urbano, Pontificia Universidad Católica Madre y Maestra, Santiago, DR.

Rosenau, James. (1992). "Governance, Order and Change in World Politics." In James Rosenau and Ernst-Otto Czempiel, eds., *Governance Without Government*. Cambridge: Cambridge University Press, pp. 1–29.

———. (1995). "Governance in the Twenty-first Century." *Global Governance* 1(1)(Winter): 13–14.

Rostow, Walt Whitman. (1960) *The Stages of Economic Growth: A Non-Communist Manifesto*. Cambridge: Cambridge University Press.

Ross, Eric. (1998). *The Malthus Factor: Population, Poverty and Politics in Capitalist Development*. London: Zed Press.

Rowell, A. (1996). *Green Backlash: Global Subversion of the Environmental Movement*. London: Routledge.

Rowlands, Ian. (1992). "The International Politics of the Environment and Development: The Post-UNCED Agenda." *Millennium* 21(2): 209–229.

———. (1995). *The Politics of Global Atmospheric Change*. Manchester: Manchester University Press.

Rubin, Charles. (1994). *The Green Crusade: Rethinking The Roots of Environmentalism*. New York: Free Press.

Ruigrok, Winfried, and Rob van Tulder. (1995). *The Logic of International Restructuring*. London: Routledge.

Runnalls, David. (1996). *Shall We Dance? What the North Needs to Do to Fully Engage the South in the Trade and Sustainable Development Debate*. Manitoba: IISD.

Sachs, Wolfgang. (1993). "Global Ecology and the Shadow of Development." In W. Sachs, ed., *Global Ecology: A New Arena of Political Conflict*. Halifax: Fernwood Press, pp. 3–21.

Said, Edward. 1979. *Orientalism*. New York: Vintage Books.

Sale, Kirkpatrick. (1985). *Dwellers in the Land: The Bioregional Vision*. Philadelphia: New Society.

Sanger, Clyde. (1993). "Environment and Development." In Fen Osler Hampson and Christopher J. Maule, eds., *Canada Among Nations 1993–1994: Global Jeopardy*. Ottawa: Carleton University Press, pp. 154–169.

San Miguel, Pedro. (1997). *Los Campesinos del Cibao: Economía del Mercado y Transformación en la República Dominicana, 1880–1960*. San Juan: Editorial de la Universidad de Puerto Rico.

Santana, Julio. (1994). *Estrategia Neoliberal, Urbanización y Zonas Francas: El Caso de Santiago, República Dominicana*. Santo Domingo: Editora Taller FLACSO.

Sassen, Saskia. (1996). *Losing Control? Sovereignty in an Age of Globalization*. New York: Columbia University Press.

Sassoon, Anne Showstack. (1987). *Gramsci's Politics*. London: Hutchinson.

Saurin, Julian. (1996). "International Relations, Social Ecology and the Globalization of Environmental Change." In John Vogler and Mark Imber, eds., *The Environment and International Relations*. London: Routledge, pp. 77–99.

Schmidheiny, Stephan. (1992). *Changing Course: A Global Business Perspective on Development and the Environment*. Cambridge: MIT Press.

———. (1995). "Trade, Environment and Sustainable Development." Speech at SYNERGY '95, National Wildlife Federation's Corporate Conservation Council, 1 May.

Schmidt, Vivien. (1995). "The New World Order, Incorporated: The Rise of Business and the Decline of the Nation-State." *Daedalus* 124(2): 75–106.

Schrader-Frechette, K. S., and E. D. McCoy. (1993). *Method in Ecology: Strategies for Conservation*. New York: Cambridge University Press.

Schulz, William G. (1999). "Cuba at a Crossroads." *Chemical and Engineering News* (11 January): 8–13.

Schumacher, E. F. (1973). *Small Is Beautiful: Economics as if People Mattered*. New York: Harper and Row.

Sellers, Christopher. (1997). *Hazards of the Job: From Industrial Disease to Environmental Health Science*. Chapel Hill: University of North Carolina Press.

Sen, Amartya. (1981). *Poverty and Famines: An Essay on Entitlement and Deprivation*. Oxford: Clarendon Press.

Sessions, George, ed. (1995). *Deep Ecology for the 21st Century*. Boston: Shambala.

Shackley, Simon. (1999). "Epistemic Lifestyles in Climate Change Modeling." Prepared for P. Edwards and C. Miller, eds., *Planetary Management and Political Culture: National Perspectives on Climate Science and Policy*. Unpublished manuscript.

Shaw, Martin. (1994). "Civil Society and Global Politics: Beyond a Social Movements Approach." *Millennium* 23(3): 647–667.

Shiva, Vandana. (n.d.). "The Neem Tree: A Case History of Biopiracy." At Third World Network website: http://www.twnside.org.sg/souths/twn/title/pir-ch.htm.

——. (1989). *The Violence of the Green Revolution: Ecological Degradation and Political Conflict in Punjab*. Dehra Dun, India: Research Foundation for Science and Technology.

——. (1993). *Monocultures of the Mind*. London and Atlantic Highlands, NJ: Zed Books.

——. (1997). *Biopiracy: The Plunder of Nature and Knowledge*. Boston: South End Press.

Shiva, Vandana and Radha Holla-Bhar. (1996). "Piracy by Patent: The Case of the Neem Tree." In Jerry Mander and Edward Goldsmith, eds., *The Case Against the Global Economy*. San Francisco: Sierra Club Books, pp. 146–159.

Simon, Julian L., and Herman Kahn, eds. (1984). *The Resourceful Earth: A Response to Global 2000*. Oxford: Basil Blackwell.

Singer, Peter. (1990 [1975]). *Animal Liberation*. New York: Avon.

Slater, Gilbert. (1968). *The English Peasantry and the Enclosure of the Common Fields*. New York: A.M. Kelly.

Smith, Kirk R., and Yok-Shiu F. Lee. (1993). "Urbanization and the Environmental Risk Transition." In J. D. Kasarda and A. M. Parnell, eds., *Third World Cities: Problems, Policies and Prospects*. London: Sage, pp. 161–179.

Smith, L. D. (1976). "An Overview of Agricultural Development Policy." In J. Heyer, J. K. Maitha, and W. M. Senga, eds., *Agricultural Development in Kenya: An Economic Assessment*. Nairobi: Oxford University Press, pp. 111–151.

Smith M. (1996). "Looking Beyond Singapore on Trade and Environment." *ICME Newsletter* 4(4): 1–4.

Smith, N. C. (1990). *Morality and the Market: Consumer Pressure for Corporate Accountability*. London and New York: Routledge.

Smith, Zachary A. (1995). *The Environmental Policy Paradox*, 2d ed. Englewood Cliffs, NJ: Prentice Hall.

Smouts, Marie-Claude. (1998). "The Proper Use of Governance in International Relations." *International Social Sciences Journal* 50(1): 81–89.

Soroos, Marvin. (1986). *Beyond Sovereignty: The Challenge of Global Policy*. Columbia: University of South Carolina Press.

Spear, Thomas. (1981). *Kenya's Past*. Burnt Mill, UK: Longman.

Sprinz, Detlef, and Tapri Vaahtoranta. (1994). "The Interest-Based

Explanation of International Environmental Policy." *International Organization* 48(1): 77–105.

Stauber, John C., and Sheldon Rampton. (1995). *Toxic Sludge Is Good for You*. Monroe, ME: Common Courage Press.

Stevenson, Glenn G. (1991). *Common Property Economics: A General Theory and Land Use Applications*. Cambridge: Cambridge University Press.

Stevis, Dimitris. (2000). "Whose Ecological Justice?" *Strategies* 13(1): 63–76.

Stevis, Dimitris, Valerie J. Assetto, and Stephen Mumme. (2000 [1989]). "International Environmental Politics: A Theoretical Review of the Literature." In Wolfgang Rüdig, ed., *Environmental Policy*. Vol. 2, *International Environmental Policy*. Cheltenham, UK: Edward Elgar, pp. 3–37.

Stevis, Dimitris, and Stephen Mumme. (Forthcoming). "Rules and Politics in International Integration: Environmental Regulation in NAFTA and the EU." *Environmental Politics* 9(4).

Stillwaggon, Eileen. (1998). *Stunted Lives, Stagnant Economies*. New Brunswick, NJ: Rutgers University Press.

Stoker, Gary. (1998). "Governance as Theory: Five Propositions." *International Social Science Journal* 50(1): 17–27.

Storper, Michael. (1997). "Territories, Flows, and Hierarchies in the Global Economy." In K. R. Cox, ed., *Spaces of Globalization*. New York: Guilford Press, pp. 19–44.

Strange, Susan. (1996). *The Retreat of the State*. Cambridge: Cambridge University Press.

Streeck, Wolfgang. (1998). "The Internationalization of Industrial Relations in Europe: Prospects and Problems." *Politics and Society* 26(4): 429–459.

SustainAbility. (1996). "Strange Attractor: The Business-ENGO Partnership Strategic Review of BP's Relationships with Environmental NGOs, Summary of Findings: Trends," July.

Sutcliffe, Robert. (1995). "Development After Ecology." In V. Bhaskar and A. Glyn, eds., *The North, the South and the Environment: Ecological Constraints on the Global Economy*. New York: St. Martin's Press, pp. 232–258.

Switzer, Jacqueline, and Gary Bryner. (1998). *Environmental Politics: Domestic and Global Dimensions*. New York: St. Martin's Press.

Taylor, Peter, and Frederick Buttel. (1992). "How Do We Know We Have Global Environmental Problems? Science and the Globalization of Environmental Discourse." *Geoforum* 23(3): 405–416.

Teeple, Gary. (1995). *Globalization and the Decline of Social Reform*. Toronto: Garamond Press.

Terry, Kathleen R., and Warren D. Woessner. (n.d.). "Bring Them Back Alive! Patents on Products of Nature." At the Schwegman, Lundberg, Woessner and Kluth, P.A., website: http://www.slwk.com/paper9.html.

Thomas, William. (1995). *Scorched Earth: The Military's Assault on the Environment.* Gabriola Island, BC: New Society.

Tignor, Robert L. (1976). *The Colonial Transformation of Kenya.* Princeton: Princeton University Press.

Tolba, Mostafa K., Osama A. El-Kholy, E. El-Hinnawi, M. W. Holdgate, D. F. McMichael, and R. E. Munn, eds. (1992). *The World Environment 1972–1992: Two Decades of Challenge.* London: UNEP, Chapman and Hall.

Trepl, L. (1994). "Holism and Reductionism in Ecology: Technical, Political, and Ideological Implications." *Capitalism, Nature, Socialism* 5(4): 13–31.

Turner, R. Kerry, David Pearce, and Ian Bateman. (1994). *Environmental Economics: An Elementary Introduction.* Hemel Hempstead, UK: Harvester Wheatsheaf.

UNEP (United Nations Environment Programme). (1992). Convention on Biological Diversity, 1992. Reproduced in *International Legal Materials* 31: 818–841.

UNESCO. (1950). *Proceedings and Papers of the International Technical Conference on the Protection of Nature,* August 1949. Paris: UNESCO.

United Church of Christ, Commission on Racial Justice. (1987). *Toxic Wastes and Race: A National Report on the Racial and Socioeconomic Characteristics of Communities with Hazardous Waste Sites.* New York: Public Data Access.

United Nations. (1956). *Proceedings of the United Nations Scientific Conference on the Conservation and Utilization of Resources (UNSC-CUR).* 17 August–6 September 1949 (I) A/Conf. 10/7. New York: United Nations.

———. (1972). *Founex Panel Report.* A/Conf 40/10, Annex 1. New York: United Nations.

van der Pijl, Kees. (1984). *The Making of an Atlantic Ruling Class.* London: Verso.

———. (1998). *Transnational Classes and International Relations.* New York: Routledge.

Veras, Leyda. (1991). *Río Yaque: Vives o Mueres?* Santiago: Sociedad Ecológico del Cibao.

Victor, David, Kal Raustiala, and Eugene Skolnikoff, eds. (1998). *The Implementation and Effectiveness of International Environmental Commitments: Theory and Practice.* Cambridge: MIT Press.

Vidal, John. (1996). *McLibel: Burger Culture on Trial.* Basingstoke, UK: Macmillan.

———. (1997a). "Industry Terrified at the Outbreak of Ethics." *The Guardian,* 23 April.

———. (1997b). "Kids Love Him. But What Do They Know?" *The Observer,* 6 April.

Vig, N. J., and R. S. Axelrod, eds. (1999). *The Global Environment: Institutions, Law, and Policy.* Washington, DC: CQ Press.

Virilio, Paul. (1995). *The Art of the Motor*. Minneapolis: University of Minnesota Press.

————. (1997). *Open Sky*. London: Verso.

Vogel, David. (1978). *Lobbying the Corporation: Citizen Challenges to Business Authority*. New York: Basic Books.

————. (1995). *Trading Up: Consumer and Environmental Protection in a Global Political Economy*. Cambridge: Harvard University Press.

Vogler, John. (1996). "The Environment in International Relations: Legacies and Contentions." In John Vogler and Mark Imber, eds., *The Environment and International Relations*. London: Routledge, pp. 1–22.

Vogler, John, and Mark F. Imber, eds. (1996). *The Environment and International Relations*. London and New York: Routledge.

Vogt, William. (1947). *Road to Survival*. London: Victor Gollancz.

Walker, Gordon. (1994). "Industrial Hazards, Vulnerability and Planning in Third World Cities, with Reference to Bhopal and Mexico City." In H. Main and S. W. Williams, eds., *Environment and Housing in Third World Cities*. Chichester, UK: J. Wiley and Sons, pp. 49–64.

Wallerstein, Immanuel. (1974). *The Modern World-System: Capitalist Agriculture and the Origins of the European World-Economy in the Sixteenth Century*. New York: Academic Press.

Waltz, Kenneth. (1986). "Reflections on the *Theory of International Politics*: A Response to My Critics." In Robert Keohane, ed., *Neorealism and Its Critics*. New York: Columbia University Press, pp. 322–345.

Wapner, Paul. (1996). *Environmental Activism and World Civic Politics*. Albany, NY: SUNY Press.

————. (1997a). "Environmental Ethics and Global Governance: Engaging the International Liberal Tradition." *Global Governance* 3(2):213–231.

————. (1997b). "Governance in Global Civil Society." In Oran Young, ed., *Global Governance*. Cambridge: MIT Press, pp. 65–84.

Watkins, Kevin. (1992). *Fixing the Rules: North-South Issues in International Trade and the GATT Uruguay Round*. London: Catholic Institute for International Relations.

Watson, Paul. (1993). *Earthforce! An Earth Warrior's Guide to Strategy*. Los Angeles: Chaco Press.

WBCSD (World Business Council for Sustainable Development). (1998). *Trade, Environment and Sustainable Development: A Briefing Manual*. Geneva: WBCSD.

WCED (World Commission on Environment and Development). (1987). *Our Common Future*. Oxford: Oxford University Press.

Weale, Albert. (1992). *The New Politics of Pollution*. Manchester: Manchester University Press.

WEFA Group, and H. Zinder and Associates. (1996). *A Review of the Economic Impacts of AOSIS-Type Proposals to Limit Carbon Dioxide Emissions (Prepared for Global Climate Coalition)*. Eddystone, PA: WEFA Group.

Wendt, Alexander. (1999). *Social Theory of International Politics*. Cambridge: Cambridge University Press.

Wendt, Alexander, and Raymond Duvall. (1989). "Institutions and International Order." In Ernst-Otto Czempiel and James Rosenau, eds., *Global Changes and Theoretical Challenges*. Toronto: Lexington Books, pp. 51–73.

Wengert, Norman. (1972). "Environmental Policy and Political Decisions: The Reconciliation of Fact, Values, and Interests." In Phillip Foss, ed., *Politics and Ecology*. Belmont, CA: Wadsworth, pp. 39–49.

Wettestad, Joergen. (1995). *Nuts and Bolts for Environmental Negotiators? Designing Effective International Regimes*. Lysaker, Norway: Fridtjof Nansen Institute.

Wettestad, Joergen, and Steinar Andresen. (1991). *The Effectiveness of International Resource Cooperation: Some Preliminary Findings*. Lysaker, Norway: Fridtjof Nansen Institute.

Williams, Marc. (1996). "International Political Economy and Global Environmental Change." In John Vogler and Mark F. Imber, eds., *The Environment and International Relations*. London: Routledge, pp. 41–58.

Williams, Marc, and Lucy Ford. (1999). "The WTO, Social Movements and Global Environmental Management." *Environmental Politics* 8(1): 268–289.

Wirth, Timothy E. (1996). "Statement by Timothy E. Wirth, Under Secretary for Global Affairs, on Behalf of the United States of America, at Convention on Climate Change, Second Conference of the Parties, July 17 1996." Geneva: United States Mission, Office of Public Affairs.

Woods, Ngaire. (1996). "The Uses of Theory in the Study of International Relations." In Ngaire Woods, ed., *Explaining International Relations Since 1945*. Oxford: Oxford University Press, pp. 9–31.

Woodrow, R. Brian. (1980). "Resources and Environmental Policy-making at the National Level: The Search for Focus." In O. P. Dwivedi, ed., *Resources and the Environment: Policy Perspectives for Canada*. Toronto: McClelland and Stewart, pp. 23–48.

World Resources Institute, United Nations Environment Programme, United Nations Development Programme, the World Bank. (1996). *World Resources 1996–97, A Guide to the Global Environment: The Urban Environment*. New York: Oxford University Press.

Worster, Donald. (1979). *Nature's Economy: The Roots of Ecology*. Garden City, NY: Anchor Books.

———. (1994). *Nature's Economy: A History of Ecological Ideas*, 2d ed. Cambridge: Cambridge University Press.

WTO (World Trade Organization). (1996a). *Procedures for the Circulation and De-Restriction of WTO Documents*. WT/.L/160/Rev.1. Geneva: WTO.

———. (1996b). *Guidelines for Arrangements with Non-Governmental Organisations*. WT/.L/162. Geneva: WTO.

———. (1998a). *Ruggiero Announces Enhanced WTO Plan for Cooperation with NGOs*. WTO Press Release 107, 17 July. Geneva: WTO.

———. (1998b). *United States—Import Prohibition of Certain Shrimp and*

Shrimp Products: Report of the Appellate Body. WT/DS58/AB/R. Geneva: WTO.

———. (1998c). "WTO: Relations with NGOs—Meetings." October. At WTO website: http://www.wto.org/wto/ngo/meeting.htm.

WWF (World Wide Fund) International. (1996). *Terms of Reference for an Assessment: Impact of the Uruguay Round Agreement on Environment and Sustainable Development.* Gland, Switzerland: WWF International.

Yearley, S. (1991). *The Green Case.* London: HarperCollins.

———. (1996). *Sociology, Environmentalism, Globalization.* London: Sage.

Young, Oran. (1989). *International Cooperation: Building Regimes for Natural Resources and the Environment.* Ithaca: Cornell University Press.

———. (1992). "The Effectiveness of International Institutions: Hard Cases and Critical Variables." In James Rosenau and Ernst-Otto Czempiel, eds., *Governance Without Government: Order and Change in World Politics.* Cambridge: Cambridge University Press, pp. 160–195.

———. (1994). *International Governance: Protecting the Environment in a Stateless Society.* Ithaca: Cornell University Press.

———. (1997). "Rights, Rules and Resources in World Affairs." In O. Young, ed., *Global Governance: Drawing Insights from the Environmental Experience.* Cambridge.: MIT Press, pp. 1–23.

Zimbalist, Andrew S., and Claes Brundenius. (1989). *The Cuban Economy: Measurement and Analysis of Socialist Performance.* Baltimore: Johns Hopkins University Press.

Zimmerman, Michael. (1994). *Contesting Earth's Future: Radical Ecology and Postmodernity.* Berkeley: University of California Press.

Zürn, Michael. (1998). "The Rise of International Environmental Politics: A Review of Current Research." *World Politics* 50(4): 617–649.

The Contributors

Valerie J. Assetto is associate professor of political science at Colorado State University. Her current research focuses on the impact of international financing on energy, water, and environmental policies in Central and Eastern Europe and the capacity of local government in Hungary to formulate, implement, and enforce environmental policies. Her most recent work appears in *Ökológia.Környezetgazdálkodás.Társadalom* (in Hungarian), the *Budapest University of Economic Sciences Paper Series*, and *International Boundaries and Environmental Security: Frameworks for Cooperation* (Kluwer Press 1997).

Frederick Buttel is professor and chair, Department of Rural Sociology, and professor of environmental studies, University of Wisconsin, Madison. His research focuses on relations among technology, agriculture, and environment, and he is currently exploring the role of international trade regimes in shaping controversies over genetically modified organism (GMO) crop varieties and other agricultural biotechnology products. Buttel is past president of the Rural Sociological Society and of the Agriculture, Food, and Human Values Society, and he is currently president of the Environment and Society Research Committee (RC 24) of the International Sociological Association. He is a fellow of the American Association for the Advancement of Science and received the Excellence in Research Award of the Rural Sociological Society. Buttel is coeditor of *Environment and Global Modernity* (Sage 2000).

Valérie de Campos Mello received her doctorate in political science from the European University Institute, Florence, Italy. She is presently on leave from the Candido Mendes University, Rio de Janeiro, and is working as a political affairs officer in the

Department of Political Affairs of the United Nations. Her research interests center on global environmental politics, development, and globalization. Her work has appeared in *Contexto Internacional, Revista Brasileira de Política Internacional, Revista Internacional de Estudos Políticos,* and *Human Ecology Review.*

Daniel Egan is assistant professor of sociology at the University of Massachusetts–Lowell. He is currently conducting research on the Multilateral Agreement on Investment and on government subsidies for business. His most recent work (coauthored with David Levy) has appeared in *Politics and Society* and in *Non-State Actors and Authority in the Global System* (Routledge 2000).

Rosalind Irwin is a doctoral candidate and teaches political science at York University. Her dissertation examines issues of global environmental policy in multilateral institutions. Her current interests include global environmental policy, multilateralism, peace studies, and ethics in Canadian foreign policy. Most recently she has been contributing editor to *Ethics and Security in Canadian Foreign Policy* (UBC Press 2001).

Gabriela Kütting is lecturer in international relations in the Department of Politics and International Relations at the University of Aberdeen. Her research interests include the global political economy of the environment, issues of environment and development, and the political economy of textile production and consumption. Her most recent work is *Environment, Society, and International Relations: Towards More Effective International Environmental Agreements* (Routledge 2000).

Eric Laferrière is cochair of the Department of Humanities, Philosophy, and Religion at John Abbott College, Ste-Anne-de-Bellevue, Quebec. He recently published (with Peter J. Stoett) *International Relations Theory and Ecological Thought: Towards a Synthesis* (Routledge 1999), which reflects his continuing research interest in the philosophical roots of international relations theory and ecopolitical thought, and the relation between political and ecological order.

David Levy is associate professor of management at the University of Massachusetts–Boston. He has received a grant from the Consortium on Environmental Challenges at MIT and the Dutch Climate Program to research corporate strategic responses to climate change. His most recent work has appeared in *Politics and Society* and in *Non-State Actors and Authority in the Global System* (Routledge 2000, coauthored with Daniel Egan), *Organization and Environment,* and *California Management Review.*

Timothy Luke is University Distinguished Professor of Political Science at Virginia Polytechnic Institute and State University in Blacksburg, Virginia. He is completing a book-length critique of the politics at play in a number of major museums in the United States entitled *Museum Pieces: Probing the Powerplays at Culture, History, Nature, and Technology Museums* (University of Minnesota Press, forthcoming). His most recent books are *Capitalism, Democracy, and Ecology: Departing from Marx* (University of Illinois Press 1998) and *Ecocritique: Contesting the Politics of Nature, Economy, and Culture* (University of Minnesota Press 1999).

Barbara Lynch is currently director of the Program on International Studies in Planning and visiting associate professor in the Department of City and Regional Planning at Cornell University. She came to Cornell from the Ford Foundation where she was program officer for the Caribbean environment and development program. She is currently working on an edited volume on urban environmental issues in Latin America and the Caribbean and a comparative study of environmental management in Santiago, Dominican Republic, and Havana, Cuba. Her most recent work has appeared in *Creating the Countryside* (Temple University Press 1996) and in *Social Problems.*

Marian A. L. Miller is associate professor in the Department of Political Science at the University of Akron. Her major areas of research interest are environmental politics and the politics of development. Her book, *The Third World in Global Environmental Politics,* received the International Studies Association's 1996 Sprout Award for its contribution to international environmental politics. She has also authored numerous papers on various aspects of environmental politics. Current research projects include an assessment of the Caribbean Environment Programme and an examination of how transnational corporations influence the evolution of global environmental politics.

Peter Newell is a research fellow at the Institute of Development Studies, University of Sussex. His work on the international politics of climate change has appeared in the *Review of International Political Economy* and in *Environmental Politics* and his book *Climate for Change: Non-State Actors and the Global Politics of the Greenhouse* is forthcoming with Cambridge University Press. He also has coauthored a book, *The Effectiveness of EU Environmental Policy,* forthcoming with MacMillan Press, and recently edited and contributed to a special issue of the *IDS Bulletin* on *Globalization and the Governance of the Environment* (1999). He continues to work in the area of business regulation and the environment and is involved in a project on the governance of crop biotechnologies in the developing world.

Dimitris Stevis is associate professor of political science at Colorado State University. His current research interests focus on global and regional environmental and labor politics and policy with an emphasis on their political purpose. His most recent work has appeared in *New Political Economy, Work and Occupations, Journal of World-System Research* (http://csf.colorado.edu/wsystems/ jwsr.html), *Strategies: Journal of Theory, Culture and Politics, Review of Political Sociology,* and *Environmental Politics.*

Marc Williams is professor in the School of Political Science, University of New South Wales, Sydney. He has written widely on international economic organizations, North-South relations, and international political economy. His most recent research has focused on global social movements and multilateral economic institutions. His most recent work has appeared in *Environmental Politics* and the *Journal of World Trade.* He is also coauthor of *Contesting Global Governance: Multilateral Economic Institutions and Global Social Movements* (Cambridge University Press 2000).

Index

About the Book

When considering the nature of environmental problems, many scholars and practitioners assume that—while there may be disagreement about solutions—we know what the problems are. In contrast, the authors of this volume investigate the framing of both problems and solutions to clarify the particular political dynamics and preferences that they reflect and legitimate. They test their analytical tools on the real world of international environmental politics, combining theory with empirical research.

All of the chapters raise theoretical questions at the core of research and policymaking that value social equity and environmental health. In combination, they tell a cohesive, substantive story about the IPE of the environment at the beginning of the third millennium.

Dimitris Stevis and **Valerie J. Assetto** are associate professors of political science at Colorado State University.